To Sue with
wishes,

Christina

£29.99

CONCEIVING OF EUROPE: DIVERSITY IN UNITY

Conceiving of Europe: Diversity in Unity

Edited by

ANDREAS MUSOLFF
University of Durham

CHRISTINA SCHÄFFNER
Aston University, Birmingham

and

MICHAEL TOWNSON
Dublin City University

Dartmouth
Aldershot • Brookfield USA • Singapore • Sydney

© Andreas Musolff, Christina Schäffner and Michael Townson 1996

All rights reserved. No part of this publication may be reproduced, stored in a retrieval system or transmitted in any form or by any means, electronic, mechanical, photocopying, recording, or otherwise without the prior permission of Dartmouth Publishing Company Limited.

Published by
Dartmouth Publishing Company Limited
Gower House
Croft Road
Aldershot
Hants GU11 3HR
England

Dartmouth Publishing Company
Old Post Road
Brookfield
Vermont 05036
USA

British Library Cataloguing in Publication Data
Conceiving of Europe : diversity in unity
   1. European Union 2. Europe - Economic integration 3. Europe - Politics and government
   I. Musolff, Andreas II. Schäffner, Christina III. Townson, Michael
   337.1'42

Library of Congress Cataloging-in-Publication Data
Conceiving of Europe : diversity in unity / edited by Andreas Musolff, Christina Schäffner, Michael Townson.
      p.   cm.
   ISBN 1-85521-742-2
   1. Europe–Politics and government–1989- 2. European Union.
3. Europe–Languages. 4. Nationalism–Europe. 5. Europe (The word)
I. Musolff, Andreas. II. Schäffner, Christina. III. Townson, Michael.
D2009.C653   1996
320.94–dc20   96-1353
                                                                         CIP

ISBN 1 85521 742 2

Printed in Great Britain by the Ipswich Book Company, Suffolk

Contents

Acknowledgements — vii

Abbreviations — ix

Diversity and Unity in European Debates
Christina Schäffner, Andreas Musolff, Michael Townson — 1

False Friends Borrowing the Right Words? Common Terms and Metaphors in European Communication
Andreas Musolff — 15

Building a European House? Or at Two Speeds into a Dead End? Metaphors in the Debate on the United Europe
Christina Schäffner — 31

The Enlargement Negotiations in the West-European Press: A Study of Information Flow in the EU
Lieve van de Walle — 61

Team Europe? Stereotypes of National Character in European Sports Reporting
Hugh O'Donnell — 79

Cultural Convergence and National Stereotyping: The Future of Advertising in the United Europe
Helen Kelly-Holmes — 97

Political Communication and Political Culture in Germany
and Great Britain: Some Differences and Similarities
Colin Good   109

Indirect Speech and Conversational Implicatures: The Case
for Contrastive Pragmatics
Frank Liedtke   121

The Concept of Work in Europe
Wolfgang Teubert   129

The 'other' Europe on the Threshold of the Twenty-first
Century: The Political and Cultural Consolidation of the
Baltic States' New Sovereignty?
Francis Knowles   147

'Den festen Kern festigen': Towards a Functional Taxonomy
of Transnational Political Discourse
Nigel Reeves   161

Contributors   171

Acknowledgements

Earlier versions of most of the chapters in this book were presented at a conference "Conceiving of Europe - Diversity in Unity" held at Aston University, Birmingham, September 1994. Support for this conference was provided by the Aston Modern Languages Research Foundation.

Abbreviations

CDU	Christlich-Demokratische Union (Christian Democratic Union Party in Germany)
CIS	Commonwealth/Community of Independent States
CPSU	Communist Party of the Soviet Union
CSU	Christlich Soziale Union (Christian Social Union, Party of Germany)
DDR	Deutsche Demokratische Republik (German Democratic Republic)
EC	European Community
ECU	European Currency Unit
EEC	European Economic Community
EFTA	European Free Trade Area
EG	Europäische Geminschaft (European Community)
ERM	Exchange Rate Mechanism
EU	European Union / Europäische Union
EWS	Europäisches Währungssystem (European Monetary System)
FDP	Freie Demokratische Party (Liberal Party of Germany)
MEP	Member of the European Parliament
MP	Member of Parliament
PDS	Partei des Demokratischen Sozialismus (Part of Democratic Socialism)
SBZ	Sowjetisch Besetzte Zone (Soviet Occupation Zone)
SED	Sozialistische Einheitspartei Deutschlands (Socialist Unity Party of Germany
UNO	United Nations Organisation
USSR	Union of Socialist Soviet Republics

Diversity and Unity in European Debates

CHRISTINA SCHÄFFNER, ANDREAS MUSOLFF,
MICHAEL TOWNSON

Introduction

At the end of the twentieth century, the entire post-Second World War settlement in Europe is undergoing a complex change as the development towards a united European Community (EC) or European Union (EU) and the movement towards a post-bloc Europe are having to be combined.

Up until the peaceful revolutions in Eastern Europe, the idea of a united Europe focussed mainly on Western Europe, but the collapse of Communism has now opened up new and hitherto-undreamed of possibilities for the formerly divided continent of Europe.

At the outset of the move towards West European integration in the late 1950s, the goals of the then European Communities (re-named EU from February 1993) were comparatively modest and consisted mainly in the creation of a customs union and a partial common market. Further progress was made between the 1970s and 1990s, for example with the establishment of a common agricultural policy (CAP), a European Social Fund, a European Investment Fund, and with the development of a common transport policy and the free movement of people and capital. At Maastricht in December 1991, the EC Heads of Government approved the idea of a political union to complement the single market. These developments were accompanied and influenced by a continuous enlargement of the EC. Britain, Denmark and Ireland signed their membership Treaty in 1972, Greece joined in 1981, Spain and Portugal in 1986, and Austria, Sweden, and Finland became EU members in 1994.

The Maastricht Treaty on a European Union includes a number of important aims which will, in time, change the political complexion of the Community. Its aims include, for example, the adoption of common foreign and defence policies, the development of an economic and monetary union (EMU), and EU-wide regulations in the area of social policies (the Social Charter). Ratification of this treaty by all the member states (which is an interesting story in itself) has been the subject of various levels of heated and antagonistic debate in the national parliaments as well as in the media and the public at large. From its inception, this treaty had been the subject of wide-ranging debates. One focus of these debates had been, for instance the wording of the aim of European integration. The formulation in the preamble of the Maastricht Treaty as moving towards an 'ever closer union among the peoples of Europe, in which decisions are taken as closely as possible to the citizen', was a compromise solution because the British government rejected the original proposed formulation of a 'federal Europe'. Likewise, the phrase 'state identity' was replaced by 'national identity' in the preamble of the Maastricht Treaty to avoid further misinterpretations. Such terminological and conceptual changes can be seen throughout the history of the EC/EU. For example, in one draft for the founding document of the EEC, the Treaties of Rome (1957), the term the 'United States of Europe' was used to describe the aim of the projected integration process, but this phrase was later deleted because it had met with fierce opposition in some member states, due to different national interpretations of the word 'union'.

Agendas of European integration

The public debates about the whole range of EU issues, such as currency, labour law, European army, European parliament, reform of the EU institutions and their procedures, are far from over. One complex of questions debated concern the final aim of a European Union, i.e., should it be a structured community or free trade area? Although most politicians officially support further integration, many political scientists, economists and historians argue that different outcomes are still possible (cf. Pinder, 1995). They base their arguments on the obvious diversity in the political and economic philosophies of EU member states. For example, in comparing the political cultures of Britain, France and Germany, Pinder (1995) argued that Germany wants federal institutions and federal instruments, the French do not want federal institutions but do want federal instruments, whereas Britain does not want either.

The diversity within the EU is also a diversity of economic performance (there are strong and weak economies, and this diversity may further increase with East European countries joining the EU). Various solutions (more regulation or more deregulation?) are under discussion. Another example of diversity is the existence of strong and weak currencies. All these diversities may lead to diversion, but, as Pinder (1995) argued, the diversion threats are counterbalanced by an increasing interdependence of the member states caused by political pressures from outside (especially Russia), by economic pressure from outside (especially USA, Japan), and by the internal pressure of recession. These pressures have an effect on the disintegrative forces within the EU.

Pinder (1995) sees three possible scenarios for the future development of the EU: (i) the diversity will overcome the interdependence, and this will lead eventually to disintegration; (ii) a core group (France plus Germany plus a few others) will move to a more federal EU; or (iii) the whole EU will be moving into a federal direction. In Pinder's view, this third scenario is only possible if British political thinking changes radically.

Such discussions are accompanied by a debate about deepening and/or widening of the EU. Can both processes take place at the same time? Or can only one of these be achieved, but not the other? Should one (which one?) be completed before the other? The British preference is for widening before deepening, the French would like to see a deepening first, the German government wants to have both at the same time. Would deepening the community mean more regulation and standardisation, and, thus, less sovereignty for individual member states? The enlargement debate has been given new impetus with the end of the Cold War and with Eastern European countries applying for membership. Over the years, criteria have been set up which must be fulfilled if a country wishes to be considered for EU membership. These criteria are the following:

1. They must be European countries.
2. They must be multi-party parliamentary democracies.
3. They must be market-type economies.
4. They must respect human rights (Coffey, 1995, p. 7).

These criteria are modelled on the current characteristic features of the EU. In other words, they point to a continuation of the EC/EU policy as it was devised at the end of the 1980s. This can be compared to an observation by Preston (1994). He argues that the events of 1989-91 in Eastern Europe have called into question the comfortable political certainties and official ideologies of the Cold War. But talking about the West having 'won the Cold War' has also had "the consequence that further developments within the global system would necessarily follow the western model" (Preston, 1994, p. 155).

The fundamental question of the EU, concerning the alternative or combination of deepening and widening, is reflected in the debates about new models for the future development, such as the creation of a loose European Confederation, concentric circles, variable geometry or a Europe à la carte. These debates, just as those about the terminology in the main European treaties, show a marked differentiation across the member states and their respective party political and media spectra. They, in turn, are closely linked to national stereotypes and characteristics of political culture and symbolism.

It is linguistic aspects of the political debates about the future of Europe that the different contributions in this volume focus on. The discussions of and comments on EC/EU issues that provide the material for the analyses, are not evaluated from the point of view of the social or political sciences, but from the perspective of critical discourse analysis.

Linguistic aspects of the European debate

Politics is constituted in discourse, both in written texts and in oral debates, which in turn shape and modify material political developments. There are a number of issues in relation to Europe and European integration that are of interest for linguistic research, especially in the fields of text analysis, sociolinguistics and critical discourse analysis. Some of them will be mentioned here, some are discussed in more detail in the following chapters.

What is Europe?

A first point of interest is the term 'Europe' itself and its meaning in political discourse. 'Europe' is often used in a rather vague sense and its meaning is negotiable, depending on the context in which the term is deployed. On the one hand, 'Europe' can denote continental Europe in a geographical sense. In a political perspective, on the other hand, it can denote, metonymically, only Western Europe, or even only the EC/EU. This synonymy was reflected, for example, in slogans for the 1994 Europeans elections that said 'we are for Europe'. The same differentiation applies for the term 'European', which can refer to somebody living in the geographical area of Europe or to a supporter of the EC/EU (cf. Hardt-Mautner, 1995, p. 183-4).

Even the use of the term to denote the geographical area is problematic. Where should the boundaries be drawn: where does Europe start, where does it end? Who belongs to it? A familiar phrase in this context is 'Europe from the Atlantic to the Urals'. Apart from being a geographical concept, Europe is also a political concept, and it is mainly in this respect that such specifications as 'Eastern' or 'Western Europe' can be explained (just to give an example: before the end of the Cold War, Czechoslovakia was considered to be part of Eastern Europe, although geographically, Prague is to the west of Vienna). Now, after the end of the Cold War, new labels are used to give a more refined definition of geo-political areas, therefore, the Czech Republic is now re-allocated to 'Central Europe'. But the place at the centre of Europe is highly contested. For example, in the slogans for the 1994 elections to the European Parliament, the CSU in

Germany referred to 'our Bavarian homeland in the centre of Europe', and the CDU argued that Germany had moved from the fringe into the centre and had become the geographical and economic centre of Europe.

The matter is further complicated by the multiplicity of 'European' institutions with differing membership. The European Union (EU) is not identical with the Western European Union (WEU), which again has a different membership from the Council of Europe, which in its turn has a different membership from the European Broadcasting Union (EBU), which, for example, has for some time allowed Israel, but not the (then) Soviet Union to take part in the European song contest, whereas the CIS states take part in the European football championship and the various European club competitions, from which Israel is excluded.

'Europe' itself has undergone a massive change and re-evaluation. Whilst some countries are fervently demanding admission to the European Union in order to be recognized as 'fully' competent and ranking Europeans, others, notably within the 'Union', have started re-assessing the high esteem in which they have previously held our continent. For example, in a leading article, *The Economist* claimed:

> Europe is perilously close to becoming a term of abuse throughout the European Union. (*The Economist*, 21 May 1994)

New labels have been 'invented' to illustrate different attitudes towards Europe, i.e. the EU: 'Euro-sceptics' versus 'Euro-optimists', 'Euro-realists' versus 'Euro-idealists', 'Europhiles' versus 'Europhobes'. Such coinings have strong connotations (cf. Brozich Lipizer, 1993, p. 6) and they can mislead unless we define clearly what we are talking about when we use them. The term 'Euro-sceptic' has even been included in the newly published ninth edition of the *Concise Oxford Dictionary*, defined (on p. 465) as "n. a person who is not enthusiastic about increasing the powers of the European Union." The main criterion for the inclusion of a word in a dictionary is its regular contemporary usage (cf. *Concise Oxford Dictionary*, p. vii, p. xii). This criterion must not be confused with a word's longevity, a fact which prompted *The Guardian* to argue:

> The inclusion of 'Euro-sceptic' may seem to some a dismaying nod to topicality, but the ease with which it currently spills from lips and keyboards is precisely what gained it admission. If it rapidly ceases to be a meaningful definition of certain kinds of Conservative, it will be for the guillotine. (*The Guardian*, 5 July 1995)

In a slightly more sarcastic way the term 'Eurocrat' was defined in *The Guardian's* 'Eurospeak: a beginners' phrasebook' as follows:

> Official with the openness of the Briton, the sense of humour of the German, the discipline of the Italian, the charm of the Belgian, the world

outlook of the Luxembourger, humility of the French, language of the Greek. (*The Guardian*, 22 June 1991)

Language policy

Another area that lends itself to linguistic research in terms of unity and diversity is the whole aspect of language policy. This can be discussed at three levels: firstly, language policies within the individual EU member states, secondly, language policy within the EU institutions, and thirdly, the attempts to establish EU-wide language policies by, for example, promoting the so-called 'minority' languages.

The number of languages - as defined in linguistic terms - exceeds the number of nation states by far: in Europe as a whole about 80 to 90 languages are spoken, and about 35 of them in the EU, with many more dialects (cf. Nelde, 1994, p. 170). This means that for most countries it is bi- or multilingualism that is normal, not monolingualism. This will have consequences for language planning within each country, and it affects, for example, the role of national languages, compared to vehicular languages (linguae francae), regional languages, majority and minority languages. Political decisions in this respect are related to promoting or restricting languages and language use, as well as to language teaching (cf. Coulmas, 1991, Truchot et al., 1994, *Current Issues in Language and Society,* vol. 1, nos 1 and 2, 1994). The teaching of languages is not only an issue for education authorities within a country (i.e. concerning the choice of the vernacular languages spoken in the country) but is also of relevance when it comes to the choice of languages to be offered and taught as foreign languages.

The language policy within the EU institutions is one of equality. Everybody has the right to speak in their own language. All languages are equal, and all are "working languages". The continuous enlargement of the EEC/EC has, however, resulted in an increase of languages, which is posing practical problems for an effective working of the institutions (cf. Dollerup, 1993). For the original six EEC members, there were four official languages, French (spoken in France, Belgium, Luxembourg), Dutch (spoken in the Netherlands, and also in Belgium), German (spoken in Germany, and also in Belgium and Luxembourg), and Italian (spoken in Italy). The total number of official languages increased to six in 1973, when the United Kingdom, Ireland (with English - although this is only the second official language of the Irish state) and Denmark (speaking Danish) became members of the Common Market. It increased again in 1981 (when Greece joined, adding Greek) and in 1986 (when Spain and Portugal joined, adding Spanish and Portuguese), resulting in nine official languages for the Community of twelve. With each enlargement there is also an increase in the number of languages, a further possible increase to 20 members will mean 15 languages, and to thirty members even 25 languages.

In order to facilitate communication, a few languages function as principal working languages within the EU institutions, thus fulfilling supranational functions. But since not every official in these institutions is competent in several languages - to say nothing of the politicians - another feature of the internal EU communication is the constantly high demand for translating and interpreting. For example, in 1993 the European Commissions employed 2500 translators (some texts were sent to external translation agencies), 600 interpreters in-house, and 2500 free-lance interpreters (cf. Dollerup, 1993; Born 1992, 1993; Ickler, 1991). "The Joint Interpreting and Conference Services in Luxembourg and Brussels reported 9,720 meetings in 1989, the equivalent of 110,000 interpreter days" (Sager, 1994 p. 299). In the European Commission, draft documents are translated into the languages of all the member states. After national hearings, Community meetings try to reach an agreement. The document is then finalized at the Commission and the final decision is taken by the Council of Ministers. Sager (1994, p. 295) gives an indication of the changing role of individual languages in these translation processes:

> For example, the translation services of the Commission of the EC in Brussels reported for the year 1976 that 58% of translations were from French, 19% from English and only 11% from German. As expected the distribution of translation into the official languages of the EC member states was much more balanced, namely, 20% into English, 20% into German, 15% each into French, Italian, Dutch and Danish.

With Austria, Sweden and Finland having joined the EU in 1994, the number of language combinations for the Commission's translation service increased from 72 to 132. It can be expected that with more countries joining in future, the translation service will also balloon. To make these services more efficient, certain standardizations of terminologies have been attempted and terminology data banks have been created. Considerable resources were invested into developing computer-assisted translation systems, for example, the multinationally co-ordinated project *Eurotra* (for a critical evaluation of this project cf. Schuurman, 1994).

In some of the EU institutions, official texts are created by way of multilingual negotiation, which constitutes a new type of interlingual and intercultural communication (cf. Schäffner, in print). Some linguists have discussed consequences for the linguistic structure of such texts. Schütte (1993) illustrates the specific textual make-up of such 'Eurotexts', in his case, legal texts. They are set up by several authors of different mother tongues, they have to exist in all languages of members states, and each text is legally binding.

This developing linguistic convergence is seen by some as a threat to the national language. In both France and Germany, for instance, there is a heightened awareness - and sometimes, deep resentment - of an alleged neglect of their national idioms, mainly to the advantage of English (cf.

Ammon, 1990; Falter, 1991; Bister-Broosen, 1992). But even 'within' national languages - or rather, the national speaking communities - the influence of linguistic 'Europeanization' sometimes stirs strong feelings. For lovers of 'plain English', for instance, Gowers (1986, pp. 186-7) complained about the resulting 'Euro-English':

> The most recent threat to British English has developed since we joined the European Economic Community, and the threat is particularly menacing for official writers. They are exposed to a flood of documents in English from the European Commission and other community institutions. The English in the Community's publications, which has been derisively called Euro-English, is distorted under the influence of other European languages and displays a bureaucratic jargon of its very own. The impositions of Euro-jargon should be firmly opposed and the Europeanisms resisted.

Others (cf. e.g. Wandruszka, 1990) see the mutual influence between different European languages as a huge experiment in linguistic cross-fertilization that should only be encouraged (and that could not be avoided anyway). Others again, foreseeing a linguistic and political confusion similar to the one caused by the Tower of Babel project, argue for a new unified language. Some authors, for instance, would argue for the introduction of Esperanto as a possible solution to language problems within the EU. From a more pragmatic point of view, Dollerup (1993) characterizes 'Eurospeak' as a certain jargon, i.e. as a language of Eurocrats and known to delegates and EU staff (including translators and interpreters). It is not only a sociolect but also a language for specific purposes, i.e. negotiations within the EU.

Texts created by way of multilingual negotiation provide material for new perspectives in comparative linguistic research. One central question concerns their language status: do they represent a new type of text, as the result of a true pan-European discourse? It would be interesting to study some of the texts jointly created by, for example, the political groupings in the European Parliament, such as the European People's Party (EPP, i.e., a pan-European organization of Christian Democratic politicians), the Party of European Socialists (PES), or the European Liberal, Democratic and Reform Party (ELDR), in order to see whether they provide evidence of a pan-European discourse. Apart from such product-oriented research, it would be necessary to study the processes involved in them, for example, an analysis of the actual debates on different versions of the text, and the mechanisms underlying the consensus finding, within these groupings. This might provide answers to such questions as whether something like a supranational Euro-discourse is emerging, whether it is an imitation of a dominant national discourse (meaning that political discourse in general is culture specific) - or a truly new type - or a hybrid.

As previously stated, all languages used in the European Union states are supposed to have equal status, i.e. every EU citizen has the right to use their mother tongue - which can have far-reaching consequences for such areas as educational policy. In order to promote the use of 'minority' languages, the EU has set up an agency to promote the use of 'lesser-used' (or 'less widely spread') languages, and there are supporting measures from other organisations, for example from the Council of Europe, which is fostering the use of such languages (e.g. Welsh, Gaelic) in broadcasting.

The support for minority languages also has to be seen in the context of EU regional policy. One vision of Europe is that of a 'Europe of the regions', and new regional groupings are developing which cut across previous national boundaries - for example the SAAR-LOR-LUX region comprising the Saar, Lorraine and Luxembourg, or the moves towards a new regional grouping centred on the Irish Sea, and which is already seeing both official and unofficial collaboration between Welsh, Irish and Scottish communities, with accompanying measures to promote the use of Welsh, Irish and Gaelic.

The promotion of diversity represented by EU regional policy also extends to certain nomadic groups; for example, the new SOCRATES programme has a special chapter to support the educational needs of travellers and their children. At the same time, however, the support given to 'minority' languages also has its limits. It appears that the languages to be supported are those which are 'native' to the EU member states, and therefore official support is not granted to languages such as Arabic (in France), Turkish (in Germany) and Urdu, Gujarati and Hindi (to name but a few) in Britain, and this is also reflected in national language policies, even though, for example, the native speakers of languages from the Indian sub-continent in Britain probably outnumber those of Welsh.

Political discourse

The term 'discourse' has been used in several different ways in language study (for a discussion on this cf. van Dijk, ed., 1985; Fairclough, 1992), e.g. initially as a description of language above the level of the sentence (Harris, 1951), as analysis of spoken dialogue (discourse here is contrasted to 'text' for written documents), as a genre or a language style (e.g. newspaper discourse, advertising discourse, Thatcher's discourse). 'Discourse', as used in this book means the socially situated and purposeful use of (written or spoken) language.

Political discourse is a very wide concept, it covers both internal discourse (politicians talking to other politicians, the production of texts that are instrumental in policy making) and external discourse (politicians talking to the wider public, mainly argumentative and persuasive texts). The latter aspect fits into the more general category of 'public discourse' that comprises the language of media in general, as well as advertising and any kind of linguistically manifested social activity that is not restricted to a particular group of addressees. We can, however, ask how 'public' public discourse in fact is. Speaking of European integration, we can enquire how politicians, and also the media, are 'selling' the EU to the public, which arguments are presented and how, whether the information presented is backed up by background arguments, and whether government decisions are explained to the public.

Europe is very often not yet seen as a unity, but rather as a conglomerate of individual states, which are more often defined in terms of differences (diversity) than in commonalities (unity). With regard to political discourse, this would imply that fundamentally there are as many discourses as there are political unities, and that any talk of a 'European discourse' would be a mere abstraction. With reference to the UK polity, Preston (1994) criticizes that "UK public political discourse in respect of EC integration has been severely restricted in character", namely "national, economistic, and unreflexive." In his view, this "narrow and pragmatic focus has blocked discussion of the likely changes which the broader processes of complex change will occasion within the UK" (Preston, 1994, p. 130). The development of a 'European discourse' that deserves its name would need a 'European public' as its discursive agent.

On the other hand, the emergence of new Euro-specific text types, as well as the reactions to a perceived European influence on national public discourse mentioned earlier, could be interpreted as signs of unity - sometimes dreaded as uniformity - of discourse structures. Moreover, from a historical point of view, such convergence phenomena and the resulting question of common European discourse are by no means new. The French Revolutionaries were probably not the first to claim that they spoke not just for their nation, but for the whole of Europe (sometimes even for the whole of humanity), and despite political opposition from the rest of European states at that time, they were successful in shaping much of international political terminology, witness the modern meanings of terms and phrases such as 'democracy', 'revolution', 'to put an issue on the (political) agenda', etc. (cf. Brunot, 1969; Furet and Ozouf, eds, 1989). Many cultural stereotypes and discourse features that are still in use today, derive their relevance - as communicative 'bridges' and as 'barriers' between speech communities - from this 'background' of previous usage. Has the European public been in the making for several hundred years, rather than just since the negotiations for Treaties of Rome?

Regarding current political discourse both within individual EU member states and between them, as well as the discourse within the EU institutions, we can enquire into typical, culture-specific versus universal or culture-overlapping discursive strategies. How are texts structured? How are arguments presented? Which concepts are used, by whom, when, where, why, and how? Some strategies might be genre-specific and thus functionally equivalent, for example, speeches in parliaments, speeches by party leaders. Others might be more culture-specific, for example, negotiating strategies. Concepts and terms may be interpreted and/or used differently in their different cultural environments (as, for instance, the term 'federalism'). We could indeed ask whether communication and mutual understanding within and across the EU can be assured in view of a diversity both in the interpretation of various terms and in discursive practices - these are in fact the main topics of this book.

Unity and Diversity

Questions about commonalities, similarities, and differences in the European debate have not yet often been asked in discourse analysis. European debate is to be understood in two senses here: firstly, the debate about Europe/EU and European integration/European unity, and secondly, discourse within and among the European countries. This second perspective concerns discourse structures (text type conventions), ideas and concepts (conceptualization and verbalization of experience), and communicative/discursive strategies (which are based on and determined by political strategies, by political cultures, and by communicative cultures). Linguistic differences, i.e. differences in languages as systems are well-known, from research in contrastive linguistics. Such systemic differences are not, however, our main concern here. We are particularly interested in language use, and more specifically, in diverse concepts and discursive strategies in the unity of the EU.

Earlier versions of most of the chapters in this book were presented at a conference "Conceiving of Europe - Diversity in Unity" held at Aston University, Birmingham, September 1994. The chapters address on the one hand questions of what hinders communication between the member states and their linguistic communities, and on the other hand, what promotes this communication. Communication can be hindered by different discourse traditions that inform the current usage of political terms (Musolff), different conceptualizations of domains (Schäffner, Reeves), national stereotypes (O'Donnell), differences in the political culture (Good), different strategies in the press (van de Walle). Similar discursive strategies can be seen, for example, in the strategic use of implicatures (Liedtke).

Communication can be promoted and made easier by converging economies, converging ideologies, and converging lifestyles, as evidenced in pan-European advertising (Kelly-Holmes). This raises the question of what Europeans are supposed to have in common. Is it mainly that lifestyles and material interests converge, especially among young people? Is the European citizen then not much more than a Euro-consumer? Or do Europeans also share other features and interests, for example, in their attitudes and values towards environmental protection, security, peace keeping, etc.? Is the Euro-citizen, for example, also a Euro-ecologist?

How are interests and problems presented as common interests and problems? How are European citizens made aware of the fact that there are quite a number of issues they share? For example, the growing structural unemployment requires Europeans to reflect whether the traditional notion of work should remain the central value of an industrial society (Teubert). What role do the media play in making the public aware of common identities and problems? Do they focus on the identities or on the differences? What role do newspapers, such as *The European* or international TV stations such as *MTV* and *Eurosport* that broadcast across Europe, play in this respect? Another aspect most not be overlooked when we think of Europe growing together: In parts of Eastern Europe, especially in the newly emerging states formerly belonging to the Soviet Union, linguistic 'autonomy' is promoted and used as a vehicle for asserting national and cultural independence, with 'reverse' discrimination of the previously dominant (Russian) group as a potential consequence (Knowles).

Conclusion

Obviously, the questions raised in the contributions to this volume - and even more so the tentative answers outlined - can do little more than indicate some issues of the analysis on European discourse that need much further research. The dialectics of European diversity and unity are certainly not a topic that will soon be settled 'once and for all'. Even the basic premises, i.e. the assumption of 'common topics' for European discourse are still far from clear. Are common solutions advocated for problems that are perceived as common to the EU, e.g. coping with unemployment, immigration? One possible line of research seems to us to be the comparative analysis of texts that are produced in the individual EU member states, showing how national and supra-national European problems and interests are being reflected. Certainly, other avenues of research into this area are required, too. We hope the discourse on such methodological and conceptual questions of discourse analysis will be developed further just as the discourse on the future of Europe will continue.

References

Ammon, Ulrich (1990), 'Deutsch unter Druck der englischen Sprache', *Sprachreport*, no. 2, pp. 6-8.
Bister-Broosen, Helga (1992), 'Frankreichs Sprachgesetzgebung', *Sprachreport*, no. 4, pp. 13-14.
Born, Joachim (1992), 'Eurospeak + Eurotexte = Eurolinguistik? Anmerkungen zu sprachlichen Gewohnheiten im Brüsseler "Euro-Alltag"', *Sprachreport*, no. 2-3, pp. 1-4.

Born, Joachim (1993), 'Bauen wir Babel?, Zur Sprachenvielfalt in der europäischen Gemeinschaft', *Sprachreport*, no. 1, pp. 1-3.

Brozich Lipizer, Giuliana (1993), 'The Compatibility of Immediate Solutions with Socio-cultural Differentials in the Interpretation of Political Discourse', *The Interpreters' Newsletter*, no. 5, pp. 3-7.

Brunot, Ferdinand (1969), *Histoire de la Langue Française des Origines à nos Jours. Nouvelle édition.Tome XI: Le Français au dehors sous la Révolution, le Consulat et l'Empire*, A. Colin, Paris.

Coffey, Peter (1995), *The Future of Europe*, Edward Elgar, Aldershot.

Concise Oxford Dictionary (1995), Ninth Edition, Oxford University Press, Oxford.

Coulmas, Florian (ed.) (1991), *A Language Policy for the European Community. Prospects and Quanderies*, de Gruyter, Berlin and New York.

Current Issues in Language and Society, vol. 1, nos 1 and 2 (1994).

Dollerup, Cay (1993), 'Translation, Interpreting and Negotiations as Forces in Language Change in Member States of the EC', paper delivered at the AILA Congress, Amsterdam 1993.

Fairclough, Norman (1992), *Discourse and Social Change*, Polity Press, Cambridge.

Falter, Christina (1991), 'Sprachgesetzgebung in Frankreich', *Sprachreport*, no. 4, pp. 1-3.

Furet, François and Ozouf, Mona (eds) (1989),*The French Revolution and the Creation of Modern Political Culture*, 3 vols, Pergamon Press, Oxford.

Gowers, Ernest et al. (1986), *The Complete Plain Words*, London, HMSO.

Hardt-Mautner, Gerlinde (1995), 'How does one Become a Good European?: The British Press and European Integration', *Discourse & Society*, vol. 6, no. 2, pp. 177-205.

Harris, Zelig (1951), *Methods in Structural Linguistics*, University of Chicago Press, Chicago.

Ickler, Theodor (1991), 'Zur Sprachenpolitik der EG', *Sprachreport*, no. 1, pp. 17-18.

Nelde, Peter (1994), 'Languages in Contact and Conflict: The Belgian Experience and the European Union', *Current Issues in Language & Society*, vol. 1, no. 2, pp. 165-82.

Pinder, John (1995), 'Convergence and Diversity: Economic and Political Forces', paper delivered at the conference 'Is European Union Irreversible?', Bath, 30 June - 1 July 1995.

Preston, Peter (1994), *Europe, Democracy and the Dissolution of Britain. An Essay on the Issue of Europe in UK Public Discourse*, Dartmouth, Aldershot.

Sager, Juan (1994), *Language Engineering and Translation. Consequences of automation*, Benjamins, Amsterdam/Philadelphia.

Schäffner, Christina (in print), 'Where is the Source Text?', in Wotjak, Gerd and Schmidt, Heide (eds), *Festschrift für Albrecht Neubert*, Narr, Tübingen.

Schuurman, Ineke (1994), 'Eurotra: The Philosophy Behind It', *Meta*, vol. xxxix, no. 1, pp. 176-83.

Schütte, Wolfgang (1993), '"Eurotexte" - Zur Entstehung von Rechtstexten unter den Mehrsprachigkeitsbedingungen der Brüsseler EG-Institutionen', in Born, Joachim and Stickel, Gerhard (eds), *Deutsch als Verkehrssprache in Europa* (Institut für deutsche Sprache, Jahrbuch 1992), de Gruyter, Berlin and New York, pp. 88-113.

Truchot, Claude, et al. (1994), *Le Plurilinguisme Européen - Théories et Pratiques en Politique Linguistique. European Multilingualism - Theory and Practice in Language Policies. Europäische Mehrsprachigkeit - Theorie und Praxis in der Sprach(en) Politik*, Editions Champion, Paris.

van Dijk, Teun A (ed.) (1985), *Handbook of Discourse Analysis* (vols 1-4), Academic Press, New York and London.

Wandruszka, Mario (1990), *Die europäische Sprachengemeinschaft*, Francke, Tübingen.

False Friends Borrowing the Right Words? Common Terms and Metaphors in European Communication[1]

ANDREAS MUSOLFF

Introduction

The British newspaper *The Guardian* is used to making a meal of the Tory government's problems. In September 1994, though, it extended its menu to European politics. Referring to statements by the French Prime Minister and the ruling German Conservative Parties CDU and CSU calling for a new structure of the European Union that would entail a division of the Community into several 'tiers' or 'circles' of political and economic integration, the paper's political commentator Martin Kettle saw a new menu being offered at the EU 'restaurant': "Europe à la carte" was his summary of the proposals (*The Guardian* [from now on quoted as *G*] 3 September 1994). A week afterwards, the *Economist* joined in the culinary feast with a cover page that showed a plate with the EU symbolic stars, and the motto: "All you can eat" as well as a 'menu' presenting the dishes on offer: "Monetary, Social, Defence, Agriculture, Regional, Fiscal, Foreign" (*The Economist*, 10 September 1994). The leading article inside took up the menu metaphor, interpreting and differentiating it further by distinguishing the British ideas about a new EU structure as an 'à la carte' model from the more dirigistic French and German plans for a prescribed 'table d'hôte course' of European integration leaving little room for individual variation.

Although the metaphors of different 'courses', 'tiers', 'circles' or 'speeds' of political integration in Europe were at that time clearly designated as having 'international' status, their pragmatic-political meanings seemed to differ substantially in different languages. The metaphor of several 'tiers', for instance, was openly attacked by the British Prime Minister John Major in a speech in Leiden, Netherlands, on 7

September 1994, denouncing it as "dangerous" and as coming near to the negative Orwellian vision of "a union in which some [EU member states] would be more equal than others" (quoted after *Daily Telegraph*, 8 September 1994). Some German commentators saw this reading as a wrong interpretation, if not as a malicious misrepresentation of the CDU/CSU-statement (which had been published as a discussion paper), pointing out that only a few months before Major himself had advocated a "multi-track, multi-speed, multi-layered Europe".[2] In a parliamentary speech the next day, Helmut Kohl, the German Chancellor, insisted Germany did not want the "[European] convoy's speed to be dictated by the slowest vessel", but on the contrary desired a fully integrated "political union in Europe" (*Daily Telegraph*, 8 September 1994). And again a few days later, the then French president, François Mitterrand, joined the fray and distanced himself from his own Prime Minister's use of the "variable geometry" version of the multi-circled Europe concept, outlining an alternative concept for "Europe as a confederation" (*G*, 10 September 1994). Why all this fuss about a figure of speech that might, at first sight, seem to be an innocent enough description of the different aspects of the process of European integration? After all, the metaphor versions in the various European languages were literal translations of each other, with the 'à la carte' option also being an internationally accepted loanphrase from French, employed in its original form by both English and German media.

Common terminologies: bridges or walls in international communication?

International expressions, or "internationalisms",[3] which are typical of international political debate, can create special communicative problems. Terms that look or sound similar in different languages and are recognizable as etymologically 'related' expressions, such as 'democracy', 'constitution', 'capitalism', often carry different meaning aspects in their different realizations in various languages, and thus can add to problems of cross-national communication, as their outward similarity seems to suggest the existence of a 'common ground' for understanding which does not in fact exist. In today's political discussions in Europe, the case of 'federalism'/'Föderalismus'/'fédéralisme' illustrates such differences between the variants of a seemingly 'international' terminology. Whilst 'federalism', as used in public discourse in Britain, has some meaning aspects that liken it to the concept of *centralism*, these features are not as important, and often specifically excluded for the French and German terms 'fédéralisme'/'Föderalismus'.[4] The mismatch between British and continental versions of 'federalism' became an international issue in late 1991 when, at the last minute of the negotiations for the Treaty on European Union, the British government insisted on the erasure of the term 'federal', in all its versions in the EC languages, from the official text of the treaty, because using it gave "an unnecessarily wide field of competence to the community on social, industrial and cultural issues" (*G*, 11 November 1991). The British hostility to that particular term surprised some continental commentators. The German newspaper *Frankfurter Rundschau*, for instance, reported that, due to British pressure, the "dreaded F-word" had been eliminated from the treaty and had been replaced by the paraphrase of an "ever closer union of European nations" - "whatever that is supposed to mean", was the somewhat disenchanted commentary by the author of the article.[5]

In the months leading up to the signing of the treaty, British politicians and media had used the term 'f-word', which ordinarily refers to the most taboo one of all 'four-letter-words'[6], to express their disgust and horror at European 'federalism' in the sense of 'centralism' as a threat to British sovereignty, an idea that seemed to obsess particularly the so-called 'Eurosceptic' wing of the Tory Party.[7] How dangerous the f-word was thought to be can be glimpsed from a cartoon by Peter Clarke in the *Guardian* of 28 June 1991, which showed Prime Minister Major trying to cross the channel so as to join EC-Europe. In the water, three shark fins are visible with the labels "ERM", "ECU" and "F-word" painted on them, there was also the head of Major's predecessor Margaret Thatcher, who appeared to have just been killed by the Euro-beasts. On the same day, in the *New Statesman & Society*, the pro-EC leader of the Liberal Democrats, Paddy Ashdown, defended the "F-word" against alleged attempts by both the Conservative government and the Labour opposition to confuse the meaning of 'federalism' so as to hide their own centralist orientations. In the *Observer*, Michael Ignatieff contended that signing the Maastricht Treaty would take "Britain another step towards a federal Europe" in any case - the "F-word may or may not be in it".[8] However, the British media's perspective of the 'federalism'-word was by now simply parochial. As early as in June 1991 *The Guardian* quoted an adviser to the German Chancellor, who highlighted the discrepancy between the British fear of 'federalism' as "a concept that could lead to more centralism" and the Germans' understanding of 'Föderalismus' as meaning "exactly the opposite"; *The Guardian* also reported that the then president of the EC commission, Jacques Delors, defined 'federalism' in neutral terms as a "system of co-ordination of autonomous activity of a number of superimposed entities", but that he was willing to 'surrender' the word to the British side and at the same time still keep the content: "The label doesn't matter, what matters is what is in the bottle" (*G*, 28 June 1991). This strategy was put in practice by the then Dutch Prime Minister, Ruud Lubbers, leading the negotiations in Maastricht, who 'traded' the term 'federalism' for British concessions on some substantive points of the Treaty (*G*, 28 June 1991, 1 July 1991).

Does this make the 'föderal-federal-fédéral' terminology a case of 'false friends' ('faux amis'), in which high degree of similarity on the expression side of the variants in different languages is not matched on the content side, as, for instance, in German 'sensibel' and French 'sensible' (= "sensitive") versus English 'sensible', or, on the political level, 'Chancellor' (of the Exchequer) being the title of the Finance minister in Britain and 'Kanzler' in German being the title of the head of government?9 Such false friends descriptions are based on a semantic model that assumes stable definitions for 'core' meanings of the words in question (which then are mistakenly identified by naive language learners). But the assumption of such single stable meaning units does not work for 'federal' because its vagueness, allowing for different interpretations is an essential characteristic, as it is typical for the terminology of political debate in general, due to its interdependence with socio-economic change.10 Partly polysemous and vague terms may be anathema for scientists looking for well-defined terms denoting one and only one referent, but they are useful for politicians who employ them in order to gloss over embarrassing differences of opinion or potential conflicts at a particular point in time. Thus, the show-fight over 'federalism' in the Maastricht Treaty in 1991 gave the British government an opportunity to placate the Eurosceptic wing of the Tory Party with the 'concession' from the partner states to surrender that term in the Treaty text; and similar tactics were being employed in the election campaign for the new European Parliament in 1994, when the Tory Party Chairman Norman Fowler used it to stigmatize the Labour and Liberal Democrat Parties' manifestoes. Later, again to the applause of the Tory right, it was a handy label to be put on the Belgian Prime Minster Jean-Luc Dehaene who was barred by a British veto from becoming the successor of Delors as president of the EU Commission because of alleged excessively strong 'federalist' sympathies.11

However, the use of 'federalism' in its pejorative meaning could also be an embarrassment the British government, when they wanted to play to the pro-European side. In October 1993, for instance, the British leader of the Conservative group in the European parliament, Sir Christopher Prout, reminded government officials that Tory MEPs "wanted it established that the F-word" was "either banned or always interpreted", in order to prevent conservative 'Euro-bashers' from denouncing it as meaning a European "super-state", whilst conservative MEPs employed it as referring to the opposite aspect of 'decentralisation', in line with uses of 'federalism' cognates in other European countries (*G*, 15 October 1993). Nevertheless, an unambiguous and fixed definition of 'federalism' would perhaps not be in the interest of the Tory government, as it would remove the opportunity to fit their usage to changing circumstances and political priorities. Its vagueness makes the Euro 'f-word' a convenient terminological test-case to try out various interpretations without a commitment to a definitive answer to the question of whether a future Union should take the form of a 'superstate', in which the old nation states retained only the status of provinces or regions, or whether it should be a looser 'confederation' of principally independent countries, which for reasons of convenience cooperate in some areas of common political or economic interest. This might help to explain why the Tories continued to use 'federalism' as an important Euro-word even after its elimination from the Maastricht Treaty, as the use of this term will not bind them to a particular policy, while at the same time giving them space to be seen "at the heart", if not of Europe itself, then at least of the European debate.

The debate about cohesion of the European Union is not inextricably tied to 'federal' and its cognates, of course. In Germany, for instance, it is being conducted under the heading of a pair of antonyms: 'Bundesstaat', 'Staatenbund'.[12] But 'federalism', as an internationalism that exists in many different languages, serves all sides as a convenient focus to try out the different versions of the future European structure that need to be discussed widely and publicly if there is to be a legitimate political reformulation of European identity across the EU member states. The quotations of reflections on the term 'federal' in the Maastricht negotiations showed that at least some European politicians and media know very well which are the semantic nuances of 'federal'/'fédéral'/'föderal' etc. in the respective European languages. Thus, the superficial similarity of 'federal'-words can be utilized so as to hide substantial differences of opinion and political strategy under the blanket term of a 'federal Europe', which means different things to each of the 'partners'. A tongue-in-cheek illustration of such a bogus 'agreement' was presented in a cartoon in the *Guardian* on 9 July 1994, showing the British, French and German 'heads' of government with thought bubbles stating each one's understanding of the 'f-word'. To Kohl, 'Federalismus' [sic] means "The Principle that Germany runs Europe", to Major it is the same - "unless we stop it [Germany]", and Mitterand's 'Federalisme' [sic] is being explained as the "Principle that France will run along behind Germany".[13] This cartoon would be pointless if it could not be understood as an allusion to the strategic uses that Major, Kohl und Mitterrand made of their respective 'federalism'-words so as to create a politically convenient terminological agreement over potentially dangerous political ground. Such word-play may seem frivolous, but if its usage were consensus-orientated, it might help to 'talk' Europe - rather than, as so often in the past, force it - into a union.

International metaphors: images à la carte?

Metaphorical phrases shared by different languages may appear, at first sight, to be less likely to become the objects of such 'definition battles' as individual terms, as their lexical elements are translated, thus creating a rough word-for-word equivalent. There seem to be no essential meaning differences, for instance, between the variants of popular 'international' metaphors, such as 'fortress Europe'/'Festung Europa', 'the European house'/'das Gemeinsame Haus Europa' or the image of European integration as a 'journey' or 'Reise'.[14] The concrete aspect of such imagery lends itself also to pictorial translation by cartoonists into the universal language of caricature. The 'journey' or 'transport' image as an illustration of the process of European integration in particular, inspired many articles and cartoons, e.g.: in 1990, of Germany's Kohl and France's Mitterrand as riders on the front horses of the EC-coach, driven by Delors, with Britain's Thatcher as an irate, but helpless passenger on the backseat (*The Economist*, 5 May 1990). The 'transport' image is so well established in many European languages, that parts of its conceptual frame have become dead, lexicalized metaphors, some of which were employed also in the EU context, such as, in English: 'the path/road to Europe' (or, in 1991, to Maastricht)[15] or, in German, 'die Weichen [für Europa/die europäische Integration] stellen' (= to determine points of reference for new developments, literally, 'to set railway points').[16]

Whilst such lexicalized background metaphors[17] are politically relatively uncontroversial, the phrase of a 'two-speed Europe', also taken from the field of 'transport' metaphors, has proved to be more contentious. The 'two speeds' or, as often used, 'two tiers', refer to the differing time schedules for social, economic and political integration of the EU, with one group of states moving swiftly towards a unified Europe, leaving others 'behind' that might join in this process later. This image was especially useful for those critics of the British government's 'sceptic' approach to Europe who tried to encourage a 'faster' integration. Thus, *New Statesman & Society* criticized the Tory government for putting Britain in the 'second tier' of the European Community, condemning her "to 'track' the policies of the first-tier countries" (16 November 1990). Almost a year later, during the Maastricht negotiations, *The Guardian* warned against Britain being "cast in the second rank of a two-tier monetary Europe", if Major failed to "join the new system of locked exchange rates" (6 September 1991). In reports on the last stages of the Maastricht negotiations, the hierarchical notion implied in the 'two tier' phrase was integrated in the frame of the 'transport' metaphor.

After Britain had secured the acknowledgement of its special right to reserve its decision on monetary union for future legislation (in addition to the elimination of the 'f-word'), Will Hutton, the *Guardian's* economic correspondent, commented on this "opt-out" clause: "This is the two speed Europe that EC leaders have continually said they are against" (11 December 1991). Similarly, the German *Frankfurter Rundschau* (12 December 1991) asked: "and this is supposed not to be a two-speed Europe?"[18] However, here it was not the British 'opt-out' from the currency union, but of the Social Chapter, which, again as a concession to the British side, had been excluded from the text of the treaty proper and made into a separate extra protocol, signed by all other governments. The German weekly *Die Zeit* also saw the United Kingdom 'lagging' behind the rest of the EC countries in regard to social policy integration.[19] In both German texts, the social aspect is seen as an integral part of the process towards European Union. The *Rundschau* report uses it as the point of reference for the rhetorical question of whether the British opt-out was 'not' constituting a 'two-speed Europe'; in the *Zeit*-article, social policy was given at least the same weight as the financial side. In contrast to this, the 'two-tier'/'two-speed' images used by *The Guardian* and *New Statesman & Society*, only concern the monetary aspect. It would be rash, though, to conclude that the contrast of reference to social versus financial policies constitutes the main difference between British and German usages of the 'two-tier'/'two-speed' metaphor. On other occasions, British newspapers, too, made use of the 'two-speed' imagery in reporting and commenting on Britain's social opt-out.[20]

The differences between British and German usage of the 'two-speed'-image increased further, however, in Euro-debates after 1991. When the Pound Sterling was forced out of the European Exchange Rate Mechanism on 16 September 1992 (popularly dubbed 'Black Wednesday'), the then Chancellor of the Exchequer, Norman Lamont, became in the eyes of Eurosceptics a "neo-Thatcherite hero" who "had freed the pound" and had "opened the road to a Ridleyite two-tier Europe" (*G*, 26 September 1992).[21] The 'two-tier' concept now was attractive even for continental politicians and commentators who had rejected it previously. On 28 September 1992, *The Guardian* quoted German parliamentarians from SPD and CDU as well as the former president of the Bundesbank, Karl Otto Pöhl, arguing for a distinction between an "inner core" or "fast track" group of European countries that would move quickly towards monetary union, and other countries, notably the United Kingdom, that would have the option to join later. The same quotations were used by *Die Welt* that day, asking if France and Germany "should go it alone", building the advance party of an "Europa der zwei Geschwindigkeiten". On 25 September 1992, in a front page article in *Die Zeit,* Theo Sommer had already argued that the 'slower' EC member states should not hold up the 'faster moving' ones, reinterpreting the 'two-speed' image through an analogy with a convoy. As if suspecting that this scenario (and its peculiar version of the fastest ships leaving the others behind - in contrast to usual practice) might be offensive to non-German European nations that had relied on supplies from convoys in periods of the 20th century when Germany had tried to assume hegemonial power on the Continent, Sommer combined this 'convoy' image with the more abstract concept of a "variable Geometrie" as the new structuring principle for the EC.[22]

The 'convoy' metaphor was taken up by Chancellor Kohl in a speech quoted by *The Guardian* on 28 October 1992: "We don't want a two-or-three-speed Europe [...] but nor do we want a Europe in which the speed of the slower ship determines the pace of the entire convoy." This phrase, which Kohl also used in a letter published in the *Financial Times* on 4 January 1993, appears to contain an odd contradiction. If there are 'faster' and 'slower' ships in a convoy and if the slower ones are not to hold up the leaders, we are confronted with exactly the different-speed scenario, which Kohl explicitly rejects in the first part of his statement. Assuming that this violation of what in H. Paul Grice's theory of "conversational implicatures" is called the Maxim of Manner: "avoid ambiguity",[23] one can deduce that the German Chancellor was being deliberately ambiguous in order to convey a message of warning to potential 'slower ships' in the convoy, and at the same time avoiding committing himself to the phrase of the 'two speed Europe'.[24] His warning is all the more poignant because he introduces the new notion of a 'two-or-three-speed Europe', albeit in the denial part of his statement. Thus, a 'more-than-two speed' scenario has become the main issue, instead of the two-way-division that previously had structured uses of the 'tier/speed'-imagery. Was there a possibility - however remote - of Britain falling back to a 'third' rank in the EC? If Kohl was too diplomatic to fully assert this implicature, one Bundesbank board member was not so shy. In an article published in *Die Zeit* on 29 October 1993, Ulrich Cartellieri openly argued for the formation of two main groups within the EU, with an extra set of one 'left behind'. In his opinion, France and Germany should move swiftly towards monetary union, with other 'hard currency' states to follow suit. Italy and Spain were deemed not to be capable of joining this group immediately due to their slower ('second') speed, but Cartellieri was convinced that they were committed to 'catching up' with it later. Only Britain, whose government 'did not want such a community at all', was the 'odd man out', thus constituting an extra 'tier' of Europe all by herself.[25]

Alternatively, instead of the hierarchical notion, the notion of more than two 'tracks/speeds' of European integration could also be used to emphasize differences between principally equal approaches to the Union. It was this version of a multitude of tracks that the British government chose to make it their motto for the campaign in the elections to the European Parliament in the summer of 1994. Prime Minister Major now sang the praises of "a third European path besides total integration and a two-speed Europe, one which involved different alliances of states choosing to opt out on different issues. [...] A multi-speed, multi-track, multi-layered Europe was a Conservative idea in line with the mood of the people everywhere" (*G*, 1 June 1994). But the Prime Minister's idea, supposedly 'in line' with everyone's mood, was immediately challenged by the political opponents. Labour's response came in the form of 'football' imagery: their election campaign co-ordinator, Jack Cunningham, portrayed Major as being "willing to offer voluntary relegation to the second division in Europe" (*G*, 1 June 1994); the Liberal leader and "F-word" defender

Ashdown admonished the Government that it ought to play "a full part in shaping Europe's future" rather than prepare "for Britain being in the outer lane" (*G*, 3 June 1994). There was no open dissent within Major's cabinet, but attempts to defend a pro-European interpretation against the applause from the Eurosceptics who had seen it as an endorsement of their favourite idea of minimal integration; thus, the Environment Secretary, John Gummer, stressed that the Premier's words had meant that Britain "was not going to be at a slower speed than the rest of Europe" (*G*, 7 June 1994). Despite such attempts at semantic damage-limitation, the Tory governments' stance towards full British commitment for Europe was perceived as being at least scepticist, if not totally negative; it earned them a disastrous election result of only 27 per cent. Neither did Major's veto at the Corfu summit meeting in late June 1994, against Jean-Luc Dehaene's candidacy for the presidency of the EU commission, help to convey an image of Britain being in the 'fast Euro-lane'. On the contrary, the perception of the British government as 'slowing down' the speed of European decisions had gained so much ground internationally by this time, that the Foreign Secretary, Douglas Hurd, had to reiterate the pro-European interpretation of Major's "multi-track" speech in order to avoid being branded as being hostile to Europe. The phrase of the "multi-track, multi-speed, multi-layered Europe", he claimed, had "clearly struck a chord, not just in Britain", but had nothing to do with a notion of Europe "as one in which there would be a highly integrated core with other countries left on the periphery", leading to "second class citizenship for countries outside a chosen few" (*G*, 2 July 1994). But the need to reiterate this interpretation exposed the problematic status of the 'multi-speed' metaphor resulting from its contradictory implications of being committed to European integration and at the same time having a 'track' of one's own.[26]

Why then, one may wonder, did Major make use of the 'multi-track' slogan at all and risk humiliation in elections and conflict with the EU partners? - just in order to sweet-talk some 'Europhobes' or 'Eurosceptics' in the Tory Party? Their (temporary) pacification certainly did play a role in the British government's strategy, but the main problem Major and Hurd were facing was that of regaining some initiative in the debate on European Union so as to avoid being completely sidelined or excluded from it. Since 1990, the 'two speed/tier' metaphor had increasingly become a catchphrase in the discussions on European integration both in the British public and on the diplomatic level. Since 1992/93, the German government had combined official denials of the 'two-or-more speed' image with thinly veiled warnings to 'slower' EU countries being 'left behind' by the EU core countries. There was no chance to protest officially against this undeclared policy as long as the two-speed metaphor remained a sub-text of Euro-debates, officially appearing only in denials. Moreover, a strong part of the Tory party that had been the driving force behind Britain's several opt-outs, favoured the isolationist notion, thus helping the two-speed metaphor almost to become a self-fulfilling prophecy. Tentatively, I would therefore interpret the British government's enthusiasm for the 'multi-track' slogan in summer 1994 as an attempt to kill two birds with one stone: placate the 'Eurosceptics' at home and regain the initiative in the international debate by starting a debate about the 'multi-speed' metaphor that could replace the two-way distinction and thus give them room for political manoeuvres and interpretation.

The row, in September 1994, over the above mentioned German CDU/CSU's 'discussion paper' that openly argued for the 'hard core' moving ahead on European economic and political integration,[27] seems to corroborate this conclusion. Major now could, and did, claim that his 'multi-track' idea was less problematic than the CDU's Euro-elitist position. Of course, the continental politicians had their own multi-layered agendas for using the 'core'-metaphors, as the *Guardian's* commentator Martin Woolacott acknowledged:

> There has to be a distinction here between rational arguments about the future of Europe and populist recipes for the winning of elections. The trouble is that one level of communication borrows from the other, and the prime task must be to disentangle them. At the rational level, most serious people in all member countries of the European Union have for some time assumed that the solution must lie in some kind of multi-speed system for the future. But Helmut Kohl and Edouard Balladur, both involved in vital election campaigns, are not running a think tank, but crafting signals to their electorates that they think will be successful. The signal in each case is of a return to the old Europe of the Six, but shedding a worryingly different Italy, [...] (*G*, 14 September 1994).

It thus became obvious that the British government was not the only one of the EU governments that was prepared to play to Eurosceptic parts of the public by using vague terminologies and metaphors in crucial debates. It would be both unrealistic and futile, I think, to chide them for this language use, as it is the only one that can serve several purposes at the same time. All governments have to play to the 'home' public, as well as to particular factions within the ruling party or coalition, and, in addition to this, they have to keep, and possibly gain, some bargaining ground for immediate and future negotiations with the other 'partner' governments. As in the case of international 'federalist' terminology, semantic vagueness proves to be an essential functional element for the use of metaphors in such debates. The semantic indeterminacy of the metaphor field of 'tracks'/'tiers'/'speeds'-images gave all participants opportunities to make their respective political preferences and inclinations known, whilst keeping several options open. Thus it was possible to use and discuss freely dichotomic 'two-tiers' images, hierarchical as well as non-hierarchical versions of 'more-than-two tiers' models, dynamic images of 'speeds' and more static 'geometric' concepts of 'circles' or 'core' and 'periphery'; even the 'pick-and-choose' version of a loose EU-confederation seemed more palatable, if dressed up as an 'à la carte' menu.

Conclusion

The differences of interpretation and evaluation of these metaphorical Eurovisions were not semantic shortcomings or pragmatic mishaps, but constituted the main purpose of the debates. A description of 'fédéral'/'föderal'/'federal' or of the 'tier/speed'-metaphors as false friends on the grounds of difference in their interpretation in national debates would not capture the politico-semantic function of these terms and phrases. Their meaning differences cannot be explained exclusively as the contrast between one interpretation in German and a different one in English, or among more than one interpretation in either language; nor is it just a case of confusion or misunderstanding between opposing interpretations that can be solved by 'proper' translation or consistent usage of this term by politicians. It is precisely its vagueness and polysemic potential that make 'federalism' or the 'multi-track' phrase prominent symbols of political differences among British and continental politicians on the issue of European integration. The meaning contrasts of the 'Federalism'-words and 'tracks', 'lanes', 'tiers' and 'menus' in the different national debates express different underlying systems of reference and discourse traditions, i.e. those in which transfer of central legislaive and perhaps also executive powers from a national government to EC bodies has long since been regarded as an aim and even as a probable outcome of the EEC-/EC-/EU-process since the 1950s, and those discourse traditions, of which the British Euro-debate is but one example, where such an objective is seen as a possibly problematic or even dangerous topic. The only way to combat these dangers seems to me to lie not in a stigmatization of these terminologies or metaphors, but in explaining and discussing them up to a point when their implications for political recipes have become clear to all those sitting round the European table, ready to participate in the communal dinner or lunch.

Notes

1 Parts of this paper have been presented to the 1994 ISSEI conference at Graz University, Austria. I wish to express my thanks to the British Academy for their support for the preparation of the Graz presentation.

2 Cf. e.g. *Die Zeit*, 9 September 1994 and especially in the following week: "John Major hat den CDU/CSU-Fraktionstext, den er doch gelesen haben will, entweder nicht verstanden oder plump verfälscht. Dort heißt es klipp und klar: 'Die Kerneuropa-Gruppe muß prinzipiell allen EU-Mitgliedern -

vor allem dem Gründungsmitglied Italien, aber auch Spanien und selbstverständlich Großbritannien - ihre uneingeschränkte Bereitschaft glaubhaft machen, sie einzubeziehen, sobald sie bestimmte derzeitige Probleme gelöst haben und soweit ihre Bereitschaft reicht, sich in dem beschriebenen Sinne zu engagieren'." (*Die Zeit*, 16 September 1994).

3   For discussions of linguistic internationalisms cf. Braun, Schaeder and Volmert, 1990; and Barbour and Stevenson, 1990, p. 257; for 'ism'-words as a special semantic group of international expressions cf. Strauß, Haß and Harras, 1989, pp. 188 ff.

4   French and German dictionaries, for intance, refer to 'centralisme'/'Zentralismus' as antonyms of 'fédéralisme' and 'Föderalismus', cf. Robert, 1977, p. 767; Duden, 1982, pp. 256-7. Moreover, in French, 'fédéralisme', 'fédéraliste' have specific historical overtones, dating back to the French Revolution, when they were used by the Jacobins as terms of accusation against their internal enemies (cf. Cellard, 1989, pp. 199-207). In English, 'federal' appears to be a partly polysemous lexeme that allows for several interpretations, which may contradict each other with respect to the 'centralist' aspect. Thus, the *Concise Oxford Dictionary* (1979, p. 381) has as the two main definitions of 'federal': "1. Of a system of government in which several States form a unity but remain independent in internal affairs; concerning this whole and not the separate parts. 2. Relating to or favouring central government, as distinct from government by separate provinces etc."

5   *Frankfurter Rundschau*, 12 December 1991: "Überraschung nach der Beichtstuhl-Runde. [...] [Es] wurde das 'gefürchtete F-Wort', genau wie Major beim Eintreffen am Tagungsort prophezeit hatte, aus dem Vertragsentwurf zur Europäischen Union eliminiert: deren 'föderale Ausrichtung'. Ersetzt wurde der Begriff durch das komplizierte Gebilde 'immer engere Union der Völker Europas, in der Entscheidungen so nah wie möglich an den Bürgern getroffen werden' - was immer das konkret bedeuten mag." Another German daily newspaper, *Die Welt*, presented the British 'centralist' interpretation as a result of terminological confusion or misinterpretation on the part of English speakers: "Das jenseits des Kanals irrtümlicherweise als zentralistisch abgelehnte Wort 'Föderalismus' verschwand aus der Vertragsvorlage" (11 November 1991).

6   Cf. McDonald, 1988, p. 56; Thorne, 1994, p. 193.

7   *The Guardian* referred to these reactions as "Pavlovian responses of British Conservative politicians, who see in European federalism the shadow of a centralised super-state," evoking "puzzlement in the EC" (*G*, 19 June 1991).

8   Cf. *Observer*, 17 November 1991: "Grand illusions of the island race". For further usages of *federalism* in this sense in the British press at the time of the Maastricht discussions cf. also *G*, 11 November 1991; *The Times*, 27 November 1991; *European*, 21 June 1991.

9   For analyses of false friends in European languages, especially between English and German, cf. Malone, 1985; and Wandruzska, 1990, pp. 16f., pp. 121f.

10 For discussions of the functional vagueness as a characteristic of political language use cf. Wilson, 1990, pp. 77ff.; Townson, 1992, pp. 28ff.

11   Cf. *G*, 24 February 1994: "Fowler predicts jobs famine in 'federal Europe'", *G*, 28 February 1994: "Lib Dems ready for 'federalist' election charge"; *G*, 2 May 1994: "Federalism's final farewell", *G*, 12 July 1994: "Weak candidate leads Euro-field".

12   For the discussion between German Europhobes on the right wing of the CDU/CSU (calling for no more than a 'Staatenbund') and the 'Unionists' (calling for a 'Bundeststaat' after the model of the USA) cf. e.g. *Die Zeit*, 5 November 1993, 12 November 1993, *Der Spiegel*, 13 December 1993, *Frankfurter Allgemeine Zeitung*, 15 December 1993.

13   For an earlier version of such caricaturization of Euro-terminology cf. "Eurospeak: a beginners' phrasebook" in *The Guardian*, 22 June 1991 with the following definitions: "Federalism: Building a United States of Europe. Confederalism: What they do in Switzerland. Federalisme: Building a Europe that is run by the French (translates what they do in Switzerland). Föderalismus: Moving the German parliament down the Rhine from Bonn to Strasbourg (on the Swiss model)."

14   For the range of metaphors employed in German debates on Europe cf. Bachem and Battke, 1991; Vogt, 1991; and Schäffner, 1993. The 'journey' imagery is by no means restricted to European topics, but belongs in the wider field of *transport* metaphors focusing on developmental aspects of political processes. Thus, for instance, the media often portrayed German unification as a 'train journey' with varying 'passengers', 'engine drivers', 'points', 'stations', 'starting times', 'routes' and 'destinations' (cf. Schäffner, 1991).

15   Cf. e.g.: *G*, 3 October 1991, 30 October 1991, 13 November 1991, 26 November 1991, 3 December 1991, 10 December 1992, 4 January 1993; for the German media cf. *Die Zeit*, 13 December 1991; *Der Spiegel*, 16 December 1991: "Über den Rubikon". For discussions of the notion of metaphorical frames cf. Lakoff and Johnson, 1980, pp. 87ff.; Lakoff, 1988, pp. 135ff; and Schäffner, in this volume.

16   Cf. e.g. *Frankfurter Allgemeine Zeitung*, 12 August 1989; *Die Zeit*, 6 December 1991; *Die Welt*, 9 December 1991.

17   For the distinction of 'weak' background versus salient metaphors in public discourse cf. Küster, 1983; and Musolff, 1993.

18   *Frankfurter Rundschau*, 12 December 1991: "Und das soll, wie Kohl und Major unisono beteuern, kein Europa der zwei Geschwindigkeiten sein?"

19   *Die Zeit*, 13 December 1991: "Großbritannien [...] wird den möglichen Fortschritt in der europäischen Sozialpolitik, wie schon in der Wirtschafts- und Währungsunion, wenn überhaupt, nur mit Verspätung fördern."

20   Cf. e.g. *G*, 1 July 1991 and 13 October 1993.

21   The term 'Ridleyite' referred to Thatcher's robustly anti-European Minister for Trade and Industry, Nicholas Ridley, who was forced to resign after polemically attacking the EC and in particular France and Germany.

22   *Die Zeit* was not the first German newspaper to use the 'convoy' metaphor; *Die Welt*, for instance, had argued for an 'advance group of nations to sail on', on 11 December 1991: "Es kommt, wie es immer gekommen ist: Wirtschaft und Währung eilen voraus, die Politik folgt hintennach. Der Geleitzug der Europäischen Union - so heißt das Gesamtwerk nun - ist

auseinandergerissen. Die schnellsten Schiffe, Deutschland und Frankreich, haben sich das Privileg gesichert, das Ziel einheitlicher Währung von 1998 an allein anzukreuzen, falls die Mehrheit dazu 1997 nicht bereit ist."

23 Cf. Grice, 1975, p. 46, pp. 54ff.; and Levinson, 1983, pp. 112ff.

24 In further statements from the same period, Kohl avoided mentioning 'zwei Geschwindigkeiten', while still conveying the 'convoy'-message. Commenting on 'delays' of ratification of the Maastricht Treaty on the part of Britain and Denmark, he said that if ratification was not completed by all twelve EC states within six months, the Community would "go ahead to pursue European unity with 10 nations" (*G*, 23 February 1993). *The Guardian* pointed out that Kohl's statement "was all the more significant", for until then he had insisted on ratification by all member states as a precondition for any implementation of the Treaty, while some German government officials had already unofficially endorsed "French talk of a two-tier EC" (*G*, 23 February 1993).

25 Cf. Die Zeit, 29 October 1993: "Und dies ist die politische Dimension der Währungsunion: Sie muß gewollt werden. Die übrigen Länder des bisherigen Hartwährungsblocks - die Benelux-Staaten, Dänemark und gegebenenfalls Irland - sollten und können hier von Anfang an einbezogen werden. [...] Italien [...] wird sich einem solchen frühen Vorstoß zur Währungsunion derzeit nicht anschließen können. Dennoch gibt es jetzt auch dort Unterstützung für diese Idee. Bei nüchterner Analyse sollte auch Spanien seine Aversion gegen ein Vorgehen in zwei Geschwindigkeiten überwinden können. [...] Daß die jetzige britische Regierung eine solche Gemeinschaft nicht mehr will - sich und ihre Bevölkerung in der kurzsichtigen Annahme wiegend, der Konjunkturanschub durch die Abwertung des Pfundes belege die Richtigkeit diese Politik -, darf die Kontinentaleuropäer nicht daran hindern, aufgrund ihrer geschichtlichen Erfahrungen als dicht beieinanderlebende Nachbarvölker diese Gemeinschaft mit aller Kraft anzustreben." For further uses of the two-speed image in 1993 cf. e.g. Hugo Young in *The Guardian*, 2 November 1993 and Giovanni Spadolini (president of the Italian Senate) in *Die Zeit*, 3 December 1993.

26 Immediately after Major's *multi-track* speech Young, in *The Guardian*, had already identified this dilemma: the Prime Minister's claim that Britain could "opt for the slowest speed while still decisively influencing the direction and velocity of the fastest" was irrealistic, and "one day the choice between the centre and the fringe" would "become inescapable" (*G*, 2 June 1994).

27 Cf. *G*, 10 September 1994, *Daily Telegraph*, 8 September 1994.

References

Bachem, Rolf and Battke, Kathleen (1991), 'Strukturen und Funktionen der Metapher *Unser Gemeinsames Haus Europa* im aktuellen politischen Diskurs' in Liedtke, Frank, Wengeler, Martin and Böke, Karin (eds), *Begriffe besetzen. Strategien des Sprachgebrauchs in der Politik*, Westdeutscher Verlag, Opladen, pp. 295-307.

Barbour, Stephen and Stevenson, Patrick (1990), *Variation in German*, Cambridge University Press, Cambridge.
Braun, Peter, Schaeder, Burkhard and Volmert, Johannes (eds) (1990), *Internationalismen: Studien zur interlingualen Lexikologie und Lexikographie*, Niemeyer, Tübingen.
Cellard, Jacques (1989), *Ah! ça ira ça ira ... Ces Mots que nous devons à la Révolution*, Balland, Paris.
Concise Oxford Dictionary (1979), 6th ed., Oxford University Press, Oxford.
Duden (1982), *Fremdwörterbuch*, Bibliographisches Institut, Mannheim, Wien and Zürich.
Grice, H. Paul (1975), 'Logic and Conversation' in Cole, Peter and Morgan, Jerry L. (eds), *Syntax and Semantics 3, Speech acts*, Academic Press, New York, San Francisco and London, pp. 41-58.
Küster, Rainer (1983), 'Politische Metaphorik', *Sprache und Literatur*, vol. 51, pp. 30-45.
Lakoff, George (1988), 'Cognitive Semantics', in Eco, Umberto et al. (eds), *Meaning and Mental Representations*, Indiana University Press, Bloomington and Indianapolis, pp. 119-54.
Lakoff, George and Johnson, Mark (1980), *Metaphors we Live by*, University of Chicago Press, Chicago.
Levinson, Stephen C. (1983), *Pragmatics*, Cambridge University Press, Cambridge.
Malone, Dagmar E. (1985), '"Faux amis" in English and German' in Brunt, Richard J. and Enninger, Werner (eds), *Interdisciplinary Perspectives at Cross-Cultural Communication*, Rader (Alano), Aachen, pp. 103-18.
McDonald, James (1988), *A Dictionary of Obscenity, Taboo and Euphemism*, Sphere Books, London.
Musolff, Andreas (1993), 'Die Sprache der Medien und wirtschaftliche "Realitäten" - Sprachgebrauch in öffentlichen Debatten um den Daimler-Benz-Konzern' in Grewenig, Adi (ed.), *Inszenierte Kommunikation*, Westdeutscher Verlag, Opladen, pp. 31-55.
Robert, Paul (1977), *Dictionnaire Alphabétique & Analogique de la Langue Française (Le Petit Robert)*, Dictionnaire Le Robert, Paris.
Schäffner, Christina (1991), 'Der Zug zur deutschen Einheit', *Sprachreport*, no. 4, pp. 1-3.
Schäffner, Christina (1993), 'Die europäische Architektur - Metaphern der Einigung Europas in der deutschen, britischen und amerikanischen Presse' in Grewenig, Adi (ed.), *Inszenierte Kommunikation*, Westdeutscher Verlag, Opladen, pp. 13-30.
Strauß, Gerhart, Haß, Ulrike and Harras, Gisela (1989), *Brisante Wörter von Agitation bis Zeitgeist: Ein Lexikon zum öffentlichen Sprachgebrauch*, de Gruyter, Berlin and New York.
Thorne, Tony (1994), *Dictionary of Modern Slang*, Bloomsbury, London.
Townson, Michael (1992), *Mother-Tongue and Fatherland. Language and Politics in German*, Manchester University Press, Manchester.

Vogt, Rüdiger (1991), 'Die Karriere "Europas". Vom Eigennamen zum europäischen Schlagwort' in Liedtke, Frank, Wengeler, Martin and Böke, Karin (eds), *Begriffe besetzen. Strategien des Sprachgebrauchs in der Politik,* Westdeutscher Verlag, Opladen, pp. 276-94.

Wandruszka, Mario (1990), *Die europäische Sprachengemeinschaft,* Francke, Tübingen.

Wilson, John (1990), *Politically Speaking,* Blackwell, Oxford.

Building a European House? Or at Two Speeds into a Dead End? Metaphors in the Debate on the United Europe

CHRISTINA SCHÄFFNER

Introduction

> British political life bristles with ephemeral wittering about Europe. Are we *at the heart* of it? Can we *leave* it? Is *it moving towards us or we towards it*? (*The Guardian*, 6 May 1994)

This quotation from *The Guardian* reflects in a very succinct way the various arguments that were (and are) in use in political debates about Europe. As a linguist I am interested in how political discussions and political concepts are reflected in language, and how language, i.e. texts, reflect underlying cognitive and conceptual structures. One way to find out how politics is conceptualized is to analyse texts for metaphors and metaphorical reasoning processes. As can be seen from the example above, political arguments are often couched in the form of metaphors. Metaphors are a very powerful and efficient device both for cognition, i.e. to understand a phenomenon, and for communicative interaction, i.e. to communicate an idea and to structure an argument. Metaphors are in fact basic models for thought processes in human society.

I am interested in metaphors that are commonly used to speak about Europe, and about European unity and integration. Apart from getting access to the mental (conceptual) structures underlying these metaphors and thus explaining them, I am also interested in the question of whether there are cultural differences in the preference for particular metaphors and their use. In the long term, I want to find out which metaphors are preferred in which country, in which contexts, by whom; whether there are common European metaphors; by whom and how a metaphor is brought into national or international (political) discussion; whether it incurs changes when transferred from one culture/language into another; and I am also interested in the role which translating plays in this process.

After a more general illustration of the cognitive and communicative potential of metaphors, two of the most frequently encountered metaphors in the European debate, i.e. construction and movement metaphors, will be discussed in more detail on the basis of English and German texts. The aim of this interlingual comparison is to provide tentative answers to one of the questions mentioned above: which metaphors are preferred in which country and in which contexts?

The cognitive potential of metaphors

Cognitive and interpersonal functions

Metaphors are not just decorative elements. Cognitive linguistics (cf. Lakoff and Johnson, 1980; Lakoff, 1986; Chilton, 1989; Chilton and Lakoff, 1995) describes metaphors as means to understand a new, unknown domain (a target domain) in terms of another, a familiar one (source domain). The source domain is mapped onto the target domain.

There are two features of metaphor, one cognitive, the other interpersonal (cf. Chilton and Ilyin, 1993). From the cognitive point of view, metaphors are used in communication to understand more abstract, sometimes problematic, situations in terms of more concrete situations, situations we understand and are familiar with. For example, Kövecses (1986) illustrates that the conceptual metaphors of 'anger' are derived from everyday knowledge about physiological effects. One such metaphor is 'anger is the heat of a fluid in a container', which is reflected, for example, in the phrase 'you make my blood boil' (cf. Kövecses, 1986, p. 14).

Metaphors provide the necessary schemata for producing new thoughts about the complex or abstract phenomena. When a base conceptual schema is used as the source for a metaphor, the structural components of that schema are transferred to the target domain. Once we start to think in the source conceptual domain, all kinds of entailments are possible (though of course not necessary). For example, the source domain 'heat of a fluid in a container' allows for knowledge based entailments in the target domain 'anger', such as 'when the intensity of anger increases, the fluid rises' (e.g., 'his pent-up anger welled up inside him'), 'intense anger produces steam' (e.g., 'I was fuming'), or 'when anger becomes too intense, the person explodes' (e.g., 'we won't tolerate any more of your outbursts') (cf. Kövecses, 1986, pp. 15-16).

Ontological and epistemic correspondences

Kövecses makes a distinction between ontological and epistemic correspondences. Ontological correspondences are "correspondences that obtain between entities in the source domain and corresponding entities in the target domain" (Kövecses, 1986, p. 8), for example, the container is the body, the heat of fluid is the anger. "Epistemic correspondences are those that obtain between our knowledge of the source domain and our knowledge of the target domain. They arise as a result of a process whereby we carry over some of our knowledge of the source domain onto the target domain" (Kövecses, 1986, p. 8). For example, the knowledge that when the fluid is heated past a certain limit, pressure increases to the point at which the container explodes (source domain), is carried over to the target domain as: when anger increases past a certain limit, pressure increases to the point at which the person loses control (cf. Kövecses, 1986, p. 18).

Metaphors combine declarative knowledge (knowing what) and procedural knowledge (knowing how). In their structure they are, thus, similar to schemata or frames (cf. Fillmore, 1976).

From the interpersonal point of view, metaphors are used to establish mutual knowledge between the communicative partners. Also in political discourse, metaphor is not an empty rhetorical device, but can be an important diplomatic device. Here, metaphor can ease interpersonal contact, one of the reasons being that it leaves room for the negotiation of specific meanings and references. The metaphor of the 'common European house' introduced into political discourse in the mid-1980s by the then leader of the Soviet Union, Mikhail Gorbachev, can serve as an example.

A case in point: The common European house

The 'house' is an example of an artefact. In a taxonomy of categories and terms it can be seen as a sub-category of buildings, with a house probably being a good exemplar of the category 'building', in other words, a prototypical building (cf. Rosch, 1977).

The metaphor *obshchejevropejskij dom*, the common European house, had entered the international political debate after a speech by Gorbachev in April 1987. This metaphor was a reflection of the 'new political thinking' in the Soviet Union and the Communist Party under Gorbachev. It was a concept that reflected the political realities of the mid-1980s and was meant as a model for setting up a new policy. The metaphor of the common European house was to represent the idea of all European states, East and West of the 'Iron Curtain', living and working together on the basis of peaceful coexistence.

In speeches and articles by Gorbachev, the house metaphor was elaborated in terms of its structural, architectural, aspects (ontological correspondences) as well as in terms of aspects that concern the inhabitants living together and respecting certain rules of the house, a certain code of conduct (epistemic correspondences). The basic idea for Gorbachev's use of the metaphor was a multi-storey apartment block with several entrances, in which several families live, each in their own flats (i.e., the prototypical house in larger Russian towns). The rules of the house have to guarantee that every family can live their own lives, without interference from their neighbours. In addition, sensible norms or rules of living together in this house ensure that the common house is protected from fire or other accidents and kept in order. Such rules of conduct involve rights and duties for the inhabitants (for example, preserve the house, improve it, make it safer), as well as opportunities for their interaction (for example, cooperation and communication). In Gorbachev's discourse, the focus was above all on these functional aspects rather than on the visual, structural, ones.

Gorbachev's idea of the 'common European house' was not readily welcomed in Western European countries. It was even rejected, for example in official political circles in France, with the argument that the French word 'maison' had a connotation of conviviality which, however, did not apply to the situation in Europe in the mid-1980s (cf. Lesage, 1990). The French interpretation of 'L'Europe notre maison commune' would be based on the one-family house (the French prototypical house) with free movement from one room to the other.

More often than being rejected outright, the metaphor was taken up and conceptually challenged. In other words, not the base schema as such was contested in political debate, but rather the entailments. For example, an analysis of texts in the British weekly *The Economist* (March 1985 till September 1989) showed that structural aspects dominated in the argumentation (cf. Schäffner and Trommer, 1990). At the beginning, there was not yet an established English phrase, both 'common European house' and 'common European home' were used, even, although extremely rarely, 'shared house of Europe'. These structural aspects are reflected in the examples below (italics in all examples are mine, C.S.):

> Despite much Russian and East German talk about the "*shared house of Europe*", old European fears are plainly far from disappearing (Poles like to point out that *the shared European house* is the one where they have to lie *in the corridor* and get trodden on). (*The Economist*, 31 October 1987)

The argumentation in the leading article "One roof, two houses still" (*The Economist*, 23 April 1988) built around the idea of detached and semi-detached houses (i.e., prototypical English houses):

> Good *fences*, they say, make good neighbours. Mr Mikhail Gorbachev prefers fencelessness. He claims to believe that the 700m inhabitants of the place the atlas calls Europe - divided between two military alliances, with

conflicting political philosophies and economic systems - can *live happily under one roof* in a "*common European home*". [...]
But Europe is still a pair of *semi-detached houses*, in which two different sorts of people live two different kinds of life. (*The Economist*, 23 April 1988)

This critical reception and even rejection of Gorbachev's metaphor was determined by the activation of different (culture specific) prototypes of a house, that is, different characteristic features and, thus, different metaphorical entailments. This shows that metaphors can be explained as prototypes.

The house metaphor was expanded in specific ways, depending on the intentions and preferences of the respective speakers (cf. Schäffner and Trommer, 1990; Bachem and Battke, 1991; Chilton and Ilyin, 1993). Such developments of the metaphor in discourse were evidence of conceptual shifts such as particularisation and expansion, as can be seen in the following two examples in the context of a divided Germany:

Mikhail Gorbachev's "*common European house*" may have many *mansions* but it has no *room* for a reunited Germany. (*The Economist*, 29 October 1988)

[...] Soviet officials said privately they [...] hoped that one day there would be two "comfortable German *apartments* with lots of *doors* between them" in the *common house*. (*The Economist*, 17 June 1989)

In his book *Perestroika*, Gorbachev himself recounts a conversation with the then German federal president Richard von Weizsäcker. Gorbachev asked Weizsäcker how the idea of a 'common European home' ('home', and not 'house', is used in the English translation of the book) is understood in West Germany. The dialogue continued as follows:

Richard von Weizsäcker: It is a reference-point which helps us visualize the way things should be arranged in this *common European home*. Specifically, the extent to which the *apartments* in it will be *accessible for reciprocal visits*.
Mikhail Gorbachev: You are quite right. But not everyone may like receiving *night-time visitors*.
Richard von Weizsäcker: We also aren't especially pleased to have a *deep trench passing through a common living-room*. (quoted from Gorbachev, 1988, pp. 184-5)

This dialogue reveals a general phenomenon in connection with the house metaphor: when the Russian word 'dom' got translated into other languages, its meaning was not typically interpreted by reference to the communal block model. Ironically, as the exchange with Weizsäcker shows, it was Gorbachev's own metaphor that had the potential to provide one key conceptual and discursive tool for the Germans to contest and conceptualize the possible forms of unification.

However, with the collapse of Communism and the end of the Cold War in Europe, the metaphor of the European house has lost some of its political potential. Although, in the course of time, the metaphor has again and again been made use of, it has changed (most noticeably, the 'common' has disappeared). Its productivity is related to the richness of entailments and inferences this metaphor allows for, both in terms of ontological and epistemic correspondences.

Moreover, the cognitive ability "to structure the more abstract in terms of the more concrete" (Nikiforidou and Sweetser, 1989, p. 27) systematically links ontological and epistemic correspondences. Ontological correspondences are embedded in more complex knowledge domains, thus focussing on situational and functional aspects of structures. So we have not only the 'house' as an architectural structure, but rather as a dynamic organism, for which it might be more appropriate to speak of a house frame or a living-in-a-house frame. The political use of the metaphor is not only based on a (constructed) analogy of walls, roofs, doors, or windows. Metaphorical entailments are cognitive processes that operate on the basis of more complex knowledge structures, such as frames. And it is by virtue of such frames, that metaphors allow for continued elaboration, due to changing social situations and political intentions. Such a metaphorical entailment of the living-in-a-house frame became obvious in an editorial in *The Economist* in the autumn of 1989, reflecting on the political changes in East Germany and the possibility of German unification:

> [...] the strengthening of Germany looks unstoppable. To borrow Mr Gorbachev's terminology, in the "*common European house*" the Germans will be *landlords*. (*The Economist*, 14 October 1989)

More recent uses of the metaphor of the European house within the debate on European integration will be discussed below.

Metaphors in the debate about Europe

My empirical research is based on English and German texts, mainly newspaper texts, speeches by politicians and material from various political parties, such as leaflets for the 1994 elections to the European Parliament. The analysis so far has shown that there are a few metaphors which seem to dominate political thinking about European integration. It has also shown that these metaphors are very often combined and get linked or even mixed up in political discourse, so that we actually have a whole network of interrelated metaphors and, thus, a network of metaphorically based reasoning (cf. Schäffner, 1994a). The dominant metaphors in the texts analysed are the following: construction, movement, container, birth and death, illness, marriage. The most frequent ones are the construction and movement metaphors which will be presented in more detail below. The other metaphors will just be briefly illustrated.

Container metaphor

The container metaphor is frequently used in political discourse. Very often, the state is metaphorically described as a container (cf. Chilton and Lakoff, 1995), so it is only logical to extend this description to a community of states. This metaphor allows for inferences of being inside or outside the container, getting into it, entering or leaving it. In the texts analysed, both the European Community and the ERM are often represented as containers. This can be seen in phrases such as 'enter the EU', 'enter into Europe', 'EU entry', 'admission', 'admit to the EU', 'the pound left the ERM', 'sterling should not re-enter', 'keep the pound inside the ERM', and correspondingly in German, 'Beitritt', 'Zutritt zur EU', 'Eintritt', 'das EWS verlassen', cf. also the following examples:

> The British application was twice rebuffed. Britain was eventually allowed *in* only after 12 whole years had passed, [...] It is hardly surprising that the British felt uncomfortable *in a body* where they were accused of being 'un-European' whenever they expressed their own views about the way the things should be run. (*The European*, 15 October 1992)

> Once a country has *entered the EU* (and, before it, the European Community), the others are stuck with it, however fervently they might wish it *out*. [...] Once *ejected*, a country could apply for *readmission*. (*The Economist*, 5 March 1994)

This metaphor is often used in arguments about a widening of the EU, i.e. the admission of new members. In this context, 'take them in' and 'bring them in', on the one hand, and 'let them in', on the other hand, reflect different attitudes as far as willingness on the part of the present member states is concerned. The above mentioned links between the metaphorical domains become obvious, for example, with the ideas of 'moving in or out', 'entering or leaving', where we clearly see the link to a movement schema.

Birth, death, and illness metaphors

Metaphors related to birth and death, to sickness and revival were particularly frequent in the summer of 1993 when the European currency system had to be drastically changed. Here we have a case of the container metaphor being used in an anthropomorphic sense: the containers Europe, EU, or ERM, are seen as human beings. These metaphors are reflected in the following examples: *"revive* the Community" (*The Times*, 7 October 1992); "Can soothing words *heal* the European Community's *wounds?*" (*The Economist*, 7 August 1993); "Economic and monetary union [...] has had *a difficult birth* [...] the ERM was effectively *pronounced dead*" (*Time*, 16 August 1993); "[...] there is a *corpse* [...] ERM is *dead* [...] the currency system *breathes on*. [...] The alliance will *live on* [...] this currency crisis marked the *death* of Europe's federal illusions." (*The Economist*, 7 August 1993); "Europa *lebt* [...] eine *Leiche* [...] die Währungsunion, ist schon heute so gut wie *tot*" (*Der Spiegel*, 18 October 1993) [Europe lives [...] a corpse [...] monetary union today is almost dead]; "*Beerdigung* des EWS [...] EWS ist *tot* [...] EWS *erhängte sich* am eigenen Strick" (*Der Spiegel*, 9 August 1993) [funeral of the ERM [...] ERM is dead [...] ERM hoisted itself with its own petard.]

Another example for organic metaphors, linked to the idea of human beings, is John Major's reference to 'being at the heart of Europe' (also some of the movement metaphors, discussed below, are organic metaphors):

> I want Britain to mould that change, to lead that change in our own national interest. That's what I mean by *being at the heart of Europe*. (*The Guardian*, 10 October 1992)

However, these organic potentials were not further developed, and the 'heart' was mainly interpreted in a spatial sense, as can be seen from the following quote from an interview *Der Spiegel* had with John Major (note the change from 'heart' to 'centre'):

> Was heißt denn, *im Herzen Europas stehen?* [...] *Im Zentrum Europas* zu sein bedeutet, den Grad des Tempos und der Innovation mitzubestimmen. (*Der Spiegel*, 25 April 1994)
> [What does being at the heart of Europe mean? [...] Being at the centre of Europe means helping to determine the degree of speed and innovation.]

Marriage

The marriage metaphor too, can be related to an anthropomorphic view. It is used particularly in cases when the text deals with two EU member states and their problems. These two states are normally France and Germany. The following three examples are evidence of the marriage metaphor:

> Mrs Morris [...] condemned *the ERM 'marriage'* of 1990, saying that even the Bundesbank had struggled to *satisfy* "*ten wives at the same time*". She added: "Thank God for the *divorce*." (*The Times*, 9 October 1992)

> [...] Klagen über die selbstsüchtigen Deutschen [...] wenn auch - etwa bei den Briten - zuweilen Schadenfreude über die Franzosen anklang, die sich wie *verlassene Liebhaber* gebärdeten. Bonn und Paris führten nunmehr

eine *"offene Ehe"*, [...] und bereitwillig boten sich die Engländer für *gelegentliche Seitensprünge* an. [...] Die Irritationen eines *"Paares, das in den Herbst" seiner Ehe* [...] *eingetreten ist*, [...] (*Der Spiegel*, 30 August 1993)
[complaints about the selfish Germans [...] but sometimes, for example with the British, there was malicious joy about the French who behaved like deserted lovers. Bonn and Paris are having an 'open marriage' [...] and the English offer themselves for occasional extramarital adventures [...] irritations of a couple that has entered the autumn of its marriage.]

Construction metaphor

As already mentioned above, the construction metaphor is the one most frequently encountered in texts about Europe after movement metaphors. Here the ontological correspondences concern the concrete result of a building process and the structural elements of buildings, and the epistemic correspondences are the entailments that are related to the construction process, to the design or blueprint, and to the architects or construction workers. These components of the construction metaphor can be characterized as being embedded in an architecture schema.

Building process

The action of building is expressed either by verbs or nouns ('build Europe', 'construct the EU', 'construction'; and in German there are also prefix verbs and compound nouns to indicate a continuation of the action: 'die EU ausbauen', 'Bau einer Gemeinschaft europäischer Staaten', 'Aufbau der EU'). In the Tory Manifesto for the 1994 European elections, the EU's common foreign and security policy (CFSP) is the object of the building process: "our objective is to *build* the CFSP *brick by brick*" (Conservative Manifesto for Europe 1994), and the same image was used in German texts ('GASP [the German equivalent to CFSP] als Baustein der EU).

Structural elements

The elements of the architectural structure predominantly referred to in both the English and the German texts are 'foundations/Fundament', 'pillars/Pfeiler', 'cornerstone/Eckstein', with the additional use of 'Grundstein' in German ['foundation stone']. A few examples for illustration will suffice:

> Mr Major claims the Maastricht treaty has halted the federalist tide by establishing *"pillars"* - one organisation for co-operation on foreign and security policy, and another for interior-ministry work - [...] But Peter Shore, [...] views the *pillars* as "transitory arrangements which contain the

> seeds of their own *destruction*". [...] *the pillars' durability* [...] (*The Economist*, 13 November 1993)

> [...] the leaders can take solace from the fact that the Community's *foundations remain in place*. The single market, imperfect though it may be, exists, and no one seriously proposes *dismantling* it. (*Time*, 16 August 1993)

> Kern und *Fundament* der Einigung Europas bildet für uns die Europäische Gemeinschaft, die wir bald zur Europäischen Union *ausbauen* wollen. (Chancellor Kohl in his government declaration, 30 January 1990)
> [For us, the European Community is the core and the foundation of European unity and we want to extend it into the European Union.]

Such structural elements, particularly references to foundations, seem to be fairly common in conceptualizing politics, so that even obvious contradictions are not noticed. For example, in the manifesto of the German party Bündnis 90/Die Grünen for the European elections, economic integration is described as the foundation for political integration ("wirtschaftliche Integration [...] solides Fundament für politische Integration"), and also political integration as the foundation for economic integration ("der wirtschaftlichen Integration ein demokratisches politisches Fundament geben").

Blueprints and architects

The metaphorical entailments here are related to the designing stage of the construction process, and it is in this respect that criticism is often voiced. When the 'blueprint' does not seem to result in the desired structure, when there is a 'faulty design/Konstruktionsfehler', it may be suggested to "go back to the drawing board" (*Time*, 16 August 1993). The following two examples are evidence of these entailments:

> [...] Mr Baker had denounced the treaty as a *blueprint* for a European superstate, ... (*The Times*, 7 October 1992)

> Für Deutschland [...] macht das sture *Weiterwerkeln am westeuropäischen Haus* keinen Sinn mehr. Der *Bauplan* muß geändert werden. Aber wie? Stoibers Rat, sich auf den *Grundriß* des alten Nationalstaates zurückzuziehen, ist populär, aber falsch. (*Der Spiegel*, 8 November 1993)
> [For Germany [...] the continued stubborn building away the West European house does not make sense any more. The blueprint has to be changed. But how? Stoiber's advice to return to the ground-plan of the old nation state is popular, but wrong.]

The designers or architects can either be praised for a good design or be blamed when the construction is not solid enough or does not fulfil its function. References to architects and construction workers, lexicalized as

'Union's architects', 'Konstrukteure/Bauherren des geeinten Europa', 'Kohl, der Baumeister Europas', are more common in the German texts than in the English ones.

The European house and the fortress Europe

The result of the building process is often left more general in the texts, simply referred to as 'Europe' or 'EU'. Sometimes, however, it is further specified as 'föderatives Europa/federal Europe' - interpreted either as a desired or an undesired aim (cf. Musolff, in this volume). Another, more concrete result of the building process is a house. This metaphor is used again in discussions about Europe, albeit in a modified form, since, as said above, the 'common European house' that was originally designed for handling the Cold War is past its climax. The 'house' is either presented as already in existence or as still being under construction, as is illustrated in the following two examples:

> Es wäre verhängnisvolle Kurzsichtigkeit, das *europäische Haus*, an dem viele Generationen *gebaut* haben, wieder *einzureißen*, um einen neuen *Architektenwettbewerb* auszuschreiben. (Programme of the German party Bündnis 90/Die Grünen for the 1994 European elections)
> [It would be a fatally short-sighted decision to pull down the European house which has been built by many generations and invite bids for new architectural designs.]
>
> Der *Bau am gemeinsamen europäischen Haus* ist ins Stocken geraten (PDS Manifesto for the 1994 European elections)
> [The construction of the common European house has slackened.]

In the PDS manifesto, the focus is on all of Europe; in other words, the metaphor is used in an almost Gorbachevian sense.

The 'house' metaphor, which - based on my text analyses - seems to be more popular in Germany than in Britain, is nowadays often used to refer to the EU, or to Western Europe. It is particularly used with reference to the debate on admitting new members to the EU. When these members are welcome, for example the fairly rich EFTA countries, structural elements of the 'house' are focussed on (i.e., ontological correspondences), such as 'enter into Europe', 'open the doors to the EFTA countries'. The 'house' metaphor is, however, more frequently evoked in controversial debates about whether or not Eastern European countries should be allowed into the EU. In this case, the structural elements are combined with entailments that relate to a visitor script or to the idea of 'feeling at home':

> 1989 feierten sie ihre *"Heimkehr nach Europa"* - und wir mit ihnen. Heute fühlen sie sich draußen *vor der Tür gelassen*, und inzwischen betrachten wir sie allzuoft als lästige Konkurrenten oder *unerbetene Gäste*. (*Frankfurter Allgemeine Zeitung*, 20 October 1993)

[In 1989 they celebrated their 'coming home to Europe' - and we joined in the celebrations. Today they feel as if they have been left waiting outside the door, and much too often we have come to regard them as undesirable competitors or unwelcome visitors.]

Mit großem Jubel wurden die jungen Demokratien nach dem Kollaps des Sowjetimperiums *im gemeinsamen Europäischen Haus willkommen geheißen*. (*Der Spiegel*, 29 November 1993)
[With shouts of joy the young democracies were welcomed in the common European house after the collapse of the Soviet empire.]

Die meisten, die noch vor drei Jahren ihre Amtskollegen östlich von Oder und Neiße zur *"Rückkehr nach Europa"* einluden, haben mittlerweile ihre *Tore fest verrammelt*. (*Der Spiegel*, 8 November 1993)
[Most of those who three years ago invited their fellow heads of state to the East of the rivers Oder and Neisse to return to Europe have in the meantime barricaded their gates.]

This last example points to another specification of a building: the fortress. This metaphor is very often used, also in English texts, with reference to protecting Western Europe from non-European or Eastern European immigrants, as becomes obvious in the following examples:

Europe *slams the doors* (= Headline)
[...] the Continent echoes with the sound of *doors slamming shut*. [...] *The gates of Fortress Europe moved closer to the locked position* last week when Sweden and Denmark announced new immigration restrictions [...] (*Time*, 19 July 1993)

Fortress Europe yesterday lifted its German drawbridge to keep out hundreds of thousands of refugees from eastern Europe and beyond seeking a new life in the West. (*The Guardian*, 2 July 1993)

Durch die Politik der gemeinsamen *Abschottung nach außen* soll die Europäische Union *zu einer Festung ausgebaut* werden. [...] Bisher sind alle Bemühungen gescheitert, die *Tore der Festung EG* zumindest zeitweise für die Opfer des jugoslawischen Krieges zu *öffnen*. (Programme of Bündnis 90/Die Grünen for the 1994 European elections)
[A policy of shielding from the outside world will mean that the European Union will become a fortress. [...] Up to now, all attempts to open the gates of the fortress EC to the victims of the war in Yugoslavia, at least for a certain time, have been in vain.]

The productivity of the 'house' metaphor is particularly obvious in the following example in which structural elements are combined with a quality of living. In this text it is argued that the idea of one, united, Europe has been abandoned in the office of the German Chancellor because with Eastern European countries joining the EU, a divided European house may become a reality:

Mit dem Beitritt der Oststaaten [...] werde eine *Zweiteilung des europäischen Hauses* wahrscheinlich. Im geräumigen *Untergeschoß siedeln* demnach alle Staaten, die 1999 nicht reif für eine Währungsunion sind, dabei sind die Briten. Gemeinsam mit Süd- und Osteuropäern bilden sie eine Freihandelszone mit lockerem politischen Überbau. In der *Beletage residieren* die *Kern-Europäer,* vornweg Franzosen und Deutsche. Zusammen mit den Beneluxländern und womöglich den Österreichern verschmelzen sie ihre Währungen, betreiben fortan eine gemeinsame Geld- und Wirtschaftspolitik. Den *Vorgarten bevölkern* etwa Russen, Türken und Ukrainer. Ihnen wird die Mitgliedschaft verwehrt. Sie bleiben der EU mit Assoziierungsverträgen verbunden. (*Der Spiegel,* 6 June 1994)
[With Eastern European countries entering [...] a bipartition of the European house will be probable. On the spacious ground floor, all those states, including Britain, settle that in 1999 are not yet mature for a monetary union. Together with the South and East Europeans they form a free trade area under a loose political roof. On the elegant first floor, the core Europeans reside, above all the French and the Germans. Together with Belgium, the Netherlands, Luxembourg, and maybe Austria, they merge their currencies and have common monetary and economic policies. The front garden is thronged with Russians, Turks, Ukrainians. They are refused membership. They are related to the EU by treaties of association.]

Both the house and the fortress are concrete instances of a container. The more concrete a metaphorical base schema, the richer the possible entailments, and the greater the potential for controversial argumentation in political discourse. The visual elements of the 'house' and the 'fortress' also allow for their use in cartoons (cf. Schäffner, 1994b).

Movement metaphors

Movement metaphors, similar to construction metaphors, are preferably and widely used to conceptualize political aims and projects (cf. Schäffner and Porsch, 1993). In the debate about Europe, the starting point, i.e. the base schema, is not a concrete, visual, path with a beginning and an end, but rather the movement itself. Different aspects of the movement schema, or movement frame, are focussed upon in the texts.

Moving and steps

First, the action of moving itself is expressed, often in combination with a direction, and lexicalized by the (prototypical) verbs 'move/gehen', or by the noun 'steps/Schritte': "*move forward* with the support of our citizens" (*The Times,* 17 October 1992); "die Gemeinschaft einen entscheidenden *Schritt voranbringt.* [...] den *Weg zu einem vereinten Europa zu gehen*" (Declaration of the German government on a meeting of the European Council in Maastricht, 13 December 1991) [bring the community a decisive step forward [...] go along the way to a united Europe]; "the Community is *moving in a non-federal, British direction.* [...] *a bigger step towards ever-*

closer union [...] The EC never has and never will *stand still.*" (*The Economist*, 13 November 1993).

Destination

Metaphors highlight particular aspects of the respective knowledge domain, but they also hide others, leave them in the 'blind spot', so to speak. For example, the starting point of the path and the movement is hardly ever mentioned. All we find are references that we do not want to return to the nation state, that the way back is blocked ['die Rückkehr zum alten Nationalstaat ist versperrt']. On the other hand, the end point of the path, the destination of the movement, is variably and controversially specified. Even more than the container, house and fortress metaphors, the movement schema is used to bring the opposing attitudes towards the EU and European integration into the open, and particularly in the references to the destination. The differences are not so much between Great Britain on the one hand and Germany on the other, but they are rather of an internal nature, being reflected in the positions of the parties, and of groupings as well as individuals within the parties. Moreover, there is more variation and controversy in Britain than in Germany. In Germany, all the major, influential, political parties are in favour of European integration and of staying in the EU; the controversy concerns minor points, for example, that the Maastricht Treaty does not go far enough, or that there is not enough democracy in the EU institutions, or that it does not focus on all of Europe.

I have looked more systematically at the manifestoes for the 1994 elections to the European Parliament and other documents and leaflets produced by the major British and German political parties to find out similarities and differences. All of them make wide use of movement metaphors to argue their points. Differences occur in the lexicalization of the destination, i.e. the kind of Europe/EU they aim at, in the argumentation about a choice of direction in case of problems, in the characterization of the Maastricht Treaty, and in references to the speed of the movement. I will at first give examples from the election manifestoes, and then summarize the results and back them up with examples from the press.

> *CDU*
> destination: freiheitlich, demokratisch, föderal, subsidiär und bundesstaatlich gestaltete EU
> [a EU shaped like a federal state and based on freedom, democracy, federalism, subsidiarity)
> path: die Gemeinschaft ist auf dem richtigen Weg [the community is on the right path]; den in Maastricht festgelegten Kurs konsequent halten [keep to the course set out in Maastricht]
> Maastricht Treaty: ein Schritt in die richtige Richtung [a step in the right direction], hat eine neue Wegmarke gesetzt [has marked a new stage on the path]

CSU
destination: Staatenverbund [alliance of states]; Union europäischer Nationen [Union of European nations]

SPD
destination: Europa der Regionen [Europe of the regions]; Europa der Bürger [Europe of the citizens]
Maastricht Treaty: der erste Schritt einer gemeinsamen Außen-, Sicherheits- und Entwicklungspolitik [first step of a common foreign, security and development policy]; Schritt in die richtige Richtung [step in the right direction]
speed: Maastricht gibt neuen Schwung [gives new momentum]

Bündnis 90/Die Grünen
destination: friedliches, offenes Europa der Menschen [a peaceful, open Europe of the people]; Staatenverbund [alliance of states]; Europa steht am Scheideweg [at the crossroads]
path: Reise ohne Rückfahrkarte [voyage without a return ticket]; Weg in die Sackgasse [path into a dead end]
Maastricht Treaty: stellt die Weichen falsch [sets a wrong course]

PDS
destination: friedliches, sozial gerechtes, demokratisches und umweltbewahrendes Europa [a Europe that is peaceful, socially just, democratic, and preserves the environment]
path: PDS fordert einen Kurswechsel [PDS demands a change of course]
Maastricht Treaty: hat die Weichen in die falsche Richtung gestellt [set the course into a wrong direction/sent us down the wrong track]

Conservative Party
destination: a Europe of nation states, working together; a decentralized Europe which is flexible, responsive, open and democratic
path: move our way; Britain has shown Europe the way; the right way forward
Maastricht Treaty: important staging-post

Labour Party
destination: a Europe of freedom and social justice; a strong community; Europe of the regions; decentralized Europe; a people's Europe

Liberal Democrats
destination: a federal Europe that works for Britain; EU which is democratic, decentralized and diverse

We can see that the path is leading to a kind of Europe that is variously specified and characterized, and the examples also reflect the controversial arguments about *federalism* (cf. Musolff, in this volume).

Desirable endpoints which are found in English texts are a 'decentralized Europe of nation states', a 'union of sovereign nation states', undesirable destinations are a 'federal superstate', a 'federal Europe', a 'centralized

Europe', and 'United States of Europe'. Proponents of the Maastricht Treaty characterize it as an 'important staging-post', critics denounce it as a 'step too far', 'a step towards a superstate', 'a stepping stone to the United States of Europe'. These points are also taken up and argued in the press, as illustrated in the following examples:

> For Tebbit, Baker and others, Maastricht [...] books Britain *a place on the road to a centralised Europe*. (*The Guardian*, 7 October 1992)

> The Maastricht treaty, the penultimate *stop on the road to a federal Europe*, [...] (*Time*, 2 November 1992)

> For the time being, Mr Major has succeeded in reassuring much of public opinion and many within his party that the Community is *moving in a non-federal, British direction*. But Maastricht, at least on paper, represents *a bigger step towards ever-closer union* than he has cared to admit. (*The Economist*, 13 November 1993)

If the endpoint of the movement is something undesirable, it would be wise to go back or to choose another path. Critics of the course call for 'setting a new course', 'following a new path', "necessary for Europe's leaders *to set a new course*. [...] a summit intended to *put the EC back on track*" (*The Times*, 17 October 1992); "Europe will have to *follow a new path*" (*The Economist*, 7 August 1993).

Desirable endpoints which are found in German texts are a 'föderatives Europa' [federal Europe], 'Staatenbund' [union of states]; undesirable ones are 'europäischer Bundesstaat' [European federal state], 'Vereinigte Staaten von Europa' [United States of Europe] (although there have been changes in the course of time; for example, a 'europäischer Bundesstaat' was indeed the aim of the CDU in 1992 - but now it is described as an 'Irrweg' ['wrong way']). Proponents of the Maastricht Treaty characterize it as a 'Meilenstein' [milestone], a 'Schritt in die richtige Richtung' [step in the right direction]; critics denounce it as 'in die Irre geführt' [having led astray] or as 'die Weichen in die falsche Richtung gestellt' [having set a wrong course]; cf. also the following examples:

> Der Integrationsprozeß sei nun "politisch *unumkehrbar*". [...] Die CDU *hält Kurs*. (*Der Spiegel*, 8 November 1993)
> [The integration process is politically irreversible [...] The CDU stays on course.]

> Dieses Vertragswerk [...] bedeutet eine grundlegende *Weichenstellung* für die Zukunft Europas:
> Erstens: Der *Weg* zur Europäischen Union ist *unumkehrbar*.
> (Declaration of the German government on a meeting of the European Council in Maastricht, 13 December 1991)
> [This treaty [...] has decisively set the course for Europe's future: Firstly: The path towards the European Union is irreversible.]

Critics of the course call for a 'neue Kursbestimmung' [a new course], 'Kurskorrektur' [correcting the course], 'Kurswechsel' [changing the course], 'Richtungsänderung' [changing the direction]. Decisions about direction are particularly necessary when there is a crisis in the development, or metaphorically, when we arrive at the crossroads:

> Europe, [...] is "*at the crossroads.*" [...] A decision about *direction* is unavoidable. (Roy Hattersley in *The Guardian*, 10 November 1993)

> Europa *am Scheideweg* [...] Dreieinhalb Jahre nach dem Fall der Mauer *läuft die Politik* der EG-Staaten gegenüber Mittel- und Osteuropa daher *in eine tragische Sackgasse* aus Dummheit und Versagen. (*Der Spiegel*, 15 March 1993)
> [Europe at the crossroads [...] Three and a half years after the fall of the Berlin Wall the politics of the EC states towards Central and Eastern Europe is moving into a tragic dead end of ignorance and failure.]

There is an interesting linguistic point here concerning 'crossroads' and 'Scheideweg': when we visualize this metaphor, the 'crossroads' allows for a choice between four different directions (including returning the way we came), the German 'Scheideweg' (literally: a fork in the road), however, only for three directions. In the English and in the German texts I have analysed, neither of these options in the direction has actually been spelt out for the sake of political argumentation.

Speed of the movement

Other inferences that are based on the base conceptual schema of movement are related to the (un)hindered progressing along the path and to the speed of the movement:

> [...] ob nicht das *Tempo* der Veränderungen zu *schnell* sei. Doch können wir uns eine *langsame Gangart* überhaupt leisten? [...] *Stillstand wäre Rückschritt.* (Government declaration of Chancellor Kohl, 25 September 1992)
> [whether the speed of the changes is too fast. But can we actually afford a slower pace? [...] Standing still would be a setback.]

> [...] wenn die europäische Integration "*ungebremst*" fortgesetzt werden kann. (*Der Spiegel*, 29 November 1993)
> [when European integration can be continued without braking.]

> Britain is still viewed as a *stumbling block* in Europe. (*The Guardian*, 6 July 1995)

Criticism of the speed can be expressed by the choice of verbs, as in the following example:

> And all the while, as descant, the threat (again!) that the old core of the Community - Germany, France, Holland, Belgium and Luxembourg - will *plough ahead* to a single currency, leaving the rest *trailing behind*. (*The Guardian*, 26 September 1992)

In the next example, different animals are metaphorically used to give an indication of possible speeds:

> [...] we can see that Europe is *moving not at two speeds*, but at three or four [...] In Birmingham it will become proverbial that you can't *harness a bull, a mule and a racehorse*. (*The Times*, 16 October 1992)

In this example, we have also a reference to a specific elaboration of the speed idea which has become one of the basic and most controversial models for devising policies for the future development of the EU: the model of the 'two-speed Europe', or the 'multi-speed Europe'. Musolff (in this volume) discusses the pragmatic implications of this metaphor, I want to limit my comments to the linguistic and conceptual aspects. The idea of different speeds raises some questions that are based on the epistemic correspondences the movement schema allows for. A first question is linked to the destination slot in the movement schema. There are two possibilities: all bodies, moving at different speeds, may still move into the same direction, arriving ultimately at the same destination; or, on the other hand, the bodies, moving at different speeds, may actually be moving towards different destinations. Another entailment concerns the spatial position of the moving bodies towards each other: the slow moving ones will be overtaken by the faster moving ones, thus arriving late (maybe too late) at the destination. And who decides on the speed? Should the faster ones be waiting for the slower ones to catch up, so that nobody is left behind and in danger of missing a chance? These points are referred to in the following two examples:

> "There will be no *inner core*, no *fast track and slow track*, no one *left behind* and no inner groups," he [= Major] said. (*The Times*, 17 October 1992)

> [Kohl] "We don't want a *two- or three-speed Europe* [...] but nor do we want a Europe in which the *speed of the slower ship determines the pace of the entire convoy*." (*The Guardian*, 28 October 1992)

This statement by Chancellor Kohl can, of course, also be interpreted as a criticism of the speed towards European integration, and moreover, as a hidden warning (to Britain?) not to bring the integration progress to a halt. One entailment that seems to come logically with the idea of the multiple speeds are the tracks, or lanes, mentioned in the *Times* example above and also in the following two examples in which *The Guardian* first informs about Major's argumentation and then, both in an editorial and in a comment by Hugo Young, criticizes it:

> The Prime Minister last night indicated that a Conservative government would refuse to join the next phase of European integration, and held out a vision of a *multi-speed Europe* in which all member states would *proceed at a speed of their own choosing*. [...] Mr Major insisted there was *a third European path* besides total integration and a *two-speed Europe*, one which involved different alliances of states choosing to opt out on different issues. [...] "A *multi-speed, multi-track, multi-layered Europe* was a Conservative idea in line with the mood of the people everywhere." (*The Guardian*, 1 June 1994)

> If you want to *steer the European Union in a new direction*, you don't scorn all its work. You commit yourself to changing it from the inside. The last thing that you do is say that Europe is *moving our way* and then, in the same breath, invite it to *proceed as a multi-speed project* in which you *start ostentatiously from the back of the grid*. (*The Guardian*, 2 June 1994, editorial)

> But what he [= Major] offers is at bottom quite deceptive. He talks about many *speeds* and dual layers as if Britain can always have the best of all of them. He makes the same dud claim as Douglas Hurd, that Britain can opt for the *slowest speed* while still decisively influencing the *direction and velocity of the fastest*. (*The Guardian*, 2 June 1994, comment by Hugo Young)

On the same day (2 June 1994), *The Guardian* supported its argumentation by a cartoon which depicted a race course. In the right hand corner we see three horsemen with the European flag on their backs moving at a fast speed. Another horse is trotting along a track that is marked as 'slow lane', the rider is John Major, dressed in the Union Jack and sitting backwards on the horse. This horse is cheered on by spectators waving little Union Jacks and tossing their hats in the air. Once lanes have been introduced into the argumentation, new metaphorical domains can be opened up. For example, another cartoon in *The Economist* (11 June 1994) showed the 'Euro Highway' with two lanes. A big car with a Euro number plate is rushing down one lane, passing a small British car which is parked in the second lane, attached to its hood is a sign reading 'Running in - please pass'. Next to the highway we see John Bull sitting on a blanket (the Union Jack again) in the grass, having a picnic, and with his dog (a British bulldog) next to him. The sub-heading of the accompanying text reads "Britain's European election campaign has been dominated by claims and counter-claims about whether the country will end up in the European Union's 'slow' lane."

The 'lane' image was also taken up in a criticism voiced by the Labour politician Margaret Beckett. She "accused Mr Major of keeping Britain in the 'bicycle lane' not the fast lane" (*The Guardian*, 2 June 1994).

Means of transport

These examples also show that the movement schema allows for the introduction of a means of transport, i.e. some vehicle. In addition to the 'ship' we have seen above, in the texts analysed these vehicles were predominantly trains and bicycles:

> Bundeskanzler Kohl [...] "Wir müssen dafür sorgen, *daß der europäische Zug weiterfährt."* (*Der Spiegel*, 10 May 1993)
> [We have to ensure that the European train runs on.]

> [...] der Vertrag von Maastricht [...] hat die Mitglieder der Europäischen Gemeinschaft gespalten, [...] die Staaten selbst in *Schnellzug- und Bummelzug-Unionisten.* [...] (Ralf Dahrendorf in *Der Spiegel*, 3 January 1994)
> [the Maastricht Treaty has divided the members of the European Community [...] the states into fast train and slow train unionists]

The word 'train' need not appear itself in the text in order to see that the 'train' metaphor is at work. In the following three examples, 'timetable', 'derailed', and 'die Weichen stellen' (set the course, but literally: shift the switch, set railway points) are evidence of the underlying metaphor, i.e., examples of ontological and epistemic correspondences:

> The Maastricht *timetable* for European monetary union was "totally unrealistic", said the prime minister, John Major. (*The Economist*, 7 August 1993)

> The goal of forging a common currency by 1999 [...] appears to be *derailed*. (*Time*, 16 August 1993)

> In Europa dagegen *stellt* der Maastrichter Vertrag *die Weichen* in Richtung auf einen europäischen Bundesstaat, [...] (*Der Spiegel*, 19 October 1992)
> [In Europe, the Maastricht Treaty sets the course in the direction of a European federal state.]

The 'train' was predominantly used in the German texts, the 'bicycle', on the other hand, mainly in the English texts (could a reason for this be that bicycles might be more popular in Britain?, cf. also Margaret Beckett's reference to a 'bicycle lane', quoted above):

> Must the European Union *move ever onward* lest, like an *unpedalled bicycle*, it topple over? (*The Economist*, 5 March 1994)

Another aspect of the movement schema applied to the European discussion is to argue about a driving force, mainly a motor. And again, a motor may work, thus enabling the movement, or it may stall, thus slowing down the movement or preventing it altogether. The vehicles or the driving force introduced into the line of argument reveal underlying conceptualizations of the political issue, especially the aspect of self-propelled movement (organic metaphors) or externally generated movement (mechanical images):

> [...] the European Commission [...] the *motor driving the European Community*. [...] The motor has all but *stalled*. (*The Economist*, 10 October 1992)

> Is the treaty an *accelerator* for more political and economic union, or is it a *handbrake* for a more decentralised Europe? (*The Times*, 11 October 1992)

> We reject a centralised Europe. We reject the idea of a *conveyor belt carrying us* to a single executive and a single parliament. (*The Times*, 7 October 1992)

Mixture of metaphors

There is one phenomenon which deserves to be mentioned. Sometimes we find in the texts a mixture of metaphors. Not only a mixture in the sense that various metaphors are made use of for argumentation in a coherent and logical way, as in the following example:

> As they go about that, the leaders can take solace from the fact that the Community's *foundations remain in place*. The single market, imperfect though it may be, exists, and no one seriously proposes *dismantling* it. The *France-German couple* has survived its latest spat. And last week, on the very day that the ERM was effectively *pronounced dead*, Britain completed its ratification of the Maastricht treaty - a well-timed reminder that the *slow march toward integration* - and the European idea - continues. (*Time*, 16 August 1993)

What is much more interesting, and confusing, is that the metaphors get mixed in a rather incoherent way, as illustrated in the following two examples:

> Frankreich und Deutschland wollen beim *Aufbau* Europas die Rolle des *Motors* spielen. (*Die Welt*, 29 October 1993)
> [In the construction of Europe, France and Germany want to play the role of the motor.]

A 'motor' is a driving force, what could possibly be its function in the construction process? And why is role-play involved?

> Der *Weg* zur europäischen Stabilitätsgemeinschaft ist damit ein entscheidender *Eckstein* für die Europäische Union. (A statement by Chancellor Kohl, 13 December 1991)
> [The path towards the European stability community is a decisive cornerstone for the European Union.]

In this case, the movement and the building schemata were linked, and again in a non-coherent way. Do these incoherent uses contradict what was said at the beginning about metaphors not being empty rhetorical devices or decorative accessories? Or are they rather evidence of the fact that metaphors are so pervasive of political thinking and political discourse that such odd combinations just happen and even go by unnoticed by the audience? I would hesitate to give a definite answer, but I would risk saying that probably the second point applies.

New metaphorical models

Models for European integration were originally only designed for the Western European countries, or, to be more precise, for the EC/EU member states. In this context, the term 'Europe' was often used in a metonymic part-whole relationship for Western Europe and the EC/EU, respectively, i.e., for the prototypical Europe (cf. Schäffner, 1990, 1995). The explanatory power of the various metaphors and their value for practical politics, including their public acceptance, was constantly tested and contested. In an article in *The Independent,* Andrew Marshall commented - slightly sarcastically - on the value of the various metaphors:

> Multi-tracks, hard cores, temples, trees, pillars, convoys and hearts: it is a strange vision that politicians conjure up when they debate the future of Europe. The metaphors of Maastricht form a dream-like, surrealist landscape like those depicted by the painters Paul Delvaux or Giorgio De Chirico. (*The Independent,* 11 September 1994)

New political developments after the end of the Cold War, the changing boundaries and alliances, correspond to what Chilton (1986, p. 38) has called a "critical discourse moment [...] in that existing conceptualizations on which politics are based, no longer fit well with the new events". One of the consequences is that existing metaphors are (con)tested again to see whether they can accommodate the new developments and the opportunities for the future of the EU. In other words, the conceptual crisis is also a crisis of metaphor. One the one hand, some metaphors are modified, for example the 'house' and the 'speed' metaphors. On the other hand, new models and metaphors are introduced in the debates about the future of European integration. These new models will be illustrated below.

Core Europe

One of the new models is the metaphor of the 'core Europe', introduced mainly by the German government:

> Im Zentrum des Kohlschen Europas steht eine kleine, aber funktionsfähige Mini-EG [...] Kohl-Berater sehen bereits "eine Kern-Union, bestehend aus Frankreich, den Benelux-Staaten plus x" entstehen. (*Der Spiegel*, 18 October 1993)
> [In the centre of Kohl's Europe is a small but effective mini-EC [...] Kohl advisors see the emergence of 'a core union, consisting of France, Belgium, the Netherlands, Luxembourg plus x'.]

The idea of the 'core Europe' was elaborated in a discussion paper written by the parliamentary groups of CDU and CSU in September 1994, but it met with heated public debate in the EU member states. The main bone of contention was who was actually to make up the core. In the CDU/CSU document, a core was said to exist, with Belgium, the Netherlands, and Luxembourg listed by name, in addition to France and Germany as the firm core ['der feste Kern'] of the core. But it was also said that, in principle, the core must be open to new members:

> Daher muß sich [...] der *feste Kern* von integrationsorientierten und kooperationswilligen Ländern, der sich bereits herausgebildet hat, weiter festigen. Zu ihm gehören z. Zt. fünf bis sechs Länder. Der *Kern* darf nicht abgeschlossen, muß hingegen für jedes Mitglied offen sein, das willens und in der Lage ist, seinen Anforderungen zu entsprechen. (CDU/CSU Fraktion, *Überlegungen zur Europäischen Politik*, 1 September 1994)
> [Therefore [...] that already existing firm core of countries that orient towards integration and are willing to cooperate has to be further strengthened. At the moment, five to six countries make up this core. This core must not be closed but it has to be open for each member that is willing and able to comply with its requirements.]

> Schäuble [...] said Europe would not progress if "the *slowest ship*" determined the *speed of the convoy*. That is why a *strong core* of European states, especially France and Germany, must be the *powerful engine that pulls the others along*. (*The Guardian*, 7 September 1994)

The sharp criticism of the 'core' idea, especially in Britain, focussed on the danger of a division of the EU which would subsequently follow should a 'core' of few countries want to decide on who will be part of it and thus take decisions. This criticism becomes obvious in statements by John Major reported in *The Times*:

> No member state should be excluded from an area of policy in which it wants and is qualified to participate. To choose not to participate is one thing. To be prevented from doing so is quite another and likely to lead to the sort of damaging divisions which, above all, we must avoid. So I see a real danger in talk of a "*hard core*", *inner* and *outer circles*, a *two-tier Europe*. I recoil from ideas for a union in which some would be more equal than others. There is not, and should never be, an exclusive *hard core* either of countries or policies. (*The Times*, 8 September 1994)

Rejections of the idea of a 'core Europe' in Germany made use of the polysemy of the word 'Kern', which also denotes the atomic nucleus ['Atomkern']: it was argued that this idea will lead to a 'Kernspaltung' ['nuclear fission'] instead of a 'Kernfusion' ['nuclear fusion']. Other critical points were also building on the dangers of a division of the EU which would result in different classes of members. These arguments allowed for the introduction of new metaphors, such as sports leagues: "wer in welcher Europaklasse spielt [...], sich für die erste Europaliga qualifizieren" (*Der Spiegel*, 12 September 1994) ['who is playing in which European league division [...], to qualify for the first European division']. *The Guardian* (2 June 1994) published a "European Union league table" which listed the countries for the Premier League, for League Divisions One, Two, Three and Four, and for the Amateur League.

These examples again show the enormous productivity of metaphors. The interesting point for an explanation and description of metaphors in terms of cognitive semantics is that such linkages to other knowledge domains show that knowledge structures, such as frames, scripts, or schemata, share particular slots. These shared slots, or shared scenes, allow for spreading activation (cf. also Shank's, 1982, memory organization packets, MPOs, and thematic organization packets, TOPs).

In the textual argumentation, the 'core' metaphor is linked to the movement schema: 'der feste Kern kann allein vorangehen' ['the hard core can move on alone']; 'the hard core will move forward quickly', 'the core states pushing ahead alone'; cf. also the following example which links the metaphors of the speed, the ship, and the core:

> Da bietet das Konzept der "*zwei Geschwindigkeiten*" einen Ausweg: Wer *schleichen* will, soll das tun, aber ohne die anderen *aufzuhalten*. [...] Englands Premier Major, auch wenn er den Schäuble-Plan jetzt kritisiert, schwärmte schon vor Monaten von einem "*Europa verschiedener Geschwindigkeiten, verschiedener Gleise und verschiedener Ebenen.*" [...] "Soll sich der *Geleitzug* künftig nach dem *langsamsten Schiff* richten, oder sollen die, die *schneller voranwollen*, das auch tun? Unser Ziel ist ein möglichst starkes *Kerneuropa*, aber unsere Präferenz bleibt eindeutig, *alle* [...] mit an Bord zu haben." (*Die Zeit*, 9 September 1994)
> [The concept of the 'two speeds' offers a way out. Those who want to crawl can do so, but without holding up the others [...] Although he is now criticizing Schäuble's plan, already some months ago England's Prime Minister Major enthused about a 'multi-speed, multi-track, multi-layered Europe' [...] 'Should the slowest ship determine the pace of the convoy, or should those who want to move along faster be able to do so? Our aim is a strong core Europe, but our preference is clear: we want to have everybody on board.]

Variable geometry, concentric circles, and Europe à la carte

Three other models that take account of differences within the EU are the conceptual schemata of the variable geometry, the concentric circles, and a

Europe à la carte. These metaphors, too, are often linked to the movement schema:

> Für Kommissionspräsident Jacques Delors bedeutet die Erweiterung der Union um die Mittel- und Osteuropäer, daß sich die Gemeinschaft zu einem "Europa der *variablen Geometrie*" entwickelt: "Jene, die *weitergehen* möchten, können sich zu einer Politischen Union zusammenschließen, und die übrigen geben sich mit einem gemeinsamen Wirtschaftsraum zufrieden." Auch bei den drei Benelux-Ländern [...] zirkulieren ähnliche Modelle. Der Luxemburger EU-Vertreter Jean-Jacques Kasel denkt an einen "exklusiven Klub" von zunächst sechs oder sieben Mitgliedern, die eine gemeinsame Außen- und Währungspolitik entwickeln. *Drumherum* würden die *"Trabanten"* (Kasel) *kreisen, die in den inneren Kern aufgenommen* werden könnten, sobald sie die Voraussetzungen für ihre Integration erfüllen. (*Der Spiegel*, 28 March 1994)
> [For Jacques Delors, the President of the Commission, the EU enlargement by Central and Eastern Europeans means the development of the Community into a 'Europe of a variable geometry': 'Those who want to move on can unite to a political union, the others are satisfied with a common economic area.' Similar models are being discussed in Belgium, the Netherlands and Luxembourg. Luxembourg's EU representative Jean-Jacques Kasel thinks of an 'exclusive club' of at first six to seven members who develop a common foreign and monetary policy. 'Satellites' (Kasel) would orbit around them, and they could be taken into the inner core as soon as they fulfil the integration requirements.]

> Am Ende dieses Jahrhunderts wird Europa ein Bild *konzentrischer Kreise* aufweisen mit einem unterschiedlichen Grad der Anbindung an die Europäische Union:
> • die Mitglieder der Stabilitätsgemeinschaft
> • die weiteren Mitglieder der EU,
> • die EFTA-Staaten, die der Politischen Union nicht *beitreten* wollen,
> • die assoziierten Staaten Mittel- und Osteuropas.
> (CSU Manifesto for the 1994 European Elections)
> [At the end of the century, Europe will present an image of concentric circles, with a different degree of boundedness to the EU: the members of the stability community, the other EU members, EFTA states that do not want to join the political union, associated Central and Eastern European states]

> Ein Europa, das *voranschreiten* will, kann sich wohl besser nach dem *Muster konzentrischer Kreise* entwickeln. Die Mitglieder der engeren Stabilitätsgemeinschaft werden sich dabei *schneller* und weitgehender aneinander binden müssen. (*Die Zeit*, 9 September 1994)
> [A Europe that wants to move forward can best develop according to the model of concentric circles. The members of the closer stability community will have to unite faster and more extensively.]

> It would have to be a *Europe à la carte*, in which different members chose to join some policies and not others [...]. (*The Economist*, 7 August 1993)

> [...] Major [...] argued that Britain's opt-outs from the social chapter and single currency timetable were part of a wider trend towards an *à la carte Europe*. (*The Guardian*, 2 June 1994)

But also these new metaphorical models are not without problems and are both praised and rejected, depending on the political position of the speaker(s).

Conclusion

The analysis has shown that a limited number of metaphors - which, however, are often interlinked and which allow for a wide variety of entailments - are used and developed in political discourse on European integration. The same metaphors are used in English and German texts, and in a fairly similar way, although there are a few differences concerning the preference for a metaphor and also concerning the country and/or political party which introduced a specific metaphor into the political debate. These differences, however, are not so much of an intercultural nature, but rather they reflect different attitudes within the countries, sometimes even within the political parties themselves.

Metaphors and metaphorical frames are a form of knowledge organisation. They provide models which are based on elementary forms of how human beings conceive and experience reality, and how they behave accordingly. The phenomenon of the metaphor, thus, provides possibilities to describe and explain the interaction of communication, cognition and linguistic structures. By analysing texts and, thus describing (politically relevant) text worlds, linguistics can contribute to explaining how knowledge is structured in the human mind and how it is utilized in discourse.

Taking metaphors as models of experiencing reality also implies that they have the potential power to anticipate reality and to shape reality. They are, therefore, of relevance for practical politics in that they function in defining political problems and in drawing up possible solutions to those problems. For example, when the European Commission describes itself as the 'motor' of integration, it will pay attention that its decisions will result in a deepening of the EU; or, Germany's idea of a 'core Europe' pressing ahead includes hidden threats to other member states not to stop the progress. When they are presented in form of metaphors, both the problems and the solutions offer scope for debate and controversy. In discussing this function of metaphors to influence the shaping of political reality, Wesel (1991, p. 78) characterizes them as "kognitiv-aktive Ordnungsmodelle" ['cognitively active classification models'], and Mehan and Skelley (1988, p. 59) as "world-ordering concepts". Shore (1995) even argued that politicians have become caught into their own metaphors and trapped by their thoughts.

In a leading article, *The Guardian* criticized the lack of clear vision within the EU:

A long time ago there was a *vision* of Europe. Now there appears to be nobody who can describe it in any terms other than an *anti-vision*, or the assembling of as many clouds as possible to obscure the visions still seen and heard across the Channel. (*The Guardian*, 28 April 1994)

However, the ongoing debates, both in the EU institutions and in each member state, produce not only anti-visions but also new visions which allow for new metaphorical entailments. Language is - to use a metaphor - a living organism, and as long as there is debate about the future of Europe, metaphors will be used, and in this process they will consolidate, change, or, maybe, disappear. In his article in *The Independent*, already quoted above, Andrew Marshall argues about the future of the Euro-metaphors, albeit obscuring the EU's prospects:

> More designs will follow, from political parties, the European Parliament, think-tanks and governments, with different ideas of the pace, structure and spirit of integration. The proliferation of images reflects extraordinary uncertainty about what the picture that emerges from 1996 will look like - let alone how it will sell to the public. Try to imagine a piece of fruit with pillars made of Meccano bowling down a motorway built in concentric circles and you can see the problems. (*The Independent*, 11 September 1994)

In a more recent article in *The Independent*, the same author presents a "new generation of jargon". He argues that some of the metaphors, for example, metaphors of architecture and transport ('pillars' and 'trains') are outdated:

> The arcane language of Brussels, impenetrable even to insiders, is going through a change. New phrases are emerging; old ones are dead in the water. [...] The reasons are simple. Firstly, as the prospect of maybe a dozen or more members increases, it is evident that the EU has to find a way to accommodate different configurations of countries. (*The Independent*, 2 July 1995)

So, Marshall claims, instead of the dead architecture metaphors, the 1995-style Eurojargon is much more concerned with relationships, and new vocabulary to watch out for includes, for example, 'in-out cohabitation', 'coalition of the willing', and 'structured dialogue'. The future, for example the discourse on the 1996 Intergovernmental Conference to review the Maastricht Treaty, will reveal the fate of both old and new metaphors.

References

Bachem, Rolf and Battke, Kathleen (1991), 'Strukturen und Funktionen der Metapher *Unser gemeinsames Haus Europa* im Aktuellen Politischen Diskurs' in Liedtke, Frank, Wengeler, Martin and Böke, Karin (eds), *Begriffe besetzen. Strategien des Sprachgebrauchs in der Politik*, Westdeutscher Verlag, Opladen, pp. 295-307.

Chilton, Paul (1986), 'Metaphor, Euphemism and the Militarization of Language', Paper presented at the Biannual meeting of the International Peace Research Association, Sussex, England, quoted in Mehan, Hugh and Skelley, James M. (eds), *Discourse of the Nuclear Arms Debate*, (= *Multilingua*, vol. 7, no. 1/2), pp. 35-66.

Chilton, Paul (1989), 'Safe as Houses?', *Peace Review*, vol. 1, no. 2, pp. 12-17.

Chilton, Paul und Ilyin, Mikhail (1993), 'Metaphor in Political Discourse: the Case of the "Common European House"', *Discourse and Society*, vol. 4 no. 1, pp. 7-31.

Chilton, Paul and Lakoff, George (1995), 'Foreign Policy by Metaphor', in Schäffner, Christina and Wenden, Anita (eds), *Language and Peace*, Dartmouth, Aldershot, pp. 37-59.

Fillmore, Charles (1976), 'Frame Semantics and the Nature of Language', *Annals of the New York Academy of Science*, vol. 280, pp. 20-32.

Gorbachev, Mikhail (1988), *Perestroika. New Thinking for our Country and the World*, Harper and Row, New York.

Kövecses, Zoltan (1986), *Metaphors of Anger, Pride, and Love. A Lexical Approach to the Structure of Concepts*, John Benjamins, Amsterdam.

Lakoff, George (1986), *Cognitive Semantics*, (*Berkeley Cognitive Science Report*, no. 36), University of California at Berkely, Berkeley.

Lakoff, George and Johnson, Mark (1980), *Metaphors We Live By*, University of Chicago Press, Chicago.

Lesage, Michel (1990), 'L'Europe vue de France' in Villain-Gandossi, Christiane, Bochmann, Klaus, Metzeltin, Michel and Schäffner, Christina (eds), *Le Concept de l'Europe dans le Processus de la CSCE / The Concept of Europe in the Process of the CSCE*, Gunter Narr, Tübingen, pp. 125-45.

Mehan, Hugh and Skelley, James M. (1988), 'Reykjavik: The Breach and Repair of the Pure War Script' in Mehan, Hugh and Skelley, James M. (eds), *Discourse of the Nuclear Arms Debate*, (= *Multilingua*, vol. 7, no. 1/2)), pp. 35-66.

Nikiforidou, Kiki and Sweetser, Eve (1989), *Diachronic Regularity and Irregularity: Structural Parallels between Semantic and Phonological Change*, (*Berkeley Cognitive Science Report*, no. 60), University of California at Berkely, Berkeley.

Rosch, Eleanor (1977), 'Human Categorization' in Warren, Neil (ed.), *Studies in Cross-Cultural Psychology*, vol. 1, Academic Press, New York, pp. 1-49.

Schäffner, Christina (1990), 'The concept of *Europe* in the British weekly "The Economist" over the Years 1975-1988' in Villain-Gandossi, Christiane, Bochmann, Klaus, Metzeltin, Michel and Schäffner, Christina (eds), *Le*

Concept de l'Europe dans le Processus de la CSCE / The Concept of Europe in the Process of the CSCE, Gunter Narr, Tübingen, pp. 199-212.

Schäffner, Christina (1994a), 'The Concept of Europe - a Network of Metaphors' in Marsh, David and Salo-Lee Liisa (eds), *Europe on the Move. Fusion or Fission?* (Proceedings 1994 SIETAR Europa Symposium), Jyväskylä 1994, pp. 117-25.

Schäffner, Christina (1994b), 'Internal and External Stereotypes in Cartoons - a Semiotic Analysis' in Berting, Jan and Villain-Gandossi, Christiane (eds), *The Role of Stereotypes in International Relations* (*Studies in Social and Cultural Transformations*, no. 4), RISBO, Rotterdam, pp. 211-37.

Schäffner, Christina (1995), 'Metapher als Bezeichnungsübertragung?' in Pohl, Inge and Ehrhardt, Horst (eds), *Wort und Wortschatz*, Niemeyer, Tübingen, pp. 175-84.

Schäffner, Christina and Porsch, Peter (1993), 'Meeting the Challenge on the Path to Democracy: Discursive Strategies in Governmental Declarations', *Discourse & Society*, vol. 4, no. 1, pp. 33-55.

Schäffner, Christina and Trommer, Sylvia (1990), 'Das Konzept des *gemeinsamen europäischen Hauses* im Russischen und Englischen' in Schäffner, Christina (ed.), *Gibt es eine Prototypische Wortschatzbeschreibung? Eine Problemdiskussion* (= *Linguistische Studien*, LS/ZISW/A, no. 202), Zentralinstitut für Sprachwissenschaft, Berlin, pp. 80-91.

Shank, Roger (1982), *Dynamic Memory. A Theory of Reminding and Learning in Computers and People*, Cambridge University Press, Cambridge.

Shore, Cris (1995), 'Cultural Developments', Paper presented at the conference 'Is European Union Irreversible?', Bath, 30 June - 1 July 1995.

Wesel, Reinhard (1991), 'Entwicklungspolitische Rhetorik: Kognitive Strukturen im Phänomenbereich "Dritte Welt" und ihre "symbolische Politisierung" zwischen euphorischer Projektion und Bedrohungsängsten.' in Opp de Hipt, Manfred and Latniak, Erich (eds), *Sprache statt Politik? Politikwissenschaftliche Semantik- und Rhetorikforschung*, Westdeutscher Verlag, Opladen, pp. 66-90.

The Enlargement Negotiations in the West-European Press: A Study of Information Flow in the EU

LIEVE VAN DE WALLE

Introduction

In this book we are interested in verifying whether Pan-European discourse was a concept worth coining, i.e. whether we have indeed established a supra-national, 'European' discourse. This particular contribution focuses on the role of the press in this process simply because media discourse reaches a large audience and - to quote Fowler (1991, p. 9) - "is a major element in our daily experience of language". As a result, a pragmatic analysis of this type of discourse is more than likely to provide a key to ideological common ground in the European Union.

It seemed opportune to zoom in on the enlargement negotiations (February-March 1994) as here a number of longstanding but largely underestimated internal conflicts of an ideological nature between EU member states (e.g., federal versus supranational, North versus South, France versus Germany) unexpectedly came to a head and caused intense debate and friction.

By closely examining how leading magazines in Belgium, Holland, France and Germany (championing a Federal Europe) and Britain (advocating an intergovernmental approach) select, interpret and present information pertaining to these negotiations and uncovering which fundamental ideological processes are hidden at the implicit level, I shall try to establish whether there are such things as common ground or naturalized ideas concerning European issues. The leading question in this paper is whether one can indeed identify fairly homogeneous, centred flows of information in the West-European Press or whether Euro-correspondents are biased by national interests and fill in their version of Europe by-passing central or federal networks of power.

The selection and transformation of 'facts' in the press.

Most famous newspaper and magazine owners entered the business for more complex reasons than profit alone. They are not only in it for status, there is also the opportunity to impose a structure of values on whatever is represented, 'construct' reality in a manner congruent with their own ideological and political preferences and shape public opinion (cf. Fowler, 1991, p. 4), not to mention the temptation to influence the course of history. A common trait of powerholders is that they tend not to exercise their power openly. Strategies used to disguise power are constraining content and, as Fairclough (1989, p. 57) puts it, "favouring certain interpretations and 'wordings' of events while excluding others" (cf. also Fowler, 1991, p. 2). Hence, a critical analysis of linguistic structure is an excellent point of departure to uncover dimensions of power. A critical analysis is an enquiry into the relations between signs, meanings and the social and historical conditions which govern the semiotic structure of discourse (Fowler, 1991, p. 5). The disclosure of implicitly conveyed information in media reports helps one to trace underlying frames of reference and the ideology authors allegedly share with their readers. Media reports are never value-free, they are invariably embedded in a social, political, economic and ideological context, no matter how objective, conscientious, and scrupulous the authors aspire to be.

The corpus

Providers of my data were the January, February, March and April 1994 issues of the following Western European quality magazines: *Knack* (Belgium); *The Economist* (Britain); *Le Point* (France); *Der Spiegel* (Germany); and *Elsevier* (Holland). Two types of articles emerged: those introducing and commenting on the new applicants, and those discussing the constitutional crisis.

Background information on the enlargement negotiations

Neither the then applicant countries (Norway, Sweden, Finland and Austria) nor the then current EU member states are likely to forget the wrangling that went on between the Ministers of Foreign Affairs during the final rounds of the enlargement negotiations (February till March 1994). Certainly, the applicants, all members of the European Free Trade Association (EFTA), liberal democracies with small populations, and potential net contributors to the Union's budget, drove a hard bargain. It was not, however, the terms on which these states were permitted to join the club which formed the major stumbling block. It was an internal matter, i.e. voting procedures in the Council of Ministers, that led to a full-blown crisis.

Ever since the Single European Act (1986), issues such as the single market, the environment, health and safety and - most important - the Union's budget have been decided by a "qualified majority" of votes distributed roughly according to size rather than by unanimous accord. For the Union's twelve members in 1994, the votes added up to 76, and the qualified majority needed to make policy was 54 of those votes. That meant that only 23 votes were needed to form a "blocking" minority - which could be made up of two big countries and any small country other than Luxembourg (*The Economist*, 12 March 1994). In 1994, debates were held concerning the expected entry of four new members. If they joined the Union, the total number of votes would rise to 90 and - by extrapolation - the qualified majority would go up to 64 and the number of votes needed to form a blocking minority up to 27. Although this calculation seemed pretty unproblematic at first glance, it met with fierce opposition in the Council of Ministers. Britain, Spain and Italy would not hear of diluting their ability to block what they did not like. Whereas Italy came round rather quickly, Britain and Spain insisted to the bitter end that the blocking minority should remain at 23 votes and that important structural changes should await the intergovernmental conference in 1996, where basically everything will be up for discussion (number of commissioners, rotation of the presidency in the Council of Ministers, the joint security policy, ...).

As always, the Twelve eventually did come up with a compromise: i.e., the blocking minority in the enlarged Council of Ministers was set at 27 as planned, but with the understanding that, if countries can muster 23 votes, the challenged decision will stay in the pending tray for a while.

Discussion of the data and findings

Information flow

In this section I will quote and analyse data from various magazines in order to question the official EU stance on information flow, an outline of which we find in the paragraph on 'The Fourth Power: The Role of the Press' in the brochure *Une Communauté plus Démocratique* (1993). The gist of this text is that the relationship between the press and the Union is extremely good; that the Union is ahead of national governments in this respect; that the Union cares for its citizens and that newspaper reports on the Union are fairly homogeneous since they are based on official press releases and personal interviews with EU employees. Readers of this text in the brochure are meant to infer subconsciously that journalists paint the same picture of Europe, endorsing the view (illusion) that Europe is one, and that an uneven flow of communication is out of the question.

Attitude towards the enlargement A close analysis of my data reveals a full spectrum of judgements which, as I am about to demonstrate, are not always passed on in the form of hard statements. Reading between the lines, one can discriminate three tendencies ranging from the extremely negative stance that the applicants must be out of their mind wanting to join the decrepit EU, through the more ambivalent attitude that even if negotiations succeed, accession is not a sure thing, to the extremely positive stance that this development is profitable, full stop, to all parties involved.

The title to *Elsevier's* article ('From Paradise to EU', 12 March 1994) is a real gem. The point of departure for the applicants is 'paradise', a lexeme which evokes an ideal society in which hardship and pain are non-existent, the destination is membership of the EU. Without compromising himself the author implicates that the enlargement process is detrimental to the joining countries. The two-page article that follows is blotted with allusions that the decision taken by Austria and the three Scandinavian countries to join the EU was a very silly move indeed, witness the following lines (all quotations from non-English sources have been translated by me; all italics - if not indicated otherwise - are mine, L.vdW.):

> Zweden, Finland, Oostenrjk. Zo dadelijk misschien ook Noorwegen. Wat *moeten d e* sociale paradijzen, die horen tot de rijkste economie'n van Europa, in *de* door werkloosheid geteisterde Europese Unie die ze hun *beleids- en bewegingsvrijheid* zal ontnemen en hun paradijselijkheid zal aantasten? (*Elsevier*, 12 March 1994)
> [Sweden, Finland, Austria. Maybe soon to be followed by Norway. What are *the* social paradises, ranking among Europe's wealthiest economies, doing in *the* unemployment-stricken EU, which will deprive them of both *their freedom of movement and their freedom to set their own policies* and which will *affect* their paradisiacal nature?]

The author wants to accomplish a sense of indignation in his audience. By using the under-defined definite article 'the' in 'the social paradises', the author creates the impression that no countries equal the favourable conditions of Sweden, Finland, Austria and Norway. Similarly, the under-defined definite article 'the' in 'the unemployment-stricken EU' suggests that Europe has a monopoly on this social nightmare. To make matters worse, not only is Europe associated with unemployment, it is also linked with the curtailing of the freedom of movement of its members and of meddling with their policies. Join the EU and paradise is lost. The next fragment demonstrates further how the author avoids explicit statements but surreptitiously vents his negative feelings.

> De kleine rijke landen [...] hebben hun sociaal-economische autonomie al veel eerder *opgeofferd*. Toetreding tot de Unie in 1995 zoe niet meer zijn dan de voltooiing van een proces dat *sluipend* begon in de jaren zeventig en begin jaren negentig een *alarmerend en economisch bedreigend* tempo kreeg. (*Elsevier*, 12 March 1994)

> [The small rich countries *sacrificed* their social-economic autonomy years ago. Joining the Union in 1995 would merely amount to completing a process that *sneaked* up on them in the seventies and that gained *alarming and economically threatening* momentum in the early nineties.]

Again the article 'the' in 'the small countries' is used as a device to imply totality. In this passage, note especially the use of the word 'sacrificed'. To 'sacrifice' means to 'give up', to do something that hurts, usually in return for something. The author volunteers the information that these four countries gave up their autonomy but stops short of adding what their incentive for doing so was. Text cohesion requires readers to fill that gap either using real life knowledge or information communicated in the previous paragraphs. The most likely answer readers are going to come up with is the following: In exchange for their sacrifice they will get nothing but access to the EU, which, being ravaged by unemployment, will mean the onset of leaner years. Also, in the author's opinion, the process sneaked up on them. Those poor countries were not the authors of their own fate, they were not fully aware of what was going on. They were sort of tricked into membership.

Der Spiegel (7 February 1994), in contrast, stands out by its positive attitude towards the enlargement and emphasizes the gains only:

> Mit den 26 Millionen neuen EU-Bürgern aus den vergleichsweise reichen beitrittswilligen Staaten Österreich, Schweden, Finnland und Norwegen wächst das Wohlstandsniveau in der Union um 2.2 Prozent. Gemeinsam werden die 16 ein größeres Bruttosozialprodukt erwirtschaften als Nafta, [...]. (*Der Spiegel*, 7 February 1994)
> [Adding the 26 million new EU citizens from the comparatively rich applicants, Austria, Sweden, Finland and Norway the standard of living will go up with 2.2 per cent. Together the 16 will realize a higher GNP than Nafta, [...].]

Yet other magazines are mainly concerned with the referenda that will take place in the Scandinavian countries and Austria. As far as the article in *Knack* (9 March 1994) is concerned, it is clear from the very first line that the author (Mr Vuga) is not optimistic as to the outcome of those referenda:

> **In het positiefste** geval telt de Europese Unie op 1 januari '95 vijftien in de plaats van twaalf lidstaten. *In het positiefste geval*, omdat met het afsluiten van toetredingsverdragen, vorige week tussen de Unie en het driespan Zweden - Finland - Oostenrijk, lang niet alles in kannen en kruiken is. Drie stemronden moeten nog *vonnissen* over die verdragen, [...]. (*Knack*, 9 March 1994; bold print and italics in the orginal)
> [At best on 1 January 1995 the EU will consist of 15 member states instead of 12. *At best*, because having completed last week negotiations between the EU and the threesome Sweden - Finland - Austria, things are not exactly in the bag. Three ballots are yet to pronounce a verdict on those treaties [...].]

Doubtlessly, this passage beats us around the ears with ideological messages. The repetition of 'at best', twice with conspicuous typeset, is meant to convince the reader that the author must have a point. If everything goes as planned Europe will count fifteen members. This is presented as the best case scenario. More than likely, even this prognosis is too optimistic. Note in this respect his use of the idiom to 'pronounce a verdict' which, being a term used in court, has negative associations. The choice of this particular phrase strongly suggests that the electorate will be very critical indeed, if not downright negative. Perceptive readers will also notice that Norway is not included in the list, nor in the debate in general. This omission is not a mistake, but a deliberate move from the author to surreptitiously convey the message that Norway does not really stand a chance of joining. Later on in the text, the author volunteers his stance on Norway in more explicit terms, but by then the idea that Norway will refuse entry as it did in 1972 should have taken root in the minds of the readers.

The Economist (12 February 1994) also expresses its doubts on the successful outcome of the referendums. But unlike Mr Vuga, it does not force its view down its readers' throats by means of conspicuous techniques. It is not until the very last paragraph that the reader is told in a very subtle and implicit manner that the ensuing deals may yet turn sour:

> But what is *needed most of all* is a positive trend in the opinion polls in the applicant countries. Even if this month's deadline is met, the target date for entry will be irrelevant if the referenda go awry. (*The Economist*, 12 February 1994)

The fact that a positive trend is 'needed' implies that right now citizens are rather suspicious of entering the EU. The conditional clause 'if the referendums go awry' suggests that this is a possible scenario indeed and not just a wild conjecture. Besides, a positive attitude is what is needed 'most of all', i.e., the referendums and not the negotiations nor the approval by the EU Parliament will be the biggest obstacles on the path towards enlargement. In the last paragraph of the article 'From the Arctic to the Mediterranean', published about a month later on 5 March 1994, this doubt is repeated in a similar manner.

Although explicitly acknowledging the risks involved, *Le Point* (5 March 1994) is less concerned about the referendums. In its opinion, the European Parliament presents a more serious threat because Euro MPs in general resent the way in which negotiations have been conducted.

> Enfin, et *avant tout*, il faut que le Parlement européen donne, le 7 mai prochain, son feu vert. Bien qu'on imagine mal une censure de sa part, un tel coup de théâtre n'est pas exclu. (*Le Point*, 5 March 1994)
> [Finally, *and above all*, the European Parliament must give a green light on May 7th. Although its blocking the enlargement is hard to imagine, it is not impossible.]

The crisis: The British versus the Continental press? This crisis offers the media a very good excuse to vent pent-up frustrations about certain member states. Again the data will demonstrate, quite convincingly I hope, that authors and editors in quality magazines often abstain from presenting their opinion in a straightforward manner lest they should come across as too radical and antagonize readers, but strategically resort - be it consciously or unconsciously - to subliminal techniques "to fence in their ideas in the realm of the politically conceivable" (cf. Bourdieu as quoted in Wodak, 1989, p. 141).

The alliance between Spain and Britain in their opposition to the enlargement is an odd one to say the least, all magazines concur on this point. An advocate of free trade, Britain has always felt very strongly about the enlargement of the EU. Spain, in contrast, has never hidden its reluctance to admit new members, be they rich or poor. Afraid that the centre of gravity of the Union might shift from the south to the north, Spain is set on retaining its ability to form pacts with the other Mediterranean countries, Italy and Greece (Portugal has never been considered a reliable partner), to protect their olive-belt interests. If Spain (worth 8 votes) can muster the support of Italy (a 10-vote partner) and Greece (a 5-vote partner), those 23 votes are sufficient to deny any proposal the necessary qualified majority.

The Economist is by no means surprised by the anti-enlargement rhetoric of the Spanish and even anticipated it. The opening line of its article 'Spain drives another hard bargain', which was published as early as 19 February 1994, goes as follows:

> Is Spain becoming *as awkward* a European *as* Britain? (*The Economist*, 19 February 1994)

Both the title of this article and the opening line are rich in insinuations. The deictic 'another' in the title suggests that this is not the first time that Spain's obstinacy has surfaced and that it is all getting a bit tedious maybe. The opening line, on the other hand, presupposes that Britain is the epitome of awkwardness, the standard of comparison, a reputation which is not particularly flattering. Yet, in spite of this sarcastic comment, at that point in time Spain was still considered the sole obstacle on the road towards enlargement. The cartoon added to liven up the article shows a vicious-looking Spanish matador fighting a Viking who is storming forward like a bull.

Unlike *The Economist, Knack* (23 March 1994) does seem to be stunned by Spain and Italy's intransigence:

> De houding van die twee landen is *verwonderlijk*. Itali' behoort immers tot de stichtende leden van de Unie. Terwijl de Spaanse premier Felipe Gonzales zich altijd als een overtuigd voorstander van verdere Europese integratie heeft onderscheiden. (*Knack*, 23 March 1994)

[The attitude of those two countries is *surprising*. Italy is one of the founding members of the Union while the Spanish Premier Felipe Gonzales has always stood out as a champion of European integration.]

The second sentence is not explicitly linked to the first one, but the assumption is that the link is causal and that the second sentence explains the first one. Now, the argument that Italy is not supposed to play up because it is a founding member presupposes that the six founding members invariably agree no matter how or what. So, even when Italy thinks its interests are in peril, it is not supposed to object. As far as Gonzales is concerned, the fact that he is an advocate of European integration does not imply that he should favour enlargement as the readers are led to believe. Quite on the contrary, Gonzales has always pleaded for deepening and consolidating European Institutions before expanding. Thus, saying that his anti-behaviour is unexpected because of his past championship of European integration is conflating two lines of thought and as such creating a false paradox.

Neither *Knack* (23 March 1994) nor *Der Spiegel* (28 March 1994) for that matter ever even contemplated the idea that, in fact, it was the Spanish who were the authors of the whole conflict and that Britain jumped on its bandwagon later on. In the Belgian and German Press the British are depicted as the initiators of the trouble:

Toch ligt Groot-Brittanni' hardnekkig dwars, *uit princiep*. (*Knack*, 23 March 1994)
[Yet [in spite of the logical calculations: the more members, the more votes required to block a decision] Great Britain persists in being obstructive, *out of principle*.]

In Brüssel bahnt sich eine schwere Krise an: Die Briten wollen den Weg zur Einheit *versperren*. (*Der Spiegel*, 28 March 1994)
[A heavy crisis is in the make in Brussels: The British aim at *obstructing* the road towards Union.]

The way it is phrased in *Knack,* the reader is encouraged to conclude that the British have no good reason at all to oppose a change in the decision making process in the Council of Ministers. Britain is stereotyped as 'difficult', it 'obstructs' without thinking 'out of habit'. The subtitle in *Der Spiegel* makes it perfectly clear - although the causal relationship is left implicit - that the British are the only ones to be blamed for the crisis in Brussels. The fact that they have joined forces with the Spanish is only mentioned in passing in the third paragraph (the Italians are not mentioned at all). Even then Spain's role as an accomplice is not explicitly acknowledged. There is no sentence introducing or explaining the Spanish position at this point. So out of the blue an accomplice pops up, only to sink into oblivion again. In the next paragraph evil Britain plays it solo again :

In fact this is what *the British* want to achieve: [...] (*Der Spiegel*, 28 March 1994)

Spain crops up once more in the next paragraph but again it is quite clear that it is merely playing second fiddle to Britain:

> Nun sieht er [Major] die Chance, unterstützt von den Spaniern, [...] jeder weiteren Integration den Riegel vorzuschieben. "Die Briten", erkannte Belgiens Außenminister Willy Claes, "kämpfen um ein Konzept, das nicht das unsere ist." (*Der Spiegel*, 28 March 1994)
> [Now he [Major], backed up by the Spanish, sees the opportunity to nip any form of further integration in the bud. 'The British', acknowledged the Belgian Foreign Secretary, Willy Claes, 'are fighting for a concept which is not ours.']

Major is introduced as the instigator, the agent. He is responsible for obstructing further developments. The Spanish are backgrounded in a subordinate clause and are out of focus. By grammatical means, the author guides his readers to the conclusion that the Spanish play merely a passive role. The fact that the following sentence, not by coincidence a statement by a political heavyweight, draws all attention to the British only enforces that image.

At first glance, *Le Point* (5 March 1994, and 19 March 1994) steers a middle course. Whenever it addresses the impasse, it puts Britain and Spain on a par:

> Mais deux pays, l'Espagne et la Grande-Bretagne, refusent cette logique arithmétique et historique (puisqu'elle a toujours été appliquée). (*Le Point*, 5 March 1994)
> [But two countries, Spain and Britain, refuse to accept this logical and historical (because it has always been applied) arithmetic.]

But appearances are deceptive. Whereas Spain's motives for blocking the enlargement are invariably presented as acceptable if not honourable, Britain's motives trigger negative feelings. Note the contrast between the neutral 'line of argument' and the judgmental 'destructive pigheadedness' to refer to the Spanish and British argumentation, respectively:

> Pourquoi? Les Anglais, bien sûr, pour bloquer plus facilement la machine. Les Espagnols, parce qu'ils s'inquiètent de ce basculement de l'Union vers le nord [...] Mais céder à ce raisonnement - ou à l'entêtement destructeur de Londres - ce serait revenir des décennies en arrière. (*Le Point*, 19 March 1994)
> [Why? The English, of course, to block the machinery more easily. The Spanish because they worry about the shift of power to the North [...]. But, yielding to the latter line of argument - or to the *destructive pigheadedness* of London - would be a major setback for the community.]

There is no need to stress that *Le Point's* explanation for the intransigence of the British is all too simplistic ('The British are just being stubborn'). The official line of argument included the following points: It is necessary to halt both the erosion of national sovereignty by curtailing the expansion of majority voting; and, second, small countries hold disproportionate power as it is and should not get the opportunity of holding large countries to ransom (cf. *The Economist*, 12 March 1994). The Continental press, however, did not buy this and volunteered some explanations of its own. Compare the following quote from *Knack* (23 March 1994):

> Als de blokkeringsminderheid wordt opgetrokken, krijgen de groten het moeilijker om de besluitvorming van de Unie *naar hun hand te zetten*. De Britse konservatieven vrezen dat de nationale soevereiniteit zo *nog meer* bedreigd zal worden. Voor hen is de kwestie een staatszaak. Aan de vooravond van de Europese verkiezingen geeft het de konservatieve Euro-sceptici de kans op een *revanche* voor hun nederlaag in de strijd tegen het verdrag van Maastricht. (*Knack*, 23 March 1994)
> [If the blocking minority is raised the bigger member states will find it more difficult *to have their own way* with the Union's decision-making. The British conservatives fear that national sovereignty will thus be *even more* threatened. To them this matter is an affair of the state. With European elections coming up, it gives conservative Euro-sceptics a chance to *revenge* the defeat they suffered in the battle against the Maastricht Treaty.]

The way the author has chosen his words points to the fact that he does not approve of the attitude of large countries and Britain in particular. Large countries (including Britain) want to impose their will on the smaller countries, they want to pull all the strings. For Britain, national sovereignty has always been a sacred cow, touch that and you enter national politics. To link the concluding line of this paragraph to what precedes requires quite a bit of inferencing on the part of the reader. In fact, it reduces the conflict to an act of 'revenge' and pinpoints the conservative Euro-sceptics as the real culprits. It shifts the attention from the British in general to the Euro-sceptics and hints that this conflict is not about an honourable cause.

Der Spiegel, on the other hand, feels the British, opportunistic as they are, are after three things. First, they want to undermine the internal strength in the EU. Second, Major wants to butter up the conservative Euro-sceptics. Third, and most importantly, Major wants to push through his vision of Europe, which most certainly does not include a United States of Europe. The fact that Major refers to a Federal Europe as 'old slogans and dreams' suggests that the idea of a Federal Europe is out of date and not realistic anyway. All in all, one gets the feeling that *Der Spiegel* depicts the British as a threat to Europe in that they want no less than hegemony over Europe:

> Tatsächlich geht es den Briten darum, die Erweiterung der Union zu nutzen, um deren inneren Zusammenhalt zu schwächen. Premier John Major will sich mit seiner unnachgiebigen Haltung in Brüssel nicht nur bei anti-

europäischen konservativen Parteifreunden anbiedern. Er möchte den EU-Partnern seine "Vision von Europa aufzwingen" (*Financial Times*): eine riesige Freihandelszone [...] ohne ihre nationale Souveränität einzubüßen. Es sei Zeit, so Major, "die *alten Schlagworte und Träume*" von einem föderalen Eruopa aufzugeben. (*Der Spiegel*, 28 March 1994)
[In fact this is what the British want to achieve: They want to use the enlargement of the Union to weaken its unity. With his intransigent attitude, Prime Minister John Major not only seeks to butter up anti-European, conservative party members. He aims at 'imposing his vision of Europe' upon his EU-partners (*Financial Times*): A giant free-trade zone [...] without loss of sovereignty. It is time, according to Major, 'to give up those *old slogans and dreams*' about a federal Europe.]

Quite surprisingly perhaps, *The Economist*, which in its early articles was prepared to put at least part of the blame on Spain and Italy, displays no such mercy in its later articles (19 March 1994, and 26 March 1994). The titles and captions need no further explanation:

title: Still stuck
caption under a photo of Douglas Hurd: Britain's *blockhead*   (*The Economist*, 19 March 1994)

title: Perfidious Albion (next to a photo of Douglas Hurd)
subtitle: *Incompetent too* (*The Economist*, 26 March 1994)

The subtitle 'incompetent too' is a sarcastic comment. To me the small print evokes a person mumbling this between his teeth, just loud enough to be heard. As the following quote illustrates, *The Economist* is subtle no longer, as time goes by its tone becomes increasingly irritated:

Such self-interested arithmetic [by the Spanish] at least commands grudging respect.
Britain gets no such respect. Its prime minister, John Major, has always argued *loudly* for a larger Union [...]. Sending the foreign secretary, Douglas Hurd, to insist that the blocking minority should nonetheless stay unchanged *smacks* not so much of national selfishness [...] but of party politics. (*The Economist*, 19 March 1994)

The enlargement of the Union, *say the rest*, has become *hostage to* Mr Major's desire to *placate* the anti-European elements of the Conservative Party. (*The Economist*, 26 March 1994)

The style is direct. The attack on the prime minister is not diluted, there are no hedges, 'gets no such respect', 'smacks of party politics'. The fact that Major argued 'loudly' for the enlargement makes his present position all the more pathetic. The bottom line of the paragraph, backed up by politicians in the rest of Europe, is that Major's ulterior motive to stall negotiations is party politics (cf. *Knack*). Again the magazine does not shun the use of loaded words: the enlargement is held 'hostage to', Major 'desires to placate' [...]. The article 'Perfidious Albion' further explores this line of thought. The tone is quite savage, *The Economist* is clearly fed up and about to lose its patience.

It should be clear at this point that in spite of the official press releases by the EU authorities, people back home do get totally different messages depending upon the channels of information they rely on. Even quality magazines, which target a critical audience, people rich in cultural capital, and which take pride in their 'objective' accounts of what happened 'out there', often present a totally different picture. It is also a fact that the views presented by the media are often packaged so carefully that it takes close scrutiny of those linguistic features "which work subliminally in their ideological practice of representation" (cf. Fowler, 1991, p. 5) to grasp their full dimension.

Important at this point is that the press does seem to live a life of its own. As far as the enlargement negotiations are concerned, it is fairly safe to conclude that the West European press does not function as the spokesperson for the local Euro-politicians; rather they pick and choose arguments as they see fit. Journalists in Britain do not necessarily approve of the tactics used by Douglas Hurd, nor do their Dutch colleagues feel the need to support the moves of their Foreign Secretary. *Der Spiegel* was the only magazine that might be suspected of having German interests at heart.

The more varied the messages at the surface are, though, the more similar they are at a deeper level. The Western European press does seem to agree upon at least one thing, i.e. the imagery used to refer to certain nationalities. We will take a closer look at this phenomenon in the next section.

Shaping of public opinion: undercurrents of ethnocentrism and bigotry

Like metaphors, stereotypes are used to frame or pigeon-hole people or events. Contextualizing a person or an event by sorting him or her or it in a familiar, mental category facilitates communication for it presupposes common ground (cf. also Schäffner's and O'Donnell's contributions in this volume). In this section I am particularly interested in indirect, more or less disguised forms of stereotypes, for they are subtle and subliminal but effective (because invisible) ways of shaping public opinion. Furthermore, like overt stereotypes they lead us to common ground, ideological conceptions shared by large groups of (Western) European citizens.

As must be clear from my rather elaborate discussion of *Elsevier's* attitude towards the enlargement and of the British and Spanish attitude towards the voting procedures, national stereotypes, be they direct or indirect, are rampant in this corpus. In this section I will point out some more hotbeds of potential 'racism'. In the first fragment I will quote (*Der Spiegel*, 7 March 1994), the Greeks have the doubtful honour of being targeted. The German Minister of Foreign Affairs, Kinkel is described as a pugnacious hero, ready to go for it, whereas his Greek colleague, Pangalos, who is chairman to boot, is close to a nervous breakdown and wants to give up. There are no shades of grey in this picture. Without stating as much, the Greek is presented as a loser, the German as a winner:

> Der Bonner Außenminister, *kämpferisch* wie nie zuvor, wollte mit aller Macht den Erfolg. Er war es, der verhinderte, daß der *entnervte* Grieche Theodorus Pangalos, der den Vorsitz bei den Verhandlungen führte, den *"Basar"* (Pangalos) vorzeitig *abbrach*. (*Der Spiegel*, 7 March 1994)
> [The German Minister of Foreign Affairs, *belligerent* as never before, was determined to be successful. He was the one who prevented the *nerve-racked* Greek Theodoros Pangalos, the chair of the negotiations, from *shutting up shop* prematurely.]

The fact that the Greek minister symbolizes weakness is not a coincidence. There are numerous instances of Greek-bashing in my corpus, which brings us to one of the main ideological struggles in the EU, i.e. the North-South conflict. In the next passage (*Der Spiegel*, 21 March 1994) von Kyau, a German diplomat, has been assigned to wind up the negotiations with the Norwegians in spite of the fact that he is completely unfamiliar with the issues:

> Alles *Hekuba*, aber daran waren nur die Griechen schuld. Denn eigentlich hätten die als derzeit amtierende Ratsvorsitzende die Beitrittsverhandlungen mit Österreich, Schweden, Finnland und auch Norwegen führen sollen. Doch die Griechen hatten offenbar *irgendeinen Katastrophoulos* mit der Organisation betraut [...]
> Nachdem dann die Griechen die vergleichsweise einfachen Verhandlungen mit den Schweden und den Finnen für sich reklamierten, blieb den Deutschen der Problem-Kandidat Norwegen [...] (*Der Spiegel*, 21 March 1994)
> [He [von Kyau] couldn't care less [about these issues] but the Greeks are the ones to blame for this. As chair of the Council of Ministers they were in fact responsible for the enlargement negotiations with Austria, Sweden, Finland as well as Norway. But, apparently, the Greeks had entrusted the organization to a *Mr. Katastrophoulos*. [...]
> After the Greeks had claimed the relatively easy negotiations with the Swedes and Finns, the Germans *got stuck with* the problem-applicant Norway.]

The way the Greeks are represented is very disparaging. They are associated with negative qualities only. They are semantically linked with the following attributes: they are irresponsible, selfish, complacent and disastrous organizers. The tone is even sarcastic at times: 'apparently, they had entrusted the organization to a Mr Katastrophoulos'. This very fact, i.e. that the Greek language is held up to ridicule, particularly smacks of ethnocentrism. The effect the author is after is to firmly root this negative image of the Greeks in his audience and simultaneously strengthen the image of the successful German nationals. *Le Point* confirms this picture. In an article dated 5 March 1994, the Greeks are said to have merely plodded along and, in doing so, to have given ample opportunity to the applicants to maximize their gains. *Le Point* also confirms that it was Kinkel who saved the day:

> C'est le ministre allemand Kinkel qui a sauvé, mardi matin, une négociation depuis longtemps enlisée. (*Le Point*, 5 March 1994)
> [It was the German Minister Kinkel who, on Tuesday morning, saved the negotiations which had been deadlocked for a long time.]

According to this same magazine (29 January 1994, 'The twelve à la sauce grecque', the idea that the Greeks should have never even been allowed to join the EU is widespread, although not many officials would be ready to state this in public.

Unfortunately maybe, the Greeks are not the only bad guys in Europe. In *Der Spiegel* (7 March 1994) one can read that:

> Die Spanier, Wortführer der mediterranen *Profiteure, witterten* die Gefahr, daß sich die Zahlmeister der EU künftig zusammenschließen und die Empfängerländer kurzhalten könnten. Kinkel warnte die *störrischen* Unterhändler aus Madrid, daß die Position des Nettozahlers "zunehmend Schwierigkeiten in Deutschland" bereite. (*Der Spiegel*, 7 March 1994)
> [The Spanish, representatives of the Mediterranean profiteers, *sniffed* the danger that henceforth the *paymasters* of the EU could close their ranks and *keep in check* the nations at the *receiving end* of the bargain. Kinkel warned the *disruptive* negotiators from Madrid that the position of the net contributors is triggering 'increasing difficulties in Germany.]

The Spanish and all Mediterranean countries for that matter are reduced to 'profiteers', nations who live off the fat of the northern countries. Apart from that, the Spanish are said to have 'sniffed' the danger that their privileges might be threatened. This loaded expression encourages readers to conclude that the Spanish are cunning in a rather primitive way and indeed deserve to be 'kept in check' by the northerners. The Spanish negotiators are further discredited as being 'disruptive', which suggests that they are not honourable like the rest of the team. This dire image, which is meant to rub off on all Mediterranean nations, is all the more obvious because of the stark contrast with the contours of power surrounding the 'paymasters', who are in a position to hand out favours, control, close ranks, and threaten. In *The Economist* (5 March 1994) we run into this very same stereotype:

> Whereas the Spanish and Portuguese [...] saw accession as a chance to join Europe's mainstream *at someone else's expense*, voters in today's applicant countries are being asked to contribute to a Union which is in economic doldrums and, in comparison with their own countries, is poorer and dirtier. (*The Economist*, 5 March 1994)

The new applicants are spoken of in very flattering terms indeed, an honour which is most certainly not bestowed on the southern European countries Spain and Portugal. It is implicated that, in stark contrast with the latter, the former are not in it for the money (?) and that, in fact, they are more sound from an economic, social and ecological point of view. That Finland equals Spain's 20 per cent unemployment rate and that its social network has been on the brink of collapse ever since the Soviet Empire broke down is not mentioned at this point. Compare also the following quote from *Knack* (23 March 1994) in this respect:

> Als de vier nieuwe leden aansluiten, wordt Europa een stuk noordelijker en vrezen de landen van de Middellandse Zee veel invloed in de boeten. Met een blokkeringsminderheid van 23 stemmen kunnen Spanje, Itali' en Griekenland de zaken makkelijker onder controle houden en erover waken dat de *miljardenstroom naar het zuiden niet opdroogt. (Knack*, 23 March 1994)
> [Upon entry of the four new members, Europe will become quite a bit more northern and the Mediterranean countries fear losing a lot of influence. With a blocking minority set at 23 votes, Spain, Italy and Greece can keep things under control more easily and can see to it that *the flow of money running into billions does not dry up.*]

Finally, and this is quite unique to *Der Spiegel*, the ongoing competition (read power struggle) between France and Germany surfaces a number of times.

> Nicht nur finanziell versprechen sich die Bonner Entlastung, sie rechnen auch mit politischem Gewinn. Hatten bisher in den Brüsseler *Schaltstellen* vor allem die Franzosen die Weichen gestellt, so könnte jetzt die Bundesrepublik zum Motor des *neuen, nach Osten hin offenen Europa* werden. (*Der Spiegel*, 7 March 1994)
> [The relief of Bonn is not a purely financial matter, Bonn also counts on gaining political influence. If so far it was mainly the French who *held sway* over the *headquarters* in Brussels, now Germany could become the motor behind *the new Europe with its doors open to the East.*]

This passage makes the aspirations of Germany quite clear. As the biggest net contributor to the EU, it is looking forward to the enlargement of the EU not only because the new members, potential net contributors, will relieve Bonn financially but especially because of the influence it hopes to gain. The words used in the article to describe the present position of the French, i.e. 'headquarters', 'to hold sway over' barely hide the dormant envy of the Germans. However, the author stops short of explicitly stating that the time has come for the Germans to take over now. He merely hints at the impending transfer of power carefully hedging the verb: 'could become'. He does not use overt terminology like 'to hold sway over' but describes power in a euphemistic manner by means of the metaphor of the 'motor'. The author also imposes the German position on the future of Europe on the reader. That the 'new' Europe will open up to its neighbours from the East is presented as a fact - witness the use of the definite article and the absence of any hedges, 'the new Europe with its doors open to the East'.

The next quote, winding off this very same article, is meant to create the impression that the French are losers really and bad losers at that. Normally, people are supposed to share in the joy of their colleagues and amicably join the celebrations. Not so the French Foreign Secretary:

> Als die österreichische Delegation [...] auf den erfolgreichen Abschluß [...] anstieß, fehlte [...] ein wichtiger Gast: der französische Europaminister Alain Lamassoure. *Ihm war offenbar nicht nach Feiern zumute.* (*Der Spiegel*, 7 March 1994)
> [When the Austrian delegation raised a toast on the successful conclusion of the negotiations [...] one important guest was missing: the French minister for European Affairs Alain Lamassoure. Apparently he did not feel like celebrating.]

That he is tagged as a bad sport is emphasized by the way the sentence is constructed. You get lots of circumstantial information that is meant to build up to a climax, i.e. who is that mystery man? The question as to why he is absent is not explicitly answered. All that is offered is innuendo. As readers we are led to infer that Mr. Lamassoure is sulking or generally dissatisfied with the new distribution of power in the EU, a fact which is far from proven.

Although the Western European press seems to have difficulty reporting a seemingly uncomplicated chain of events like the enlargement negotiations in a homogeneous manner, they do fall for the same platitudes. The southerners, the ominous 'others', are commonly believed to live off 'our' fat. 'We' are the providers, 'they' owe us. What makes things worse, instead of being grateful, humble and submissive, 'they' are pushing for more and more ('Give them an inch and they'll take a mile', as the saying goes). The Greeks in particular are a sore point, 'they' are not like us and, therefore, inferior on all accounts. Then the British are obstructive, selfish and pigheaded. Even an international magazine like *The Economist*, which has its home base in Britain, admits to that, be it reluctantly. So, it must be true then! The Germans, on the other hand, are powerful, good organisers and true Europeans. The French are allegedly somewhat spiteful about their diminishing role in the EU and begrudge the Germans their influence in Eastern and Northern Europe. Smaller countries such as Belgium, Holland, Denmark and Luxembourg do not even enter the picture. This can be interpreted as an honour (they cannot be stereotyped). More than likely, though, they are considered too insignificant on the European scene to bother with.

Conclusion

On the basis of this small-scale research project, which has concentrated on one particular series of events, i.e. the enlargement negotiations, I can provide at least tentative answers to the following key questions: Do Euro-correspondents present uniform information to the public? Is the press generally supportive of the European 'Union' and does it, indeed, advocate European citizenship (whatever that may be)? Does it try to influence the course of events, and if so, how? As for the first question, the answer is simply negative at least as far as the surface message is concerned: one does get different versions of one single event. It is at the level of stereotypes and subliminal techniques that the magazines are most similar. As for the other questions, the gist is that even if the press overtly defends enlargement, it simultaneously encourages division and rivalry by innuendo and playing on stereotypes. Audiences are impressionable, and subliminal messages and stereotypes do stick. Relatively wealthy northerners are somehow urged to refuse support to those lazy Southern Europeans, who are merely after our money and who fail to perform their duties when it comes to it (e.g., The Greeks gallivant around town rather than prepare the meetings properly). Even if Europe is presented as an ideal solution from an economic point of view, this positive image is gradually but unmistakably undermined by allusions to ancient conflicts (e.g. rivalry between France and Germany, between the Continent and Britain) and innuendo about national identities, characteristics that cannot be shed easily. One cannot shake off the impression that the press is paving the path for a two-speed Europe. Some poorer (mostly Southern European) countries 'must' be left behind, and should no longer burden the development of the wealthier member states.

Of course, as far as value-judgements go, diversity does not need to be seen as an entirely bad thing. By 'adjusting' information about far-away Europe to a framework people back home are familiar with, by adding some local flavour, the press brings Euro-issues home to people and kindles debate. If the press resembled the ideal painted by the EU authorities (cf. Commission des Communautés Européennes, 1993), it might just be an absolute disaster. Sterile messages, communicated from the top down, might never reach, let alone affect, the public. The press does play an important role in bridging the gap, wide indeed, between the European authorities and the public back home, a fact which cannot, however, justify its contributing to the naturalization of stereotypes.

Be that as it may, philosophizing about the role the press should play and passing moral judgements on what is right or wrong is not the task of a linguist. What is the task of a linguist is to look behind the scenes and reveal deeper dimensions of what is being communicated so as to make people more alert. As far as European issues are concerned, the messages which have surfaced in this paper are clear: the Western European quality press is characterized by diversity at the 'factual' level and uniformity at the level of surreptitious information transfer. In short, the attitude of the press towards the Union is ambivalent at best.

References

Bourdieu, Pierre (1982), *Die Feinen Unterschiede. Zeitkritik der Gesellschaftlichen Urteilskraft*, Suhrkamp, Frankfurt am Main.

Commission des Communautés Européennes (1993), *Une Communauté plus Démocratique*, Office des publications officielles des Communautés Européennes, Luxembourg.

Fairclough, Norman (1989), *Language and Power*, Longman, London and New York.

Fowler, Roger (1991), *Language in the News. Discourse and Ideology in the Press*, Routledge, London and New York.

Wodak, Ruth (1989), '1968: The Power of Political Jargon - a "Club-2" discussion' in Wodak, Ruth (ed.), *Language, Power and Ideology. Studies in Political Discourse*, John Benjamins, Amsterdam and Philadelphia, pp. 137-63.

Team Europe? Stereotypes of National Character in European Sports Reporting

HUGH O'DONNELL

Introduction

Sports reports are among the most widely read elements of journalistic production in the European presses. In the UK, popular tabloid newspapers regularly dedicate between 20 and 25 per cent of their total space to sports coverage (Hargreaves, 1986, pp. 138-9). Continental European countries which also produce genuinely popular newspapers (Sweden, Norway, Denmark, Germany, Austria) follow a similar pattern on a slightly smaller scale, dedicating between ten and 15 per cent to sports reporting. Quality newspapers throughout Europe regularly dedicate two or three pages a day to sport, and many produce a special sports supplement on Mondays. Over and above this, many (in particular Southern European) countries have specialist daily sports newspapers: *L'Equipe* in France, *Corriere dello Sport*, *Tuttosport* and *Gazzetta dello Sport* in Italy, *As*, *Marca* and *El Mundo Deportivo* in Spain, and *A Bola*, *Gazeta dos Desportos* and *Record* in Portugal. These specialist newspapers can have huge readerships: *Gazzetta dello Sport*, for example, sells over a million copies a day, *Marca* is the second most widely-read newspaper in Spain. Over and above the dailies, weekly sports magazines abound throughout Europe.

A study of European television schedules also shows very considerable sports coverage, particularly at the weekend and also mid-week (Whannel, 1992). Sweden even has a daily early-evening sports programme: *Sportnytt* (*Kanal 1*). Major footballing fixtures can attract huge audiences. During the 1990 World Cup, the game between Italy and Argentina was seen by twenty-seven million Italians - almost half the entire population. Televised sports events - in particular international football matches - constitute an area of programming where viewers often uninterested in non-domestic productions will eagerly follow events even if their own team or country is not represented. For example, Italian football is featured three times a week on British television (Channel 4), and also on Sundays on Greek television (Σκαι) and German television (DSF), the latter also showing Spanish football on Saturdays. English football is shown live every Saturday in Sweden (TV2) and Catalonia (Canal 33), and an entire match is also shown recorded on Greek television (Σκαι). German football is shown in Norway (TVN) and so on.

Sports reporting, both in the press and on television, is characterized by the insistent use of stereotypes, particularly where international events are involved (Blain et al., 1993). These stereotypes characteristically relate a particular style of play to what is seen as the 'national character' of the team or individual with whom it is associated. For example, during the 1994 World Cup, the Spanish sports daily *As* carried an article which declared (all quotations translated by HOD):

> En casi todas las selecciones del mundo se refleja en el equipo el talante del pueblo: alemania juega ordenado y eficaz; Brasil, la samba con el balón; Argentina, temperamental; Inglaterra, coraje, casta. (*As*, 12 July 1994)
> [Almost all national football teams in the world reflect the character of their people: Germany plays in an orderly and efficient manner; Brazil is samba and football combined; Argentina, temperamental; England, courage, pedigree.]

The author went on to complain that the current Spanish team did not reflect sufficiently the character of the Spanish people, and looked forward to a time when the team would adopt "a style of play with which the country could identify."

There are many reasons for the existence of so many stereotypes in sports reporting. Some of these are in a sense technical and relate to the day-to-day requirements of journalistic practices. As Goldlust points out (1987, p. 94), a major aim of sports reporting - particularly on television - is to lend a sense of drama to events which in themselves can often be disappointing or tedious. A much-used technique is the development of narrative lines based on series of opposites, a strategy within which stereotypes - temperament versus rationality, fair play versus cheating - can be used to great effect. However, to limit stereotypes to mere functions of dramatic narratology is to misunderstand their complexity. Stereotypes of national character can also be approached from within a social psychological framework, and be seen as cognitive schemata used by all in their processes of classification of reality, but even with such a framework, as pointed out in the late 1980s by Social Identity Theory, they must, in order to be fully understood, also incorporate an element of historical analysis (Hogg and Abrams, 1988, pp. 18-19).

However, I would suggest that such stereotypes must be seen above all as dynamic and multifaceted discursive models expressing, reflecting and reproducing the power relations existing both between countries and within individual countries. The terms 'discursive' and 'discourse' are used here and throughout this chapter to refer to a manner of organizing language - or any other system of signs - in such a way that an ideological message is transmitted without that ideology either necessarily being named directly or explained in any overt or explicit way or even being consciously reproduced by those reproducing the discourse. As Dant points out (1991, p. 185): "The mode in which knowledge/ideology operates is discourse."

An outline of international sporting stereotypes

The stereotypes used in European sports reporting form three basic clusters. These are (1) the Scandinavian stereotype, (2) the Central European stereotypes, and (3) the Southern stereotype.

The Scandinavian stereotype

The major representatives of the Scandinavian stereotypes are beyond any question the Swedes. This is to some extent due to their much greater visibility over a long period of time in European sporting events. However, this predominance cannot be explained entirely in sporting terms, since in recent years Denmark has won the European Football Championship (1992) and Norway has hosted the Winter Olympic Games (1994). The greater visibility of the Swedes is, as I will argue below, due mainly to the fact that they are economically dominant in Scandinavia, and are the only Scandinavian country to present what is seen by the major European economic powers as a serious economic challenge. This view of the Swedes as dominant within Scandinavia is not simply held outside Sweden, but is part of the country's own self-view. Thus, the Swedish quality daily *Svenska Dagbladet*, previewing Denmark's match against Germany in the 1992 European Championship final, made indirect reference to Sweden's industrial giants such as Volvo and Saab when it described Denmark as 'a little nation, a little country, without prestigious industries which produce cars or aeroplanes. Denmark is anonymous out there in the big wide world' (*Svenska Dagbladet*, 28 June 1992).

The key elements of the international Scandinavian stereotype are coldness and clinical rationality (this stereotype is not confined to sport: many Swedish actresses have also carried the 'ice maiden' label). A major vehicle for this stereotype in the 1970s was the tennis player Björn Borg, regularly referred to in sports reporting as 'Ice Borg' and described as having an 'ice cold' temperament. In more recent years this mantle has been taken over by Stefan Edberg, who has also often been likened to an iceberg. Thus, during the 1991 Wimbledon tournament, Germany's best-selling daily newspaper, the tabloidesque *Bild* (6 July 1991), referred to him as "der schwedische Eisblock Stefan Edberg" ['the Swedish ice block Stefan Edberg'], and, when he lost the semi-final to the German Michael Stich, the Scottish broadsheet *Glasgow Herald* (6 July 1991) said of him: "it was almost as though the ice-cool temperament was melting away in the afternoon heat."

Though occurring most often in relation to Swedes, this stereotype does occasionally emerge in relation to the inhabitants of other Scandinavian countries. Thus, in an article on the 1993 Tour de France, the Dutch national daily *NRC Handelsblad* (19 July 1993) described one of the Tour's official 'hostesses', the Dane Ilse Petersen, as having 'blue, ice-cold eyes, like those of [Hans Christian] Andersen's ice queen'. Needless to say, the typically blue eyes of Scandinavians are no more 'ice-cold' than blue eyes in any other country (by contrast, the *Herald* of 21 June 1993 described the English athlete Sally Gunnel as having "laughing blue eyes"). The reference to ice derives from the stereotype rather than from any objectively verifiable reality.

The Centre

Rather than a single stereotype, as is the case for the Scandinavians, what we find in relation to central Western European countries is a series of related but nonetheless differentiated stereotypes which combine certain elements yet differ on others. The most visible stereotypes are those relating to Germany and England.

The German/Germanic stereotype Perhaps the most powerful of these stereotypes - certainly in terms of the insistence with which it recurs throughout the European media - is the German stereotype. It is impressive not just in the range of countries in which it is reproduced, but in the astonishing consistency of its elements. Throughout Europe, German sportspersons from all kinds of sports are presented as efficient, well organised, hardworking, powerful and indeed at times even mechanical. In extreme versions of the stereotype Germany, victories are often described using the vocabulary of war, with insistent reference to 'panzers' (Blain et al., 1993, chapters four and six). For example, in the run-up to the Germany-Denmark Euro'92 final, much was made in the Swedish press of Germany's invasion of Denmark in 1940. An article in the evening tabloid *Aftonbladet* previewing the game was accompanied by a photograph of a German tank in a Danish town, with a caption: "EM-finalen får dansken att minnas tilbaka - till 9 april 1940 då tyska stridsvagnar rullade över gränsen" ['The Euro'92 final makes the Danes think back - to 9 April 1940 when German tanks rolled over the border']

(*Aftonbladet*, 25 June 1992). And such associations are not limited to sport. A further striking example was to be found in the English press after the events of Black Wednesday in September 1992, when the lack of Bundesbank support led to a devaluation of the pound. The *Daily Express*'s comment on these events was as follows:

> The sky over London is dark with Bundesbank bombers, raining death and destruction on the poor pound. The Panzers of the deutschmark have already conquered the Low Countries, and France has made a separate peace with the Germans'. (*Daily Express*, 5 October 1992)

A few examples should suffice to establish the broad outlines of this stereotype. For example, the English broadsheet the *Observer* wrote in its *Wimbledon Special* (23 June 1991) of German tennis player Boris Becker: "the Becker serve is a triumph of natural genetics and Germanic efficiency." It went on to ascribe Becker's success on grass to the fact that "the German state, more predictable than procreation, took over", obliging him to concentrate from an early age on serve-and-volley tactics for faster foreign courts. "Here was a breathtaking piece of planning", it added. The notion of efficiency is always explicit in relation to the Germans. In the run-up to the Euro'92 final between Denmark and Germany, *Svenska Dagbladet* (26 June 1992) summed up the game as 'Danish dynamite and will power against German organization and efficiency.'

In the terms of this stereotype the Germans have, above all, the right mental 'attitude': a confidence in their ability to get the job done, and total commitment to the task in hand. In the course of the 1991 Wimbledon tournament, *La Libre Belgique* (6 July 1991) described Boris Becker in the following terms: "il a démontré que son mental était en acier trempé, en béton armé" ['He has shown that his state of mind is in tempered steel, in reinforced concrete']. And Bernhard Langer's fightback in the 1993 British Golf Open was described by the Dutch *NRC Handelsblad* (19 July 1993) as 'The German [...] fought back in familiar fashion [...] through his attitude.'

This stereotype has acquired the status of myth. It is used almost automatically - and sometimes self-consciously - in any international sporting event where Germans come out on top. Thus when the German football team Karlsruher SC beat the Spanish league-leaders Valencia 7:0 in the 1993-94 UEFA Cup, the Spanish daily *El País* (3 November 1993) wrote how 'Valencia helped to revitalise the German legend'. On the same day the Madrid daily *ABC* wrote how 'in the purest German spirit Karlsruhe needed only ten minutes to carve up the game.' Its status as myth is made clearer when the myth is deliberately questioned. Thus, following Denmark's victory over Germany in the final of the European

Championship in 1992, a journalist in the Swedish tabloid *Aftonbladet* wrote:

> Efter EM-finalens tyska nederlag mot ett litet gemytligt land i norr kan vi kanske få slippa de fetaste clicheerna om tyskarnas nationalkaraktär. Vem talar nu om deras oeverlägsna organisation och iskalla perfektionism? (*Aftonbladet*, 28 June 1992)
> [After Germany's defeat in the European Championship final by a small and pleasant little country from the north, perhaps we can now get rid of the worst clichés about the Germans' national character. Who is talking now about their superior organisation and ice-cold perfectionism?]

The Dutch can also share in this stereotype, though to a lesser extent. Like the Germans, they are also, in the words of the Swedish tabloid *Expressen* (23 June 1992), associated with 'power, strength, stamina and toughness', as two remarkably similar references to two of their sportspersons will make clear. Talking of the Dutch tennis player Brenda Schultz (whose serve has been measured at over 120 mph) the *Glasgow Herald* (1 July 1991) wrote: "The Dutch woman should be made to apply for a firearms licence for her racket." And *Expressen* described the Dutch footballer Ronald Koeman (whose shots have been measured at 108 mph) in the following terms:

> 'He should have a firearms licence when he steps on to a football field'.
> This is what they jokingly say about Ronald Koeman in Spain and Holland. But in fact the statement does have some validity.
> His right boot works like a cannon.
> If he hits an opponent with the ball, it's almost 'attempted murder'.
> (*Expressen*, 12 June 1992)

When Koeman scored against England in a World Cup qualifier in October 1993, the Dutch newspaper *De Telegraaf* (14 October 1993) described him as a 'cannon', and his goal as a 'feat of arms'.

We should note, however, that while this stereotype also applies to Holland, it does not apply to countries which from other points of view might appear to be more obvious candidates, such as the Austrians or the German-speaking Swiss or Luxembourgers: whatever their level of internal wealth, they are small players on the European stage. As in the case of Sweden, the crucial criteria for the applicability of the stereotype lie beyond both sport and what might be considered more persuasive considerations of national affinity. Holland is a country with considerable economic muscle and a history of Empire. Again, an awareness of its own importance on the world stage is part of this country's own self-view. Thus, in mid-1993 the Dutch public service television station Nederland 2 ran an eight-part series on "the international position of Holland's trade and industry" entitled *Holland's glory*.

The broader political and ideological implications of the stereotypes sometimes rise to the surface, as when *Aftonbladet* (25 June 1992) described the Denmark-Germany Euro'92 final as 'the cheerful Lilliput nation versus the ice-cold great power', or when *La Libre Belgique*, previewing the all-German final at Wimbledon in 1991, wrote:

> C'est ainsi que dimanche Michael Stich et Boris Becker [...] se recontreront dans une finale de Wimbledon qui hissera haut le pavillon de la puissance économique que l'Angleterre envie. (*La Libre Belgique*, 6 July 1991)
> [On Sunday, Michael Stich and Boris Becker [...] will meet in a Wimbledon final which will raise high the flag of economic power which England envies.]

It returned to this theme two days later, talking of 'the 100% German final of this economic power'.

The English/British stereotype Some of the main features of the English stereotype were already to be found in the quotation from *As* with which this paper began: courage and pedigree. The reference to 'pedigree' is due to the fact that England is widely seen - quite correctly - as the birthplace of modern sport, and - much more questionably - as the historic repository of certain sporting values.

The English stereotype revolves crucially around notions of hard work, total commitment, boundless energy, a never-say-die approach. Thus Berti Vogts, Germany's then assistant manager, interpreted England's 3-2 victory over Cameroon during the 1990 World Cup as follows: "Aber als die Engländer in Rückstand gerieten, haben sie sich auf ihre Tugenden Kampfkraft und Moral besonnen" ['when the English went behind they remembered their virtues: fighting strength and morale'] (*Hannoversche Allgemeine Zeitung*, 4 July 1990). Again, when the Portuguese team Marítimo lost 4-0 to Luton during a summer tournament in Sweden in 1992, the Portuguese sports daily *A Bola* carried an article on the match entitled "Um Luton 'bem inglês'" ['A 'very English' Luton']. In the text of the article it referred to Luton's 'typically British style of play', their 'very muscular, fast-paced game', their constant 'pressure'. Contrasting this with the Portuguese team's more deliberate pace, it concluded:

> A final, o único (grande) problema foi ter tido por adversário um conjunto inglês com outra preparação, outro ritmo, outro espírito. (*A Bola*, 27 July 1992)
> [In short, their only (major) problem was having as their opponent a British team with a different preparation, a different pace, a different frame of mind.]

This stereotype is extremely widespread throughout Europe. As the Basque daily *El Diario Vasco* commented on England's victory over Cameroon during the 1990 World Cup: 'while there is a Briton in the race nothing is ever decided until the winner breaks the winning tape [...] The English did what they always do, admirably, to be imitated by anyone who can: they fought to the end' (*El Diario Vasco*, 2 July 1990). The likewise Basque daily *Deia*, describing the English team as 'a team which still maintains intact the quintessence of football' added that 'their football brings pleasure to anyone who see this sport as non-stop effort during 90 minutes, where technique is relegated to a secondary level and physical ability is the basis of the victory of the team' (*Deia*, 3 July 1990).

It is perhaps not surprising that Scotland should at times share in this stereotype - as indeed it does. Thus, the Swedish broadsheet *Dagens Nyheter* (16 June 1990) described the Scottish player Murdo MacLeod as representing 'the classic hard Scottish school'. Analysing Scotland's victory over Sweden, the same newspaper spoke of 'Scotland's aggressive game', its 'stamina', and added that 'the Scottish defence played with a typical British touch, in other words extremely resolutely, to use a rather mild description' (*Dagens Nyheter*, 17 June 1990). Describing the same game, the German sports magazine *Kicker*, in an article entitled "Die Schotten geben 110 Prozent" ['Scotland gave 110 per cent'], added:

> Die schottische Mannschaft gab in puncto Einsatz alles [...] So aber reichte den spielerisch schwachen, nach vorne ideenlosen, im Angriff harmlosen, aber extrem aggressiven Schotten eine gute Leistung im Spiel nach hinten und Kampf bis zum Umfallen. (*Kicker*, 21 June 1990)
> [As far as commitment is concerned the Scots gave their all [...] In this way, despite the weakness of their play, their lack of ideas up front and the harmlessness of their attack, the extremely aggressive Scots pulled off a good performance in defence and fought till they dropped.]

While the political links between Scotland and England might to some explain their joint participation in a common British stereotype - they were, after all, partners in Empire - it is much less obvious that Ireland should also share in it. Yet the elements of the English/British stereotypes in descriptions of Ireland are often unmistakable. Thus, during the 1990 World Cup the German regional newspaper *Hannoversche Allgemeine Zeitung* wrote of Ireland's game against Rumania:

> Vor 31 818 Zuschauern hatte die Mannschaft von Trainer Jack Charlton zuvor über weite Strecken dominiert und glänzte mit ihren typischen Tugenden: Kampfkraft und einem schier unbändigen Siegeswillen. (*Hannoversche Allgemeine Zeitung*, 26 June 1994)
> [[...] Trainer Jack Charlton's team had dominated for long periods and had shone with its typical virtues: fighting strength and an indomitable will to win.]

Commenting on the same match, the French evening paper *France-Soir* - in an article in which it refers to the Irish as "les Britanniques"(!) - suggested that 'their greatest strength is their ability to pressurize without respite', adding:

Les Britanniques ont une vertu: ils ne bradent ni ne refusent le jeu, même s'ils le malmènent souvent. (*France-Soir*, 26 June 1990)
[The British have one virtue: they neither sell the game short, nor refuse it, even if they frequently mistreat it.]

What this similarity suggests is that this particular stereotype predates the establishment of at least part of Ireland as a separate state, and is a now anachronistic survival of a time when Ireland was part of Britain, and therefore a recipient of the British stereotype. This point is expanded further below.

The Southern stereotype

The internationally dominant Southern stereotype is based centrally on the notion of 'temperament', with all the positive and negative connotations which this carries with it. On the one hand there is admiration for the flair and creativity of Southern sportspersons, their footballers in particular, but on the other, and much more persistently, there is sustained criticism for their laziness, their lack of discipline, their lack of honesty, their play-acting and their irresistible tendency to cheat.

This stereotype is applied - in variations ranging from the mild to the vitriolic - to all Southern European nations, from Portugal to Greece. Thus, in a lengthy article on recent developments in European football, the Swedish in-flight magazine *Upp & Ner* (No. 5-6, 1991), referring to a match between Portuguese and Italian football clubs, told how 'in the Oporto-Juventus match in 1984 Oporto's hot-tempered goalkeeper Zebeto rushed out to the touchline while the match was in progress and broke the linesman's flag.' Throughout the 1994 World Cup an intense debate took place in the Spanish press as to whether or not the team was sufficiently 'passionate', or whether its trainer Javier Clemente had disciplined and systematized it to such an extent that it had lost its natural passionate qualities (León Solís, 1994). During the 1990 World Cup, Italy was the major target of this stereotype. Thus the Soviet daily *Pravda* (21 June 1990) assured its readers that 'the Italian team [...] reflected the explosive nature of its people.' The ultimate symbol of fiery Italianness during Italia'90 was to be Vesuvius, chosen to symbolize the allegedly volcanic nature of the Italian temperament in what was seen as 'national grief' when Italy was eliminated by Argentina in the semi-final. 'The Italians [...] went to Naples and at the edge of Vesuvius were burned by the molten lava' was the message in the Basque daily *Deia* (4 July 1990). And when Glasgow Rangers were well beaten by the Greek football team AEK Athens, an article in *Scotland on Sunday* (14 August 1994), entitled "Rangers undone by a Greek myth", commented: "All the talk of 'volatile temperament' among the Greeks is patronising twaddle." The journalist here distances himself from the stereotype - as the Swedish journalist quoted earlier in relation to the German stereotype did: it would be wrong to give the impression that all journalists simply reproduce the stereotypes unquestioningly - but in so doing he acknowledges its strength.

It is also worth noting that this stereotype is not limited to Western Europe. In its coverage of the 1991 Wimbledon tournament, the Soviet sports daily *Sovetsky Sport* (27 June 1991) described the then Yugoslav player Slobodan Zhivoinovic as being 'temperamental as southerners always are'.

Although it is not my intention to pursue this here, this stereotype also applies routinely to all Latin American sportspersons, from footballers to tennis players, and can also apply in a somewhat modified form to sportspersons from African countries (Blain et al., 1993, chapter 4).

Beyond stereotype to ideology

An initial clue to the analysis of these stereotypes is the fact that, although apparently attached to specific nationalities, they are *all* in fact capable of migration. Thus the Scandinavian stereotype can become attached to Germans, the German stereotype to Spaniards, and so on.

For example, during the 1992 European Football Championship, the Swedish team was - in view of the apparently 'disciplined' nature of its game - regularly referred to in both the Swedish and the Norwegian press as 'Scandinavia's Germans' (*Aftonbladet*, 24 July 1992/ *Dagbladet*, 27 July 1992), while for the Spanish daily *El País* (11 June 1990) it had displayed 'Prussian discipline' during the 1990 World Cup. During the 1994 World Cup the Spanish team itself - characterized as overly disciplined and systematic - was described in Spain as 'The Germans of the South': this was the title of an article in *El País* (11 July 1994), which went on to describe how, in its final game against Italy, 'Spain left the World Cup with a metallic screech' (the 'mechanical' component of the Germanic stereotype often involves such descriptions).

During the 1991 Wimbledon tournament, reports of Michael Stich's performance in the final played repeatedly on the theme of Nordic coolness. Stich comes from Schleswig-Holstein, the most northerly of the German Länder, bordering on Denmark, and for many sectors of the German press this qualified him as coming from 'the far north' (*Hannoversche Allgemeine Zeitung*, 8 July 1991). Thus *Kicker* (8 July 1991) wrote:

> Im selben Maße wie Boris Becker sich im Endspiel [...] erhitzte, kühlte sich der Lange aus dem Norden ab. Ein Mann ohne Nerven, bis in die letzte Faser eiskalt. (*Kicker*, 8 July 1991)
> [In the same way that Boris Becker [...] grew more and more heated, the tall man from the North cooled down. A man without nerves, ice cold to the core.]

The *Hannoversche Allgemeine Zeitung* (8 July 1991) described the final as follows: "Im Glutofen des Tennismekkas gelang dem eiskalten Stich bei nahezu 40 Grad bereits im ersten Spiel ein Break" ['In the oven of the tennis Mecca, ice cold Stich broke serve in the first game in a temperature of nearly 40 degrees'], and added later that "Viele werfen ihm vor, er zeige zuwenig Emotionen und strahle den Charme eines Eisbergs aus" ['many criticize him for not showing enough emotion and for having the charm of an iceberg']. *Bild* (6 July 1991) described him as an 'ice block'. Through the channel of a common language, these discourses also penetrate the Austrian press, where Michael Stich is referred to as the 'cool Hamburger' (*Neue Kronen-Zeitung*, 8 July 1991). In another article on the same page of this newspaper, Boris Becker describes him as 'ice cold'.

But not only is migration possible, the stereotypes can be combined in juxtapositions which appear contradictory. Thus, the French sports daily *L'Equipe* (19 June 1990), struggling to reconcile the obvious flair and creativity of the German team during the 1990 World Cup with the predominant stereotype of organisation and discipline, attempted to resolve this difficulty by inventing a new category, referring to their 'Saxon-Latin technique'. The Italian press created an even odder compound definition: "Wir sahen teutonische Organisation und die Phantasie der Zigeuner" ['We saw Teutonic organization and the fantasy of the gypsies in the same team]', said *Tuttosport* (quoted in the *Hannoversche Allgemeine Zeitung*, 12 June 1990). However, perhaps the most curious example of this phenomenon was to be found in *El País* (international edition, 11 June 1990), which described how the German team added to its habitual discipline 'a visceral, almost Khomeini-esque side, which will have caused fear among its future rivals.'

A further crucial difference masked by the surface uniformity of each stereotype relates to the way in which it is interpreted locally in the domestic media of the country to which it is applied. It is not necessarily the case that each country accepts its own international stereotype. Thus, Swedes - and Scandinavians in general - do not accept the 'ice cold' image of their international stereotype, but instead have their own national myths centering on closeness to nature and the healing powers of the northern summer (Dahlén, 1991). In fact, the idea of 'icy coldness' is one which Swedish journalists are more likely to attribute to Germans. Thus, in *Aftonbladet*'s coverage of Euro'92 we can find Germans described as 'icily efficient' (16 June 1992): see also other quotes from *Aftonbladet* given above.

German commentators accept - and on occasions enthusiastically exploit (Head, 1992) - their international associations with efficiency and organization, but are less comfortable with the 'mechanical' aspects of their international stereotype and its tendency to be associated with images of war. The lack of emotion of the Germanic stereotype is also at times seen as negative by those to whom it is applied. Again, such views are not restricted to sport. For example, Albert van de Heuvel, for eight years vice-chairman of the Dutch broadcasting organisation NOS, suggested in an interview in the Dutch newspaper *Trouw* (15 October 1993) that Dutch culture was 'poor in emotion [...] our culture is uncomfortable with emotion.'

By contrast, in Southern European countries emotion is felt to be a poor substitute for rationality. Thus when the Greek basketball team unexpectedly beat the Germans 68:58 in the 1994 World Basketball Championship, the Greek daily *Ελεφθεροτυπια* (5 August 1994) refused to be over-enthusiastic, pointing out that 'our team fought more with its heart and hardly at all with its brain.' Indeed, in southern countries in general, the inability to 'use one's brains' in the sense of planning, organising and carrying out projects efficiently is often presented as a negative side of the national character. For example, in Spain the negative side of the international Southern stereotype was presented during the Barcelona Olympics as keeping Spain in the periphery and condemning it to the ranks of the underdeveloped. The Olympics were presented specifically in the Spanish media as an unmissable opportunity for Spaniards to put these negative attitudes behind them and join the leaders of twentieth-century Europe. As an editorial in the weekly magazine *Cambio 16* on Spanish successes during the Games put it:

> Pero lo que no es nada curioso es que los éxitos han llegado después de mil esfuerzos, y no de milagro. Por primera vez este santo país ha organizado una gran campaña de promoción y apoyo a nuestros deportistas durante dos o tres años, y los resultados han sido espectaculares. Trabajar funciona. Magníficos deportistas hispanos han demostrado por estas tierras que la previsión y el esfuerzo organizado dan frutos.
> Justo esto es la modernidad. Y ojalá sepamos aplicar de nuevo este aprendizaje cuando nos toca ahora echar el resto para salvar a este país de la ruina en que nos hemos metido tras los fastos, los derroches y las fiestas [...] Sólo hace falta tener coraje para plantarle cara a la estupidez y al despilofarro. (*Cambio 16, 10 August 1992*)
> [But what is not curious at all is that the successes have come as a result of numerous efforts, and not by a miracle. For the first time this blessed country has organized a large campaign of promotion and support for our athletes over two or three years, and the results of the effort have been spectacular. Working works. Magnificent Spanish athletes have shown in this land that planning and organized effort bear fruit.
> This is precisely what modernity is. And hopefully we will be able to apply this learning again when we have to give our all to save this country from the ruin we have got ourselves into after the pomp, the extravagance, and the feasts ... All that is needed is the courage to face up to stupidity and waste.]

What the migrations, combinations and reworkings show is that the discursive models which these stereotypes realize are in fact models of behaviour rather than of national character. On closer examination, it can be seen that what they all have in common are notions of productivity and work. The highest work rates are concentrated in the Centre stereotypes, which combine planning with energy, commitment, tirelessness, and in the German case mechanical efficiency. Some distance behind, the Scandinavian stereotype combines rationality and organisation, but its notions of coldness rule out the robustly energetic zeal and dynamism of the Centre stereotypes. At the bottom of this gradient of productivity comes the Southern stereotype, where the entertainment value of flair and creativity cannot in the end compensate for lack of commitment, laziness, lack of focus, and even the attempt to obtain undeserved rewards by dishonest means.

The balance of negativity outlined here suggests that the origin of these stereotypes was at some point in the Centre. Since the only country of the Centre group which appears to be comfortable with its own stereotype is England (acquiescence in the British stereotype is highly problematic in both Scotland and Ireland), it may well be that the source of the stereotypes was originally England itself. But if their source was indeed England, they have since been appropriated by other national elites and adapted to meet their own domestic requirements.

As I have argued in detail elsewhere (O'Donnell, 1994), these stereotypes should be seen as part of an ultimately imperialist discourse through which responsibility for current core-periphery imbalances are placed on the periphery. This discourse has suffered invasion by other discourses (relating, most notably, to the Second World War), but its overall operation is clear. Within its terms, the periphery (the South) is presented as underdeveloped because its peoples do not work enough, and because they are more interested in enjoyment and self-indulgence rather than organisation and commitment. The economic - and therefore the political - dominance of the Centre is justified through reference to a willingness to work untiringly, good organisation and boundless energy to match.

Conclusion

The analysis outlined above lies broadly within the field of Critical Discourse Analysis. A common strand running through the many divisions and sub-divisions of Critical Discourse Analysis is the conviction that meaning is the dynamic outcome of both intra- and intertextual processes (van Dijk, 1985). For Critical Discourse Analysis meaning can never reside in a text, and is, therefore, never exhausted by the linguistic form of the text. Meaning is always to be seen as the provisional and highly local outcome of the encounter between the discourses informing (however imperfectly) the text and their relationships with other discourses with which they jostle in what might be called the interdiscursive arena (the role of the reader as site of convergent discourses and active producer of meanings is also crucial, of course, although it is not my intention to pursue readership theory at this point). In each society this interdiscursive arena is saturated with discourses of varying reach, weight and coherence and in varying stages of growth, maturity or decomposition in a mixture which is quite unique and will not be found elsewhere. 'Society' as understood here may subtend the boundaries of the nation state - as in the case of, say, Scotland or Catalonia - but it never transcends them. Seen from this point of view, supra-national discourses are never simply derivable from supra-national texts.

What would appear to be supra-national texts - taking 'text' here in the broad sense in which it is not restricted to linguistic text - are, in fact, nothing new in Europe, though they have tended to be confined to politically or culturally powerful groups in European societies. There has for many centuries been a European academic community, whose knowledge-texts have been widely shared. The ideological process whereby the appreciation of certain kinds of music or art came to be part of the self-identity of dominant social groups constituted a text of 'high culture' which is also a pan-European text of some considerable age. Ecclesiastical documents promulgated by the Catholic Church have also constituted - and continue to constitute - what would appear to be pan-European texts disseminated along more highly organized lines. Throughout their history, however, these texts have been appropriated locally by those holding political and/or economic power within their national fields of interest, and incorporated into discourses already circulating within the society in question. These local discourses effectively overwrite those which gave rise to the original texts: the transformations effected by translation may provide a visible marker of this process, but where translation is unnecessary the overwriting will still take place even if the linguistic form of the text remains unchanged. Neither 'knowledge' nor 'high culture' covers quite the same range of meanings in any two societies: their periodic appropriation by authoritarian regimes of one kind or another for overtly ideological ends merely brings to the surface and crystallizes a process which, within more consensual, hegemonic systems, is reproduced by more subtly persuasive means. The history of religion in Europe testifies vividly to the local redefinition and even rejection of ecclesiastical texts.

The stereotypes examined in this paper also form what is in a sense a pan-European text with a lengthy history in Europe (Nowell-Smith, 1978, p. 55; Hargreaves, 1986), no doubt dating back at least to the time of the Central European empires. The key elements of the linguistic form of this text have remained remarkably consistent, but it has likewise undergone a series of both national and local appropriations which have incorporated it within discourses whose meanings vary substantially to meet the needs of domestic elites. In other words, this *text* is the extrapolated linguistic form of imperialist *discourses* operating locally within the national boundaries of distinct European cultures. This can be seen from the different relationship which different societies have with the text, as was outlined above, and from the different internal purposes to which it is put, for, running side by side with the imperialistic discourse which it reproduces, we also find local reworkings of the northern and in particular the southern stereotype by domestic elites in an attempt to establish certain values within their national populations. These values are those required by domestic entrepreneurial capitalism of its workers in its attempts to remain competitive in international markets. In its most aggressive forms, this ideology constructs those who refuse to accept these values in northern countries as alien southerners whose inappropriate behaviour is slowing their country down, or, in the case of southern countries, as unreconstructed hedonists holding back countries which are attempting to become northern.

In the *Cambio 16* article quoted above the southern stereotype can be seen to provide political elites with an easy target via which they can attack the domestic population, and by extension the political and economic performance of the country in general, but such an approach is not limited to the South. This local redeployment of the southern stereotype is frequently initiated by those in political and economic power in all European countries: 'our' economy would be more competitive if 'we' (i.e.: you) worked harder, were better organized, took fewer holidays, had fewer absences through illness etc., cheated less, demanded less, were less greedy, in short, were less 'southern' in our (i.e.: your) behaviour. This micro-version of the southern discourse is, of course, also wielded in 'Nordic' Sweden. For example, *Aftonbladet* (8 June 1992) made the connection between behaviour and national economic performance clear when it carried a three-page investigation entitled 'What have you stolen today?'. It used almost its entire front page as a lead for this story, with the headline 'How the Swedes pilfer', pointing out that this pilfering from shops and workplaces was causing 'eleven billion crowns to disappear from Sweden plc every year'. But the particular ideological usefulness of the discourses under discussion here for dominant groups is greatly enhanced by the fact that the domestic discourses into which this story has been incorporated have been so successfully moulded to the contours of their various national habitats that they now operate effectively (and to a large extent autonomously) at the level of *popular* cultures throughout Europe, reaching vast audiences on a regular and reliable basis.

Local re-interpretation of linguistic and/or visual texts disseminated over national boundaries is in fact entirely unavoidable if they are to operate successfully at such a level. Domestic elites will - either directly or indirectly - always work to redirect transnational texts, linguistic, visual or otherwise, in advance if possible, *post hoc* if necessary. The inevitability of such reformulation has, of course, profound implications for even the possibility of pan-European discourses operating at the level of popular culture or even of so-called 'high culture'. Limiting ourselves to an analysis of linguistic forms, we can accept that pan-European texts relating to the idea of 'Europe' already exist. It is even possible to identify their source, since they mostly emanate from the major EU institutions such as the Commission or the European Parliament. However, they never reach the local populations of the EU directly. They go through a multi-layered process of filtration and mediation, whose major strata are domestic political elites and national media systems. This mediation fills uniform linguistic formulae with highly differentiated meaning potentials. Examples are not difficult to find. The discourse of 'the Europe of the regions' as understood (by most people) in Glasgow does not mean the same as it does (for most people) in London, though it is much closer in meaning to its dominant interpretation in Barcelona or Bilbao (Ross, 1993, p. 133). 'Subsidiarity' does not mean the same in all countries of the EU, nor to all sectors of the political classes in individual EU countries. Even the very notion of 'Europeanness' or 'Europeanism' has very different ranges of meaning in different countries: in Greece, for example, which sees itself as in some ways a 'frontier post' of the European Union, this notion is inextricably linked with this country's relations with its non-EU neighbours - in particular Albania and the former Yugoslav republic of Macedonia (Sofos and Tsagarousianou, 1993, p. 61) - in a way in which it could never be for, say, Spain or Belgium.

Language may be a complicating factor in the generation and maintenance of pan-European discourses, but it is not (for the time being at least) in any sense a critical one. French-speaking Belgians do not watch the news on French television, even though they can pick it up, nor do Dutch-speaking Flemings watch news broadcasts from Holland, even though there is no *linguistic* reason why they should not do so. The same could be said for Austrians in relation to Germany, or Irish citizens in relation to the UK. The fact that all the Arab countries speak the same language or that most South American countries speak Spanish has not made the development of pan-Arabic or pan-Latin-American discourses possible (Schlesinger, 1991, p. 145-6). The major obstacle facing those institutions attempting to disseminate pan-European discourses is the politico-cultural fragmentation of Europe, a situation which rules out the establishment of a European media system of any kind, let alone one which might have any credibility among local populations: the experiences of would-be pan-European television stations such as *Eurosport* - which has had to increase the number of languages in which it offers its commentaries - have been instructive in this respect. Other attempts at pan-European cultural forms, such as pan-European soap operas, have also failed miserably.

The output of European institutions always reaches the popular consumer many times removed, and in many countries - the UK among them - in fact fails entirely to implicate the population at large. Since such texts are invisibly rewritten at the level of the discourses produced and maintained by social and cultural elites, there is currently no mechanism whereby their original meanings can directly enter popular culture. This is not to say that national political parties in many European countries do not reproduce the linguistic forms of pan-European texts for popular consumption: indeed they do. At ritual moments such as the European elections, or more consistently in the case of regions on whose agenda the idea of 'Europe' has a particular significance - Catalonia is a clear case in point - many calls for 'common European solutions' can be read and heard. But while in this process of national or regional retransmission the words may have changed little or perhaps not at all, the potential meanings will never be the same. There seems no possibility of such a situation changing in the foreseeable future. Team Europe may be possible on Brussels headed notepaper, but will always be defeated by actual national teams.

References

Blain, Neil, Boyle, Raymond, and O'Donnell, Hugh (1993), *Sport and National Identity in the European Media*, Leicester University Press, Leicester, London and New York.

Dahlén, Peter (1991), *Sport/TV - Anteckningar Kring ett Försummat Forskningfält*, Studies in Nordic Television Culture, JMK, Stockholm University.

Dant, Tim (1991), *Knowledge, Ideology and Discourse: A Sociological Perspective*, Routledge, London.

Goldlust, John (1987), *Playing For Keeps: Sport, the Media and Society*, Longman Cheshire, Melbourne.

Hargreaves, John (1986), *Sport, Power and Culture*, Polity, London.

Head, David (1992), *Made in Germany: The Corporate Identity of a Nation*, Hodder & Stoughton, London.

Hogg, Michael A. and Abrams, Dominic (1988), *Social Identifications*, Routledge, London.

León Solís, Fernando (1994), 'Mundiales de Fútbol - el Juego de las Nacionalidades Visto Desde la Prensa', paper presented to the Conference of the Association for Contemporary Iberian Studies, University of Portsmouth.

Nowell-Smith, Geoffrey (1978), 'Television - Football - The World', *Screen*, vol. 1, no. 4, pp. 45-59.

O'Donnell, Hugh (1994), 'Mapping the Mythical: A Geopolitics of National Sporting Stereotypes', *Discourse & Society*, vol. 5, no. 3, pp. 345-80.

Ross, Chris (1993), 'Party-Nation and Region-State: The Re-orientation of Basque Nationalist Ideology in the 1980s', in Amodia, José (ed.), *The Resurgence of Nationalist Movements in Europe*, Bradford Occasional Papers no. 12, University of Bradford, pp. 122-36.

Schlesinger, Philip (1991), *Media, State and Nation: Political Violence and Collective Identities*, Sage, London.

Sofos, Spyros and Tsagarousianou, Rosa (1993), 'The Politics of Identity: Nationalism in Contemporary Greece', in Amodia, José (ed.), *The Resurgence of Nationalist Movements in Europe*, Bradford Occasional Papers no. 12, University of Bradford, pp. 51-66.

van Dijk, Teun A. (1985), *Handbook of Discourse Analysis (vols 1-4)*, Academic Press, London.

Whannel, Garry (1992), *Fields in Vision: Television Sport and Cultural Transformation*, Routledge, London.

Cultural Convergence and National Stereotyping: The Future of Advertising in the United Europe

HELEN KELLY-HOLMES

Introduction

Wills (1991) tells us that the distinguishing feature of the European Union - the prevalence of first world countries among its members - has led to the assumption that there will be no erosion of national and regional cultures and that their preservation is both a natural and desirable certainty. While it would therefore appear unlikely that well-established national personalities will merge into a Euro-person, Europeans will undoubtedly become more alike in terms of a superficial identity and culture - at least in the eyes of the rest of the world.

The problems of intercultural advertising have their roots in not only linguistic, but also cultural diversity and national preferences, and designing advertising for this heterogeneous, yet superficially uniform group has proved to be a difficult task. However advertising is defined, it has long ceased to be considered a purely commercial function. In spite - or perhaps because - of its major role in the economy, advertising has become a linguistic and visual force in contemporary culture. Indeed, many advertising texts are more familiar to large sections of the population than political speeches or works of literature (Cook, 1992). Therefore, advertising wields enormous power in terms of its ability to influence opinions and shape lifestyles and cultures, and in any consideration of the political discourse of European unity or disunity, a discussion of this potent force is necessary.

As one of the most dominant of all current discourse types, advertising occupies a salient position in the communication of all cultures today - both shaping and being shaped by the cultural space it occupies and permeates. Just as culture influences advertising communication and the type of advertising which is permitted or enjoyed in a particular culture, so too does advertising impact on culture, to such an extent that Davidson, 1992, p. 124) sees "...culture (as) the society we build with our brands".

Consequently, not only does the advertiser who is seeking to communicate with and in cultures other than his or her own have to take differences such as ideology, language and economic structure into account, but also communicative differences which simultaneously both evolve from and contribute to cultural difference. This not only applies to cultures which are geographically and linguistically distant - the subtle distinctions between cultures which consider themselves to be similar can provide very different communicative contexts. All too often, it is assumed that a culture which is perceived as 'close' is similar in attitudes, values and behaviour - something which can lead to great misunderstanding (Cherry, 1967).

This is particularly the case in intra-European communication, at least in terms of the rest of the world. Because of the superficial similarity between European cultures, particularly from an American or Japanese perspective, such differences are not expected, particularly not by advertisers.

The problems of intercultural advertising

Social scientists, linguists and cultural theorists are not the only ones concerned with culture and cultural difference. International marketing theory recommends the advertiser who is seeking to target another culture to first examine certain elements of that culture in order to gain an understanding of the prospective consumers and those people with whom the advertiser is communicating - the advertisees. Such factors are invariably listed as, material life (e.g. standard of living, state of development), social interactions (e.g. social roles), language and linguistic considerations, aesthetics (e.g. the meaning of colours and symbols), religion, and ethics and mores (Jain, 1990). The rationale behind such suggestions is that consumer lifestyles are formed by the culture of the society in which the consumer lives and that consumption decisions and choices are largely culture-based (cf. Jain, 1990).

Given the preceding discussion on culture and its role in communication, this conclusion would appear obvious. However, as the well-documented blunders of international advertising prove, companies operating in international markets have only relatively recently begun to take cultural factors into consideration in their marketing mix (price, product, place and promotion). Consequently, advertising and marketing failures are often the direct result of cultural errors and oversights (cf. Jain, 1990, p. 225). Furthermore, not only does the product have to be appropriate to the particular culture, but all aspects of the communications and promotions mix, e.g. the positioning of the product or service relative to other products or services, must tie in with the culture of the country or region.

Thus, Jain (1990) sees advertising and other forms of promotion as being most sensitive to cultural mistakes. Within advertising communication the most often cited examples of such mistakes are to do with language and are frequently the result of the inadequate translation of advertising slogans with little or no regard for local culture. One of the most famous examples, is the *Vauxhall/Opel 'Nova'* car. Only when its campaign was unsuccessful in Spanish-speaking countries did the company discover that 'nova' means 'no go' in Spanish - thus it was hardly surprising that Spanish-speaking consumers were not prompted to buy the car. A further example is *Gillette's* advertising for its *Trac II* razor. When it was discovered that 'trac' in some of the Romance languages actually implies fragile - obviously not an attribute which *Gillette* would wish to associate with the manly image of its products - the name was changed to *G II*.

Less tangible are the non-linguistic mistakes relating to advertising and the advertiser must also treat with caution the cultural minefield represented by nonverbal communication. Understanding the meaning of symbols in particular cultures requires a level of cultural knowledge which many advertising agencies are not prepared to attain. However, what most organisations do not realise is that a campaign which fails for cultural reasons is even more costly and makes the product even harder to relaunch. For example, *Carlsberg* was forced to redesign its *elephant beer* label for African audiences. The two elephants on the original label were a symbol of bad luck, so *Carlsberg* had to integrate a third one into the image. Along with such overtly 'cultural' barriers, other products of culture - legislation on advertising and regulation of competition - also impact on international advertising.

As stated previously, cultural diversity shapes consumer behaviour through national preferences, which are particularly evident in the area of consumer non-durable goods such as food. These deep-seated tastes, habits and perceptions are difficult (if not impossible) to change - imagine the difficulties of marketing horse meat in Britain. Not only consumer preferences, but also product perceptions and product functions differ between countries, e.g. whether a product such as toothpaste is considered medical or cosmetic.

Along with differences in tastes, habits, perceptions and preferences as regards actual products, we also prefer different types of advertising. For example, advertising and marketing executives at Germany's *Dresdner Bank* see the advertising for their products as a serious matter. They claim that in matters of money, consumers want serious, informative advertising and this is exactly what *Dresdner Bank* and to a large extent the other German banks offer. The contrast with British bank and financial services advertising is blatantly obvious. The 'serious' bank advertisement is the exception in Britain amidst the mythical sagas of *Lloyd's Bank*, the comedy sketches of *Prudential Insurance*, the rap music of the *Trustee Savings Banks* and the karaoke tactics of the *Midlands Bank*. This difference appears to be symptomatic of the gulf separating the style and role of advertising in Britain and Germany. As Davidson (1992, p. 94) points out, advertisements in Germany do not have the same "cultural prestige" as they do in Britain.

A further complication is manifested by the expansion of this market to include the newly emerging states of Central and Eastern Europe, which up to recently had only a very limited commercial advertising culture - totally alien to the Western European one - and, in fact, advertising was frowned upon as a particularly capitalist type of discourse (cf. Kelly, 1994). Many advertisers, who initially approached the Central and Eastern European market in an ethnocentric (see below) way, were forced to revise their advertising, taking the enormous cultural and ideological differences into account (Butler, 1992). Thus, the advertising for *Milka* chocolate using the purple cow proved perplexing for many consumers in Eastern Europe, as did the *Nike* campaign - which was incidentally very popular in Western Europe - which advertised sports shoes using wheelchair-bound athletes (cf. Reed, 1995). The demand has been above all for straightforward, informative advertising which avoids hyperbole, which can be interpreted literally, which uses images to which the advertisees can relate and which does not use overtly persuasive tactics (cf. Kelly, 1994; Atkinson, 1993; Reed, 1993). For example, while promoting their products through an image-oriented advertisement featuring a 'yuppie' couple in West Germany, *HUK Coburg*, advertised its financial services with an information-packed, plain-print advertisement in the eastern part of the unified Germany (Atkinson, 1993).

Methods of dealing with these problems

Despite the many problems associated with intercultural and international advertising outlined above, advertising continues to be the most popular method of promotion for companies operating globally. This is because it is still the most cost-effective way of communicating with mass audiences of consumers in one or more countries (Jain, 1990).

Companies advertising in countries and cultures other than their own may respond to these problems in a number of ways. Many simply adapt the ethnocentric approach, which assumes that what works in the home culture should also work in the host culture. The advertisement is then produced entirely within the context of the advertiser's culture. Others adopt an assimilationist approach, whereby they display a willingness to adapt the home culture advertising and promotion to the host culture. This would involve the global advertiser searching for 'cultural universals' - i.e. cultural phenomena common to many cultures - which require minimal local adaptation. So, for example, the visuals, music etc. for the advertisement are centrally produced, but the actual text and finer, more culture-specific points are left to local agencies, or companies opt for a simple translation of the text. For example, *Gillette*'s 'The best a man can get' campaign - the images have universal feel-good appeal, there is no text on the screen, except for the brand name, and the song is translated.

Thirdly, an organisation can opt for the most effective, but also most costly strategy, in which the host culture is considered primary. This approach involves not only finding out as much as possible about the host culture, but also feeling a certain understanding and affinity with it. An example of this was *Pepsi*'s advertising campaign in Eastern Europe. Although *Pepsi* is known for operating a global advertising strategy, the traditional young, free, beautiful, affluent, fun images were deemed to be too much of a contrast to ordinary life in the former Eastern Bloc. Thus, *Pepsi* opted instead for re-shooting the commercials using a context to which people in these countries could more easily relate (Keegan, 1989, p. 499).

The final approach, global advertising, may appear similar to the ethnocentric approach outlined above in that it espouses the 'one sight, one sound, one sell' dictum, but the underlying conception is fundamentally different. Whilst the ethnocentric strategy simply exports advertising from the home culture to other cultures without any regard for cultural difference, the global strategy attempts to create a new context for its advertising, a global context to which most cultures can relate to some limited extent. This is based on Marshall McLuhan's (1964) notion of the global village and was advocated strongly by Elinder (1961) in the 1960s. Such advertising is not intended to be specific to one particular culture, although the end effect may be the same as the ethnocentric strategy, particularly if the advertiser is unable to cast aside his or her cultural baggage. Obviously, the main advantage of the global approach is economic. Whilst the localized approach is still popular in Europe, more and more companies are tentatively moving one step further towards pan-European strategies. An example of this is the European advertising for *Natrel* deodorant which appeals to the particularly European need for natural, ecological and gentle products acting in harmony with nature.

This type of pan-European advertising is a sub-set of global advertising, in which Europe is seen as just one of many relatively homogeneous demographic and psychographic blocs. Many of these ads are the product of lifestyle advertising, and there is, in fact, growing evidence that lifestyles across Europe are beginning to converge, particularly among the young (cf. Benady, 1993). This convergence may be due to location, for example those living in London or Birmingham may have more in common with people living in other large metropolitan areas, such as Brussels, Frankfurt or Lyon, than they do with people living in a small village in Dorset or a farm in Cumbria. It may also be related to occupation. Professionals and academics may feel and actually be closer in terms of attitudes, opinions, education, lifestyle aspirations and priorities to other professionals and academics in France, Germany or Italy than to their immediate neighbours.

Young people represent a particularly important target group in these pan-European advertising strategies. Youth culture is becoming more and more cohesive across Europe. Favourite actors, pop groups and accessories, as well as economic privilege and ecological awareness are just some of the factors common to many young Europeans in different countries and European advertising agencies are keenly observing and nurturing what they hope will be the first generation of Euro-consumers (Benady, 1993). Therefore, "as the similarities in consumer behaviour across national boundaries increasingly outweigh the differences, geographic segmentation is likely to give way to pan-European lifestyle segmentation" (Malhotra et al., 1992, p. 94).

This notion of cultural convergence and erosion is often seen as particularly alarming among Europeans, since first world countries do not expect to be the victims of cultural erosion. Yet there is evidence to show that in certain consumer markets cultural diversity plays at best only a superficial role (Wills, 1991). Davidson (1992) contends that culture is whatever most motivates us at any one time, claiming that this is now consumption, rather than religion or military victories as may have been the case in the past. If this is indeed the case, then consumption can be seen as one aspect of culture which unifies Europeans.

The Euro-ad

Advertising on the many European satellite channels provides very interesting clues as to how such pan-European advertising is developing. *Eurosport* is a satellite channel broadcast across Europe which only shows sports programmes with commentaries in the major European languages. There are no interviews and we never see the presenter (presumably since she or he is different in individual countries depending on the language) and much of the information is presented in a highly visual form, for example, tables and charts without accompanying commentary. In fact, many of the words are replaced with symbols or small information chunks, usually in English. Interestingly enough, this description also applies to much of the advertising on *Eurosport*. One wonders if this is deliberate, since it appears to be an example of a relatively dated and unsophisticated, but nonetheless reliable, tactic whereby the advert attempts to take on the features of the co-text or accompanying text, presumably in the hope of improving its credibility.

A large proportion of this advertising is actually sponsoring, and the return of the sponsored programme is a feature of these pan-European satellite channels, for example *Swatch* sponsors programmes on *MTV*, the music channel. Breaks in the programme are immediately preceded by the image of the product or the brand-name. Often the brand-name is a constant symbol in the corner of the screen during the programme. Although the sponsored programme - something which up to recently was viewed as somewhat old-fashioned - lends itself particularly well to sports and pop music, this is an obvious direction for intercultural advertising to take. By simply placing a brand-name on the screen for the duration of the sports or music programme, the format of which is deliberately non-specific to the culture of any particular country, advertisers can save themselves a lot of time and money which would usually be spent on attempting to solve the problems outlined above. Naturally, this type of advertising is easier to process and to comprehend for mass-communication purposes.

Another characteristic of *Eurosport* is the high degree of direct advertising. Messages in German move across the screen urging Germans, Austrians, Swiss-Germans, Hungarians (a lot of Hungarians understand German), etc. to apply for some offer and giving them the relevant telephone number in their own country. Where the direct marketing is actually in the form of an ad, the emphasis is again on the visual, and the final part of the ad consists of a table containing the flags, country abbreviations and relevant telephone numbers. These ads contain no text on the screen, except for information chunks and imperatives in English (e.g. 'Buy!' 'Phone!') with an accompanying narrative in the relevant language. Again these ads are not culture-specific, rather they are nondescript, belonging to a kind of cultural limbo which neither insults nor excites any particular nation, but which is acceptable to the Euro-consumer. Obviously, creating advertising within this type of non-culture-specific limbo overcomes the problems encountered to-date in trying to create a pan-European setting for an ad, or a pan-European pun.

Thus, this type of advertising seeks to be effective by avoiding identifiable national styles (e.g. British humour), 'slice of life' images (e.g. *Typhoo Tea*'s latest campaign which features idealized images of Britons enjoying tea) or ads which refer specifically to the national culture and current affairs. An example of this was *Visa Delta*'s use of Norman Lamont, which erupted when it was claimed that the Chancellor of the Exchequer had gone over his *Visa* credit limit. In promoting its new debit card, *Visa Delta* used another former Chancellor of the Exchequer, Denis Healey, to demonstrate how simple it was to use the card and that it would do away with the need for cheques - so simple that in fact even chancellors of the ex-*cheque*r could use it. The amount of interrrelated cultural knowledge needed to interpret this advertisement is enormous. Not only does the advertisee need to have knowledge of the scandal, but at a more basic level, they need to know who Denis Healey was, what the Chancellor of the Exchequer does (in order to interpret the pun) and all this knowledge needs to be related intertextually to the media coverage of the Lamont scandal. It is, therefore, hardly surprising that intercultural advertisers do not even attempt anything like this level of sophistication in their advertising and opt instead for non-culture-specific graphics and images. Where language is used, it tends, of necessity, to be free of linguistic devices such as puns, or metaphors, and jokes - one of the most culture-specific aspects of any national personality - are avoided.

One of the most noticeable features of *Eurosport* is the advertising for German products. They are the only culture-specific ads on the channel. There is, for example, an advertisement for *Volkswagen* which is entirely in German. In this case, there is no recognition of cultural diversity or adherence to the Euro-ad formula of non-culture-specific images and sound-bites in simple English, free of linguistic devices which would require cultural knowledge to be interpreted. The German advertisers seem content to allow their ads to be broadcast to francophone, anglophone and other countries where German is not widely known without any translation or explanation. One could argue that these advertisers are targeting consumers in German-speaking countries and are simply not interested in viewers in other countries. Another explanation may be that this phenomenon is merely typical of the diminishing role of the verbal in the 'post-literate' society and the accompanying growth in the dominance of the paralinguistic and the visual. Hodge and Kress (1993), Cook (1992) and many others have recognized this trend and the secondary function of language in much of today's advertising. These German ads may, however, be seen as a more extreme example of this: the text is so unimportant and peripheral that it does not merit translation, since the paralinguistic and visual elements of the ad stand alone.

National and cultural stereotyping

But could there possibly be a positive effect on non-German-speaking consumers? As companies have begun to devise pan-European advertising strategies, they have at the same time been increasingly restricted from directly using the origin of the product as an advertising technique. Instead of telling us or reminding us that *Volkswagen* cars are German, the Euro-consumer sees the highly visual ad showing the car and all its attributes and at the same time she or he hears the German language which has the association of efficiency, quality and first-class engineering. So, in fact, there may be quite a positive effect (in terms of advertising goals) from this type of advert, even though many of the viewers may not actually understand the spoken part of the ad.

It could be argued further that the effect may be even greater because this ad is for a car. We are all familiar with the European heaven, where the Germans build the cars, the Italians are the opera singers, the Swiss the bankers, the French are the cooks, the British the police etc. Would there be this positive side effect if the ad were, say, for *Seat* and the text in Spanish, because that is not what we expect from the Spaniards? In fact,

Seat finds it necessary to remind us in its advertising that its cars are, above-all, German engineered, with the features of Spanish design. It is ironic that more and more European advertising in the borderless Europe draws on national and cultural stereotypes. This is the basis of *Audi*'s 'Vorsprung durch Technik' campaign. It is doubtful whether many anglophone consumers really know what the phrase means, but they know that it is German and since it is associated with a car, the stereotypical German product, the technique works. A further example is *AEG*'s adoption and use in advertisements of a new explanation of its abbreviated title, one which emphasizes the Germanness and, by association, the quality of the product - 'advanced engineering from Germany'.

Equally, we look to the stereotypical roles of other countries or cultures in advertising our own products. The German *Mercedes* engineer drives a *Rover* with Stuttgart number plates - thus the Germans, the carmakers approve of and actually choose *Rover*, so *Rover* cars must be good. A further example is an ad for the Irish butter Kerrygold, which interestingly enough is entirely in simple French, although directed at an Irish audience: The Irish au-pair arrives at the home of her French family. She has brought *Kerrygold* with her as a present, but the French housewife already has some and the ad finishes with the family and au-pair tucking into 'les spuds' covered in *Kerrygold*. Again, the association gives the brand credibility - the French, the European cooks, approve of *Kerrygold*, so should we.

The respective roles in these ads are based on our most deep-seated notions of other cultures within Europe. Imagine the British person enthusing about a new German food product, or the French family praising the au-pair's Irish-made car - it is difficult to believe that such an approach would work. Witness the well-known Czech car manufacturer, *Skoda*'s, new advertising campaign: The whole message of the ad is that *Volkswagen* approves of *Skoda* and has done a complete overhaul of the factory and the product - it was obviously felt that it was vital to make these details the core of the advertising message, in order for *Skoda*, a brand from one of the reforming states of Central Europe, to be taken seriously.

Furthermore, products are even exploiting other countries' negative perceptions of their country of origin in advertising to these countries. Thus, *Audi* advertised the open-top Cabriolet with the slogan 'Why the Germans no longer worry about getting to the beach first', presumably in order to find a sunlounger and umbrella before the other tourists. In the advertising for the *Renault Laguna*, the handsome driver of the car collects and drops off a number of women with whom he has an ambivalent relationship, thus exploiting the popular image of the Frenchman as womanizer. Finally, one of the best of these ads is the new advertising for *Beck*'s, which through the use of hyperbole turns the German reputation for punctiliousness into a funny, self-mocking ad. In the ad, Klaus the brewer from Bremen being a bit of a practical joker, arrives fifteen seconds earlier than usual to trick his co-workers. *Volkswagen*'s advertising campaign also pokes fun at the perceived lack of humour among Germans. The ad wishes that the German sense of humour could be as reliable as *Volkswagen* cars.

Conclusion

To conclude, it is perhaps worthwhile to summarize these trends in intercultural advertising and make some predictions about their further development. Firstly, cultures, sub-cultures, and intercultural advertising in the new Europe will be more concerned with lifestyle groups than with national groups. Secondly, in all sub-divisions of advertising, text is being replaced by paralanguage and image, something that would appear to be indicative of the overall trend away from literacy in public communication in today's society. It is also something which makes advertising, particularly intercultural advertising, even easier to create and it gives more audiences in different cultures and countries access to particular advertisements. Therefore, it is likely that we will see more images and, consequently, less text, particularly in pan-European advertising, in the future.

Thirdly, as culture-specific advertising in individual countries has become more sophisticated, witty, clever and creative, advertising directed at more than one culture, for example the Euro-ad, seems to have taken a backward step, in terms of design, humour, intelligence and sheer entertainment. Unfortunately, it seems we can predict an increase in this type of bland, inoffensive and uninteresting advertising and sub-forms of it such as sponsoring, as the European village becomes even bigger and more uniform. One wonders if, in trying to create the Euro-consumer, agencies and companies have concentrated too much on selecting the lowest common denominator shared by most Europeans - this would certainly appear to be evidenced by much of the advertising directed at this intangible group. This trend is bound to continue with the abundance of new media, particularly satellite channels set to become a part of European culture.

The final point follows on from this idea of European consumer lifestyles converging at the lowest common denominator. Where companies actually do wish to assert the nationality of their products or brands, rather than simply classifying them as European, national stereotypes based on our deep-rooted perceptions of the capabilities of countries will take on an even greater importance in giving credibility to products. Furthermore, there is likely to be an even greater transfer of values associated with a particular nation or region to products identified with that nation or region. This is the paradox of intra-European advertising. Malhotra et al.'s prediction about culture applies equally to advertising: We will witness most probably the emergence of a limited and, at first, somewhat superficial European identity among consumers overlaid on top of an abiding set of socialized national and local cultural norms (Malhotra et al., 1992, p. 86)

Given that these national and cultural perceptions are so firmly laid down, it will be increasingly difficult to change such stereotypes as a process of superficial convergence takes hold. Interestingly enough, the Generation '93 survey of European youth found that young Europeans held similar perceptions about the relative strengths of different countries (cf. Benady, 1993). Therefore, it would appear that the Euro-consumer in the year 2020 will be even less reluctant to relate to an advertising message which obviously and overtly conflicts with these cultural and national stereotypes.

References

Atkinson, Rick (1993), 'Ads Cater to Wary East Germans: Just the Facts, please, in a World without Yuppies', *International Herald Tribune*, 28-29 August 1993.

Benady, Alex (1993), 'European Youth still Beyond Advertisers', *Marketing*, 5 August 1993.

Butler, Daniel (1992), 'Advertising in the Former Soviet Bloc is not Simply a Case of Regurgitating Campaigns from the West', *Campaign*, 25 September 1992, p. 31.

Cherry, Colin (1967), 'Communication, Politics and People' in Thayer, L (ed.), *Communication Theory and Research: Proceedings of the First International Symposium*, Charles C Thomas, Springfield IL, pp. 429-40.

Cook, Guy (1992), *The Discourse of Advertising*, Routledge, London.

Davidson, Martin (1992), *The Consumerist Manifesto: Advertising in Postmodern Times*, Routledge, London.

Elinder, Erik (1961), 'International Advertisers must Devise Universal Ads. Dump Separate National ones, Swedish ad man Avers', *Advertising Age*, 27 November 1961, p. 91.

Hodge, Robert and Kress, Gunther (1993), *Language as Ideology*, Routledge, London.

Jain, Subash C. (1990), *International Marketing Management*, PWS-Kent Publishing Company, Boston.

Keegan, Warren J. (1989), *Global Marketing Management*, Prentice Hall, Englewood Cliffs NJ.

Kelly, Helen (1994), 'West German Banks and East German Consumers: A Study in Intercultural Advertising Communication', in Graddol, David and Thomas, Stephen (eds), *Language in a Changing Europe*, Multilingual Matters, Clevedon, pp. 55-63.

Malhotra, Naresh K., Baalbaki, Imad M., Agarwal, Janes and McIntyre, John R. (1992), 'One Market or many? An Assessment of the Degree of Homogeneity within the European Community', *Journal of Euromarketing*, vol. 2, no. 1, pp. 69-95.

McLuhan, Marshall (1964), *Understanding Media - the Extensions of Man*, Routledge and Kegan Paul, London.

Reed, David (1993), 'Europe: Campaign Report on Worldwide Advertising: Targeting the new Europe', *Campaign*, 12 May 1995, p. 29.

Wills, Gordon (1991), 'The Single Market and National Market Thinking', *European Journal of Marketing*, vol. 25, no. 4, pp. 148-55.

Political Communication and Political Culture in Germany and Great Britain: Some Differences and Similarities

COLIN GOOD

Introduction

This paper is divided into three sections. The first section focusses on attitudes towards what must be the central value in any political order, that of truth, and suggests that the Europe-wide dissatisfaction of the citizens with the political process may be related to the attitudes of the politicians towards this value. In the second section, it is suggested that certain aspects of the political debate in Germany, in particular discourse about the legitimacy of 'opposition' and the desirability of open conflict, are still shaped by recent German history. The final section investigates the reason why international communication often founders on what, on the face of things, look like common 'internationalisms', such as 'federalism' and 'state'. Whilst this paper mentions only Germany and Britain, the communication problems revealed apply arguably to the way all states talk to their citizens or to each other.

Language, politics and truth

Political communication in Britain and Germany and the beliefs and expectations of both politicians and citizens in these two countries - and presumably many other countries in Europe - underlying this aspect of political behaviour have, not surprisingly, a great deal in common. The similarities are not surprising because both systems, after all, involve political parties of a more or less conservative or progressive persuasion, who jostle for power once every four or five years by attempting to woo the voter, during what are called, in strikingly similar metaphors, 'election campaigns' or 'Wahlkämpfe'. Before going on to discuss the status of 'truth-telling', it is useful to recall some of the other, more obvious, common features. These include the black and white portrayal of events, the appeal to emotions rather than to the intellect, innuendo, vagueness of expression, simplification and avoiding the issue. These are features of political language *per se*, but they are undoubtedly particularly prominent at election time; as a result both the English word 'electioneering' and a common German phrase, 'wahltaktisches Kalkül', are negatively loaded terms, revealing that there is a level of critical reflection in both political cultures.

Politicians in both cultures invoke glorious - or, if the opponent is to be denigrated, inglorious - periods in the past. The past is invoked and instrumentalized in a variety of ways: for example, during the last *Land* election in Lower Saxony in 1994, the poster for the young right-wing candidate, Wulf, contained a small inset picture of Adenauer, the embodiment of immediate post-war German success, or, in a party political broadcast on British television, delivered by the Foreign Minister, Hurd, another voice, with a distinctly Churchillian ring about it, could be heard, joining the Minister in his endeavour to speak for Europe, whilst keeping on board the anti-Europe group in the party and among the voters by presenting Europe as a kind of extension of the British Empire, which would need defending against the rest of the world.

Even such a short catalogue would be incomplete without reference to the deliberate instrumentalization - that is, the reinterpretation or recontextualization - of significant concepts from the past or present political debate. I will instance here only the two German terms 'Weimarisierung' (roughly, the 'Weimarisation'), and 'Zerfransung' (literally 'fraying' or 'coming apart'). Both of these terms have been instrumentalized by the German right in the last few years, increasingly so in the run-up to the last Federal elections in 1994, as they have been applied to the rise, not, as might have been expected, of right, or even left wing extremism, but also to middle class protest parties. More precisely, of course, they have served the 'established parties' in their effort to obfuscate such differences. Now many of the communicative acts involved in the devices mentioned so far can be seen, on closer scrutiny, to include an element of what might be called 'evasiveness'. According to one commentator: "Evasiveness is a normal part of politics" (Hudson, 1978, p. 57). This point will not be further developed here. It is necessary, however, to add to this observation that 'evasiveness' resolves itself in turn into 'deceit' and other related concepts.

This consideration takes us to the very heart of the matter, to the *maxims* underlying what politicians say to the citizens. Political commentators and writers may be quite sanguine about this; let me quote only Keith Minogue, who makes the point that "a good deal of deceit is essential to the proper workings of any kind of institution" (Hudson, 1978, frontispiece). But not all voters have this kind of distance, not all are as cynical - unfortunately - as Hannah Arendt, who wrote that: " Wahrhaftigkeit zählte niemals zu den politischen Tugenden, und die Lüge galt doch immer als erlaubtes Mittel der Politik" [that is: 'truthfulness was never among the political virtues and it has always been considered acceptable to lie in politics'] (Hannah Arendt, quoted in *Die Zeit*, 14 May 1993). Indeed, as the recent, though short-lived, debate occasioned by the admission of a British minister, William Waldegrave, in the spring of 1994 that it was sometimes necessary to tell only part of the truth showed, many, perhaps less sophisticated citizens do not know that, as one journalist put it, "the illusion that things are different [that is, that politicians do not lie; C.G.] derives from the special mystique of parliament" (Hugo Young, *The Guardian*, 10 March 1994). The subsequent BBC phone-in on the matter, incidentally, revealed a wide range of views. But whilst there were certainly those who claimed that they did not believe a word that politicians said, very many people evinced shock and hurt or even disbelief at the minister's statement, or else insisted that things ought to be different.

From the point of view of downward - or media-mediated - political communication, two questions suggest themselves: what position do the politicians take on the question of telling lies and promising and all the other related values at stake in the political business and, assuming that they deliberately use a wide-spread and false assumption about the nature of political talk, how do they manage to do this, for some, if by no means all, of the citizens? On the first of these two points: it is in the interests of politicians to foster the illusion that they do not lie (and it must be remembered that, from the communicative point of view, there does not seem to be much difference between 'lying' and not telling the whole truth, or even allowing the truth of a given proposition to emerge obliquely, between the lines, as it were - what matters is the impression that arises). It is arguable that it would be impossible to carry on politics, in the narrow sense of communication with an appeal to the citizen, if both sides did not pretend to this illusion. The centrality of (beliefs about) 'truth' is beyond doubt. All political parties, for instance, have to position themselves in relation to 'truth' and 'truthfulness' from time to time. It is common even for smaller parties to seek to define themselves in relation to this value. Here is Paddy Ashdown, claiming, on behalf of the British Liberals, that: "we will tell the truth when the other two parties don't", because, as he goes on to say: "people out there are desperate about the truth" (*Breakfast TV*, 6 February 1994).

Truth is a touch-stone in our understanding of politics. The very maturity of the Green party in Germany was shown for one commentator in the fact that: "der Glaube verflogen ist, alle sozialen Wohltaten ließen sich versprechen" ['they no longer believe that one can promise to carry out everything that is socially desirable'] (*Die Zeit*, 4 March 1993). 'Lying' and' 'truth' have to do with the speech act of making a promise. Voter dissatisfaction with the record of the mainstream parties on this score may, not surprisingly, be instrumentalized by other parties, as when, the PDS (the successor to the old East German Socialist Unity Party, the SED) announced, in a 1994 Leipzig election slogan: "Wir versprechen nichts" ['we promise nothing']. Despite what even brief reflection on these aspects of the ethics of communication reveals, politicians nevertheless uphold the impression that the political game involves, as a leading Labour politician, Michael Meacher, put it in the context of the Waldegrave gaffe: "The principle of telling the truth is absolute" (*Daily Mail*, 9 March 1994). Another Labour politician, Harriet Harman, got in on the act in the same vein when she insisted - at a time when the furore about the Conservatives raising taxes, despite their election 'pledge' not to do so, was at its fiercest :

> No, what we are accusing the Conservatives of - they promised at the last election that they would cut people's taxes and what we've done is to expose the fact that they lied to the British electorate. What we're doing is exposing the myths and lies of the Tories. (*Radio 4*, 28 January 1994)

Plenty of similar German evidence could be given here; it will suffice to recall only what has come to be known in the German political debate as the 'Steuerlüge' [the 'tax lie'].

I turn briefly at this point to the second question posed above: how do the politicans manage to lie whilst appearing not to do so? The answers suggested here are linguistic ones: firstly, like the rest of us, German and British politicians use, with great sophistication, the complicated relationship between speech acts and their direct and indirect linguistic realizations, the mismatch, for instance, between promising in the sense of giving an explicit undertaking that a certain state of affairs will come about and the deliberate, but covert, creation of the impression that this will be the case. They also use, however, a different set of rules than that which usually applies to everyday interpersonal interaction. That is to say, politicians can frequently be seen to obfuscate the difference between political and moral action by fostering the illusion that the two are the same, or by trading on the differences between the two. Obfuscation may be made easier by the uncertain relation between 'political' activity, including talk, and ordinary, everyday (linguistic) behaviour. It is sometimes argued, for instance, that a commitment given by an individual does or does not bind the group (the principle of 'collective responsibility'). Rather than expand on this matter in the abstract, it will be helpful to take two simple examples of the way political talk can function in this sense. A leading Conservative, Michael Portillo, dealt with the accusation that the Tories had broken promises regarding tax rises by claiming that:

> The public deficit and the consequent need for much higher taxes was evidence of error in judging the length of recession rather than dishonesty towards the electorate. (*The Guardian*, 26 January 1994)

He clearly felt the need to address the 'sincerity' maxim; by thematizing it he was able to adjust it. The Prime Minister John Major's statement in the House of Commons that he regretted the "need to raise taxes" (*The Times*, 26 January 1994; note the invocation of 'need' again) was strikingly similar. In neither statement was the politician *apologizing*, that is to say, performing the speech act that might have been expected in ordinary interaction. At all events, this was clearly the reaction that some members of the public expected, as was demonstrated by the bemused reaction of a Church of England vicar, who said:

> It wasn't clear whether he [the reference here is to Portillo again, this time on the subject of the easy acquisition of university degrees in other countries; C.G.] was apologizing for the damage he had done to the countries he was talking about, or to his own party. (*Radio 4*, 7 February 1994)

Finally, the point made above concerning the 'pragmatic' meaning of utterances is reflected in the way one newspaper reported of another political figure that "Sir Robert thus at least acknowledges that a misleading effect may occur" (*The Guardian*, 10 March 1994), the point being that, in terms of the ethics of communication, making a misleading statement is tantamount to stating something outright. To return to Hugo Young's attribution of the fuss surrounding the Waldegrave 'revelation' to the illusion that a whole institution is honest, we may add that this illusion is maintained by the prohibition on the use by politicians of the word 'lie' with reference to their political opponents, laid down in the rules governing the conduct of business (known as 'Erskine May') in the House of Commons. This prohibition, too, remains on the surface of linguistic behaviour, choosing to ignore that there are, as has been argued above, many ways of 'lying'. If, as many commentators seem to think, there is a crisis of parliamentary democracy in many European countries at the moment, it seems likely that the dissatisfaction of many voters is a reaction to the 'ethics of communication', as I have interpreted this in the aforegoing.

Some peculiarities of German political culture: 'opposition' and 'conflict'

In this second section it is suggested that there are a number of elements in German political discourse which are likely to impede rather than facilitate Germany's linguistic relations with her European neighbours.

There is a discernible unease about some aspects of communication in the German political process which has taken on actual institutional form during a number of post-war elections. In 1994, again, a so-called 'Schiedsstelle' ['arbitration panel'] was set up to oversee the conduct of the election and to ensure fair play. In practice, 'unfairness' - the loan-word 'Fairness' is actually enshrined in the 'contract' signed by the various political parties - has usually involved aspects of linguistic conduct, 'verbal injury' that is, broadly speaking, defamatory statements by one side about the other. The panels have usually been composed of members of the major political parties; significantly the chairman has always been a bishop. The choice of a cleric is significant because it is the church and the Jews in Germany who were and are the prime movers behind the setting up of these institutions (cf. *Das Parlament*, 4 March 1994). They can be seen to be acting, for obvious historical reasons, as a kind of conscience, not yet quite drowned out by the many sceptics who believe this anxiety about the 'young democracy', about how Germany may appear to her neighbours and about the nature of the state is now misplaced and old hat. In other words, the 'Schiedsstellen' - and many other features of German political culture - are ultimately explainable only against a background of Weimar and National Socialism and can only be understood if one sees them in the context of the 'Obrigkeitsstaat' ['authoritarian state'].

One must not over-generalize: there are, as I have just implied, those who argue that democracy is sufficiently well-established in Germany to render concern over the conduct of political debate superfluous. One newspaper commented about the installation of an arbitration panel for the 1986 election as follows: "alle Parteien meinen, der Wähler selbst wird schon entscheiden, was fair sei und was nicht" [in a nutshell, 'leave it to the common sense of the voters'!] (*Frankfurter Allgemeine Zeitung*, 16 August 1986). A prominent political figure, Jens Reich, reacted similarly, when he judged that a written election contract was not necessary: "weil dort etwas festgeschrieben würde, was selbstverständlich sein sollte" ['because it lays down what should be obvious anyway'] (*Frankfurter Allgemeine Zeitung*, 16 August 1986). But there is a note of doubt even in his formulation ("sein sollte") ['should be']. It is the nagging doubt, that will not go away, an echo, I would contend, of what Dahrendorf called: "die Sehnsucht nach der Synthese" ['a longing for synthesis'], something he regarded as "ein Spezifikum der politischen Kultur in Deutschland" ['specific to political culture in Germany'] (Sarcillini, 1990, p. 12). Indeed, the need for a 'Schiedsstelle' is often discussed in terms of the German past. The argument runs as follows: the prevention of mud-slinging will discourage extremism, which is related, in turn, to the Holocaust and the present wave of xenophobia.

The problematic nature of certain aspects of political communication that I have identified here can be related to the demand from some quarters for a 'Streitkultur'. It is difficult to think of a satisfactory English equivalent for this term, with its odd combination of 'argument' and 'culture'. A 'culture of open debate' comes close, possibly, but is strange to our ears precisely because the British political process expects politicians to hand out as good as they get! The term 'Streitkultur' has recently, I believe under the influence of linguistic theory, been replaced in some publications by 'Gesprächskultur' ['a cultured conversation']. This term, too, relates to a mode of linguistic conduct promulgated officially by the state - to judge by the many titles emanating from the various 'Institutes for Political Education' - and betraying as much anxiety about open conflict and opposition as the earlier version:

> Gesprächskultur ist nicht allein gelungenes Arrangement eines rationalen Diskurses, sondern auch die kultivierte Begegnung von Menschen im Gespräch ['conversational culture is not just about the successful conduct of rational discourse, but also about civilized debate']. (Fürst, 1989, p. 10)

Even the description of polemics in a standard German work on elections, a description which hovers uncertainly between the descriptive and the prescriptive, is essentially 'idealistic', expressing the desire that dissension and conflict can or should be controlled by a kind of self-imposed ethic of enlightenment:

> Nicht die Zerstörung des Gegners ist in der freiheitlichen Demokratie Sinn der parteilichen Polemik, sondern die inhaltliche Abgrenzung, um die Wähler zu einer Entscheidung zu veranlassen ['polemics aim not to destroy the opponent in a democracy, but to state the differences in policy clearly, so that the voter can reach a sensible decision']. (Wolf, 1980, p. 228).

There are many other cultural phenomena which I would argue can be related to the same syndrom: the anxiety about sinking election turn-outs, their diagnosis as 'Staats-, Partei- oder Politikverdrossenheit' ['a lack of interest in and irratation with the state, the parties, and with politics'], or the lexicalization of the phenomenon in such terms as 'Wahlabstinenz' ['no participation in elections'], despite the sensible reminder that poor turn-outs at the polls, incidentally much lower in some European countries than in Germany, are in themselves quite ambivalent and can be: "sowohl Ausdruck einer Normalisierung als auch ein Symptom krisenhafter Entwicklungen" ['both the expression of normalization and a symptom of crisis'] (Wolf, 1980, p. 216).

Semantics and international dialogue

Do 'internationalisms' mean the same in different political cultures? Before turning to such international vocabulary, it will be useful to indicate some broad differences between German and British political thinking. Despite Margaret Thatcher's 'new dawn' and the epic strain in her pronouncements, I have the impression that key abstract philosophical-cum-political terms play less of a role in British politics than they do in Germany. The appeal in Britain is more often to the 'common sense' of the citizens, and both main parties struggle to occupy this 'middle ground' - although, as suggested in the statement by one Labour MP, Margaret Becket, that: "I believe that common sense and radicalism are entirely compatible terms" (*Radio 4*, 2 May 1994), the Socialists in Britain have something of a problem with ideas which clearly come from a left-wing tradition. The middle ground in Germany cannot, for obvious historical reasons, involve appeals to the national spirit in concepts such as 'Patriotismus', 'Vaterland' and 'Nation', which, despite Chancellor Kohl's partial rehabilitation of these 'ideologemes' in the early 1980s, still require careful handling in that political culture. One shrewd political journalist put my argument most succinctly when he observed that: "Patriotismus könne in anderen Ländern mit Pragmatismus durchaus koexistieren, während in Deutschland die beiden Wörter immer Gegensätze markierten" ['In other countries, patriotism and pragmatism can coexist, but in Germany, the two words always marked opposite poles'] (Dieter Buhl in *Die Zeit*, 7 September 1984). What this probably means in terms of international dialogue is that the British read German texts in which patriotic diction occurs in quite a different way than we would presume to intend our own.

I want to turn now briefly to a number of other key terms, whose tradition in British political discourse is such that their occurrence in the context of British-German dialogue seems bound to cause misunderstanding. The assumption is probably justified that such problems will be repeated in international dialogue involving other European states. Most of the differences in 'mental sets' that are discussed below clearly predate Thatcherite politics, although the fourteen or so years of Tory rule under the Iron Lady did nothing to smooth over the differences, and indeed added some more.

Problems are attached already to a term as basic within the network of concepts expressing a political culture as the idea and the word 'state' or 'Staat'. A different history and the resulting real differences in the structure of the two political orders have produced what several political scientists have called 'eine andere Weltauffassung' ['a different view of the world']. Different conceptions of the state - sharpened, as suggested, rather than reduced under Thatcherism - manifest themselves right down to the level of the syntactic and semantic shape of sentences, where, as has been shown, 'state' appears in German political language as actor in sentences significantly more often than it does in Britain, where the equivalent actor is often the 'government'. There is not a lot of hard evidence here (but cf. Seck, 1991), but I would instance as an example of the kind of communication problem I have in mind two statements. The first is from a dictionary of politics: "As a concept the State has been somewhat overlooked in the political theory and research of the last century, especially in the Anglo-Saxon world and still creates a good deal of confusion and uncertainty" (Robertson, 1986, p, 308). I would argue that the state has been 'overlooked' as a concept precisely because of the conceptual differences involved, these in turn deriving from real differences between the two political orders. The second observation comes from a political scientist with a strong interest in linguistics:

> In the US and GB neo-conservatives have no problem in combining the call for strong government with a rejection of bureaucratic and even socialist measures, which might hinder the entrepreneurial spirit, because they can do so without resorting to the use of a concept (State) which names at one and the same time the enemy and the ideal they are striving for. (Opp de Hipt, 1990, p. 217).

'State', in other words, is construed differently and embedded differently in a network of concepts in the political discourse of the two countries involved. The ideological result of the British understanding of the term emerges very clearly when one considers that Thatcherism was able to combine a paring down of the concept of state with arguably the greatest degree of centralization the British political system has seen this century.
Just as 'state' differs in German and English, so, too, does the concept of 'democracy'. The German and the English concepts are so different as to cause profound misunderstandings in Europe. However different the emphases may be across the political spectrum in Germany, there is broad consensus on the component of collective involvement and participation. The 'democratic idea' permeates political discourse right into the economic sphere; the concept that comes to mind here is 'Mitbestimmung' ['codetermination']. In Britain the dominant understanding is probably that of the exercise of power by a duly elected government, on the basis of the majority system of election. The different understandings of democracy relate, of course, to many other concepts in the two mental sets, such as 'federalism' and 'society'.

The general argument is summed up by two German linguists as follows:

> ... sollte man nicht verkennen, daß der Gebrauch einer allgemein-europäischen Terminologie wie Pluralismus, Parteienregierung, politisches System usw. keineswegs bedeuten muß, daß die entsprechenden Realitäten in gleicher Weise konstruiert werden ['it does not follow from the use of a common set of European terminology such as pluralism, party government, political system etc. that the corresponding realities are constructed in the same way']. (Dörner and Rohe, 1991, p. 57)

They go on to say that "all dies [...] rhetorisch in Rechnung gestellt werden muß", but I am stuck in attempting to translate this by the degree of difference that clearly exists between the ideas of rhetoric in the two cultures [roughly, the quote means 'all this must be accounted for rhetorically, i.e. discursively'].

A term from the vocabulary of economics is so central to our argument as to merit separate discussion: 'market economy'. In Germany, this idea has been unthinkable without the associated idea of the 'social component', which has its origins in Catholic social teaching, as espoused, for instance, by the 'Zentrumspartei' during the Weimar period and is still an important element in the programme of the right-wing CDU. In Britain, right-wing think-tanks have been at pains to stress the amorality of the market, with the result for the semantics of political discourse that 'welfare' is, according to some commentators, on the way to becoming what it already is in American English, namely a term denoting something like the pittance meted out to the poorest of poor in the USA. This different view of the nature of political morality, expressed in the discourse surrounding the market and welfare state, clearly does nothing to ease communication across borders - I need only indicate here the differences over the acceptability of the Social Chapter in the Maastricht Treaty. The response of the British to the call for a Social Charter has been, as it were, to accord rights to the new British citizen to complain to the railways if the trains are running late or to ring cone hot-lines if one is puzzled by a particular arrangement of cones somewhere along the motorways. Underpinning the concept of the 'active citizen' in Britain - the idea seems to owe much to the notion of the politically 'mündiger Bürger' [the 'mature citizen'] in Germany - is a view of the *individual* citizen as, first and foremost, a consumer, enjoying economic freedom.

Conclusion

Such differences as I have discussed here are likely to play an important role in the discussion of 'citizenship' that is going on at the moment in and between the various member states of the European Union. It might have struck the attentive reader that I used the word 'citizen' in the earlier sections of this paper in contexts where other words, such as 'voter', 'member of the public' or 'tax-payer' might have been expected to occur in English. The same observation could be made in relation to 'Mitbürger', a common term in German in contexts where the most natural English equivalent would probably have been something like 'fellow countrymen' or, again, 'tax-payers'. 'Bürger' ('citizen') is embedded in German political thinking and discourse in quite a different network of concepts and associations. Its reinstallation in British political discourse, especially under the present Prime Minister, Major, might have been taken as a sign of hope for those wishing to see a bill of rights or a written constitution, guaranteeing *political* rights in Britain, had the notion of 'citizenship' not, as I have just described, been reduced to the stunted vision of the 'citizen-consumer'.

Discussion up to this point has concerned a number of concepts basic to all democratic systems in the Western mould. The final part of this paper will focus on two terms which are more 'local', yet also significant within the discourse of European integration. Out of all the possible contenders I will select just the 'F-word' and the 'D-word', 'Federalism' and 'Devolution', in order to show how the local application of the terms, an understanding deriving from particular and different histories, interacts with their application in a European context (cf. also Musolff in this volume). (Much of what is said applies also to the term 'Subsidiarity'.)

The concept of 'Federalism' carries such negative connotations in British political discourse that communication and agreement at an European level is bound to be severely impaired. I would suggest, briefly, that the British - here 'English' would actually be more appropriate - problem with Scotland, Wales and Northern Ireland, and with the regions generally, in a very - and increasingly - centralized political order has coloured the British view of the 'federal principle' as this might function on the European level. Generally, the resonance of the term for the British in the international context can only be understood if account is taken of 'local' historical and political conditions, or, rather, the discourse in which such issues have found expression. The 'federal idea' impinges on and threatens British nationhood domestically; this inevitably rubs off on the perception of the idea in its wider European context. Only this kind of account of the semantics of 'federalism' can account for the staggering feat of Mr Hurd, the Foreign Minister mentioned earlier in this paper, who in 1992 defended Maastricht, as one political scientist wrote: "in terms which the European People's Party would have found wounding, as a significant check for federalist ambition" (Watson, 1993, p. 304). Almost as daring was the way in which Mrs Thatcher managed to uncouple the concept of 'devolution' from the question of political decentralization and to assert a new meaning for the term, in the context of aggressive 1980s-style individualism, when in July 1983, she said: "The government believes in devolution to the individual citizen - a devolution which is now being achieved." Both politicians were reacting, however different the rhetorical means they employed might be, to the - negative - meanings of 'internationalisms' in a domestic political context, and, in so doing, they were refusing to enter a - European - debate, in which those terms might have quite a different significance. The 'local semantics' of many terms, it is suggested, will continue to be the sand in the machinery of European integration.

References

Dörner, Andreas and Rohe, Karl (1991), 'Politische Sprache und Politische Kultur. Diachron-kulturvergleichende Sprachanalysen am Beispiel von Großbritannien und Deutschland' in Opp de Hipt, Manfred and Latniak, Erich (eds), *Sprache statt Politik*, Westdeutscher Verlag, Opladen, pp. 38-65.

Fürst, Gebhard (1989), 'Einleitung' in Schmidt-Sinns, Dieter (ed.), *Politische Gesprächskultur im Fernsehen*, Bundeszentrale für politische Bildung, Bonn, pp. 1-12.

Hudson, Keith (1978), *The Language of Modern Politics*, Macmillan Press, London.

Opp de Hipt, Manfred (1990), 'Mental Pictures of the State in West Germany Party Platforms: A Research Note', *European Journal of Political Research*, vol. 18, no. 2, pp. 207-19.

Robertson, David (1986), *Dictionary of Politics*, Penguin, London.

Sarcillini, Ulrich (ed.) (1990), *Demokratische Streitkultur*, Bundeszentrale für politische Bildung, Bonn.

Schmidt-Sinns, Dieter (ed.) (1989), *Politische Gesprächskultur im Fernsehen*, Bundeszentrale für politische Bildung, Bonn.

Seck, Wolfgang (1991), *Politische Kultur und Politische Sprache: Empirische Analysen am Beispiel Deutschlands und Großbritanniens*, Peter Lang, Frankfurt am Main, Bern, New York.

Watson, Keith (1993), 'The 1992 General Election and the British Party System', *Government and Opposition*, vol. 28, no. 4, pp. 290-310.

Wolf, Werner (1980), *Der Wahlkampf. Theorie und Praxis*, Verlag Wissenschaft und Politik, Köln.

Indirect Speech and Conversational Implicatures: The Case for Contrastive Pragmatics

FRANK LIEDTKE

Introduction

Indirect speech is a central phenomenon of political rhetoric. For a politician it is very advantageous to be able to convey a message indirectly, relying on aspects of utterance-meaning (Grice, 1989) which are not explicitly stated but which are implicated to a higher or lesser degree in what is said. One of the many advantages of this technique is that the communicative effects of indirect utterances can be cancelled up to a certain degree. This is one of the reasons why indirectness is a means which is widely used, not only in the area of politics, but in everyday conversation as well. One may expect, however, that this rhetorical technique is an especially important factor in political argumentation, because one of the major aims of a politician is to gain people's allegiance, and this is much easier to attain if one cannot be falsified in what one has been saying.

I want to investigate some rhetorical techniques, especially indirectness, which the German Chancellor Kohl used during his speech on the occasion of the 50th anniversary of the attempt upon Hitler's life on 20 July 1944. As we shall see, there are some characteristic devices which help orators to extend their communicative goals far beyond the limits of the special occasion of the speech - without offending against the thematic restrictions such an occasion imposes upon every speech.

Methodologically these reflections are based on the fundamentals of pragmatic theory, as they are outlined in the works of John R. Searle (e.g. 1969, 1983), Herbert Paul Grice (e.g. 1975, 1989), Stephen Levinson (1983, 1989), Gerald Gazdar (1979), and Larry Horn (1984). Very important in this respect seems to be John Wilson's (1990) book *Politically Speaking*; it is, as far as I know, the first approach to political language and language use from a pragmatic viewpoint. In this book, John Wilson deals with linguistic implications as one form of indirectness in political argumentation. I will return to this work later.

A pragmatic explanation of indirectness

Before analyzing a central passage of Kohl's speech, we have to clarify the notion of indirectness, and this I want to do in pragmatic terms.

'Indirectness' is a rather vague notion, in that it is not clear what kind of entity is said to be indirect in one's utterance - is it a word or its meaning, is it a sentence or the utterance of a sentence, or is it rather the style of a speech? I want to restrict my use of the word 'indirect' to speech acts, i.e. to utterances of sentences by speakers with certain intentions, without ruling out other notions of indirectness. The kind of indirectness I am dealing with here may at best be explained in terms of the Gricean account of conversational implicatures; these are to be identified as layers of the total signification of an utterance which are not located at the surface of the sentence uttered. Conversational implicatures are not something which is being *said*, although they belong to that what is *meant* by a speaker who performs a speech act. I am using the terms say and mean here in the sense of Grice (1989). Grice's analysis of this kind of indirectness goes as follows:

The analysis is based on the assumption that when people interact they are guided by a basic principle of co-operation, and that under this general principle a series of maxims operate which govern conversational behaviour. The cooperative principle is formulated as a quasi-imperative, so it is assumed that people behave as if they were following an imaginary imperative. It is by no means designed as a real imperative:

> Make your contribution such as is required at the stage at which it occurs, by the accepted purpose or direction of the talk exchange in which you are engaged.

Under this general principle are subsumed several maxims of conversation, of which I only mention two. The first is the maxim of Quantity, which divides into two submaxims:

1. Make your contribution as informative as required for the current purposes of the exchange.
2. Do not make your contribution more informative than required.

The maxim of Relation runs as follows:

Be relevant. (cf. Grice, 1989, p. 26-7)

Both maxims are connected, because making one's contribution as informative as required and not more so is a form of being relevant. There are other maxims which do not fit so easily under the heading of the maxim of relevance; nevertheless some recent authors have proposed reducing all conversational maxims to a single maxim, that of Relevance, claiming that all other maxims of conversational behaviour might be deduced from this central maxim (cf. Sperber and Wilson, 1986). Others have opposed that idea, arguing that the attempt to reduce all forms of speech production to one single maxim is highly exaggerated (cf. Levinson, 1989). I do not want to become involved in this widespread discussion. Instead I would like to illustrate the mechanism of conversational implicatures, based on a special treatment of the conversational maxims by the language user. Grice's assumption is that speakers deal with these maxims in a creative way in that they sometimes obey the maxims, sometimes not. Not obeying the maxims does not mean in this case simply making a mistake, but it means producing certain conversational effects, conversational implicatures. Let us consider the following example:

If I say 'Miss X sang "Home Sweet Home"', this is a simple statement about the behaviour of a person. If I say, however, 'Miss X produced a series of sounds that corresponded closely to the score of "Home Sweet Home"', this is something more. With this utterance I indicate that the performance of the person described was not so outstanding as one might expect. This conversational effect is the outcome of flouting the conversational maxim of Manner - it fails to be brief or succinct. The important point to make is that my addressee does not simply diagnose that I am not capable of obeying the maxim of Manner; he or she assumes rather that I am following the cooperative principle, and he or she begins to seek an interpretation of the utterance which is in accordance with this assumption. One of the possible interpretations of the utterance is that the person described was not able to produce the song correctly, and therefore the addressee is ascribing this interpretation to me. In that way a conversational implicature has been performed; the speaker has communicated a layer of meaning which is implicitly conveyed, not explicitly said.

Implicature in political speeches: a case study

Implicatures of this kind play an important role in our conversations as well as in political speech. My thesis is that the speech of Chancellor Kohl contains such implicatures, and that the most important statements in this speech are made in the way of conversational implicatures. I shall analyse this speech in order to see how this conversational mechanism operates. I shall analyse a section which is situated almost at the end of the speech; the subject of this section is the role of resistance for the political development in post-war Germany, i.e. the legacy of the resistance:

> [...] Wer heute konsequent unsere freiheitliche Demokratie verteidigt, wird morgen nicht in die Lage kommen, Widerstand leisten zu müssen. Wo die Bürger teilnahmslos abseits stehen und sich nicht mehr für die demokratische Ordnung einsetzen, besteht die Gefahr, daß die Feinde der Freiheit, daß Rechts- und Linksextremisten diese Ordnung unterwandern und dann zerstören.
> Das Verhängnis ist kaum noch aufzuhalten, wenn dann auch noch gesellschaftliche und politische Eliten den Extremisten die Hand reichen - womöglich in der Illusion, sie würden mit ihnen schon fertig werden. In Wahrheit gibt es keinen Kompromiß zwischen Freiheit und Unfreiheit. Jeder von uns bleibt aufgefordert, ideologisch begründeten Wahrheits- und Machtansprüchen zu widerstehen und jeglicher Form von Fanatismus entgegenzutreten. Intoleranz und Mißachtung des anderen dürfen in Deutschland nie wieder eine Chance haben.
> Die entscheidende moralische Trennlinie - das hat uns die Geschichte dieses Jahrhunderts im Übermaß gezeigt - verläuft nicht zwischen links und rechts, sondern zwischen Anstand und Ruchlosigkeit. Wer politischen Extremismus als etwas Normales verharmlost und dessen Intoleranz aus falschverstandener Großmut toleriert, der versündigt sich - gewollt oder ungewollt - an unserer Demokratie. Wenn wir jedoch allen Anfängen gemeinsam wehren, dann haben politische Extremisten nie wieder eine Chance, unser Vaterland ins Unglück zu stürzen... (Helmut Kohl, Berlin, 20 July 1994)
> [Whoever systematically defends our democratic freedom today will not find himself in a position of a resistance fighter tomorrow. But where citizens stand aside and are unwilling to defend the system of democratic order, there is a real danger that the enemies of liberty, the extremists on the right as well as those of the left, will infiltrate and then destroy that system.
> This danger turns into an almost unstoppable disaster whenever social and political elites lend support to the extremists, perhaps in the illusion they could 'manage' them. In reality, there is no middle course between liberty and oppression. Everyone of us has the duty to resist any ideologically motivated claims to exclusive truth or exclusive power, and to speak out against any form of fanaticism. Intolerance and contempt for others must never again be given a chance to rule in Germany.
> As the history of this century has shown abundantly, the all-important moral dividing line does not run between right and left, but between basic decency and wickedness. Whoever, out of mistaken liberalism, lends political extremism the appearance of 'normality', and tolerates intolerance commits - whether consciously or not - a sin against democracy. But if we stand together in the fight against all such attempts, then political extremists will never again be in a position to ruin our fatherland.]

I want to call attention to the following remark:

> Wer politischen Extremismus als etwas Normales verharmlost und dessen Intoleranz aus falsch verstandener Großmut toleriert, der versündigt sich - gewollt oder ungewollt - an unserer Demokratie.

[Whoever, out of mistaken liberalism, lends political extremism the appearance of 'normality', and tolerates intolerance commits - whether consciously or not - a sin against democracy.]

If one does not take into consideration the linguistic and situational context of this remark, it seems to be both completely correct and at the same time highly irrelevant. Everybody knows that political extremism is dangerous and that one must not underestimate it. The phrase "[...] der versündigt sich an unserer Demokratie" ['commits a sin against democracy'] is perhaps a little excentric, but there are no further problems with this assessment.

If, however, one subjects this utterance to a pragmatic analysis, one can reveal underlying aspects of meaning which are responsible for an alternative interpretation. Concerning the context, there seems to be a thematic shift in this section from 20 July 1944, the attempt to assassinate Hitler, to the general subject of 'totalitarianism' and further to the political situation in Communist East Germany (referred to as 'Sowjetische Besatzungszone', SBZ, [Soviet Occupation Zone], and later as 'Deutsche Demokratische Republik', DDR, [German Democratic Republic]). In this context, Kohl communicates the message that one has to resist any kind of dictatorship and that one has to fight against the enemies of freedom, be they socialists or nazis. This is the *linguistic context* in which the aforementioned remark is embedded, and which is the background against which this remark is to be interpreted. The *situational context* of this speech contains an event which has taken place shortly before and which is highly relevant in respect to the interpretation of the utterance in question. Following the state elections in Sachsen-Anhalt, the SPD candidate Höppner had been elected as Minister President ['Ministerpräsident']. This election had only become possible with the help of the PDS, the successor to the former SED, which had dominated the DDR until its dissolution. The CDU, under its chairman Chancellor Kohl, classified this election as a scandal, claiming that it was illegitimate to accept the help of the successor of the SED to attain high political office in Germany.

In the context of a pragmatic analysis, these features of the context have to be represented as elements of the background knowledge of the addressees, which help them to interpret utterances like the one in question. In particular, this background knowledge contributes to the solution of the following problem. On the one hand, the cited utterance does not fulfil the conversational maxim of Relevance because it seems to be, in its generality, rather irrelevant - one is tempted to ask: 'What is the point?' On the other hand, it is supposed that the addressees of this speech assume that the cooperative principle will be followed by Chancellor Kohl. The only way of getting out of this contradiction is to assume that the utterance in question has to be interpreted in a way that something is 'meant' with it which has not been explicitly said. The inferential procedure which the addressee has to perform in order to get this interpretation runs like this:

The *linguistic context* of the utterance consists in the claim that the legacy of the resistance is also to resist all kinds of dictatorship - for example that one which had been exercized in the SBZ/DDR under the rule of the party SED.

The *situational context* contains the fact that an SPD politician has attained a high political position with the help of a successor of the SED - the PDS.

The *conversational knowledge* of the addressees contains the cooperative principle. They assume that Kohl is following the cooperative principle, this means that his contribution is such as is required at the stage of the speech at which it occurs.

At this point, the addressees have to resolve the apparent irrelevancy by means of their background knowledge, which contains the two mentioned elements. They have to reinterpret the utterance and have to seek a meaning which is beyond that which has been said - an interpretation under which the utterance is in accordance with the cooperative principle. This interpretation is exactly what has been called a conversational implicature. Now, what could this interpretation be? Let us remember what Grice said about the interpretation of conversational implicatures:

> Since, to calculate a conversational implicature is to calculate what has to be supposed in order to preserve the supposition that the Cooperative Principle is being observed, and since there may be various possible specific explanations, a list of which may be open, the conversational implicatum in such cases will be a disjunction of such specific explanations; and if the list of these is open, the implicatum will have just the kind of indeterminacy that many actual implicata do in fact seem to possess. (Grice, 1989, p. 39-40)

In view of this warning, we have to refrain from identifying one interpretation as the only one which permits us to interpret Kohl's utterance in accordance with the cooperative principle. There are several possibilities, but one which is near at hand is certainly this:

> Die SPD verharmlost politischen Extremismus als etwas Normales, indem sie mit Hilfe der PDS einen Ministerpräsidenten wählen läßt, und sie versündigt sich deshalb an unserer Demokratie.
> [The SPD excuses political extremism as something normal by accepting the assistance of the PDS in electing a Minister President, and thus offends against democracy.]

If we accept the hypothesis that this interpretation is a member of the list of candidates for a conversational implicatum, we are in possession of a pragmatic explanation of Kohl's verbal behaviour at this place. Kohl's remark is no longer an irrelevant or void utterance, but it operates as a vehicle for communicating an opinion which goes far beyond the limits of the occasion for the speech as a whole. Kohl could not have said what he has implicated without being guilty of missing the topic completely. The advantage of a conversational implicature is that it may not be assessed in the way in which the explicitly uttered sentence may be assessed - it is 'cancellable' up to a certain degree, its interpretation is open, and it plays a special communicative role insofar as the implicature is not bound to conversational norms in a way explicit utterances are.

Conclusion

Is there something which is language- or culture-specific in this example? I would advance the thesis that the degree in which conversational implicatures are valued by societal or conversational norms varies from culture to culture, as the aforementioned implicatum is more or less specific for a German speech and would be problematic in other cultural contexts. From this it would follow that there is a future task in analysing indirectness in other cultures with the aim of identifying variations in the valuation of conversational implicatures. This has partly been undertaken by John Wilson, who has analysed the use of conversational implicatures during English parliamentary sessions. Furthermore, the findings of contrastive pragmatics have to be taken into consideration (cf. Oleksy, 1989). All this may lead to a sound theory of cross-cultural indirectness, for which this paper could be a starting point.

References

Gazdar, Gerald J. M. (1979), *Pragmatics: Implicature, Presupposition, and Logical Form*, Academic Press, New York.

Grice, Herbert P. (1975), 'Logic and Conversation' in Cole, Peter and Morgan, Jerry L. (eds), *Syntax and Semantics 3, Speech Acts*, Academic Press, New York, San Francisco, and London, pp. 41-58.

Grice, Herbert (1989), *Studies in the Way of Words*, Harvard University Press, Cambridge, Mass.

Horn, Larry R. (1984), 'Towards a New Taxonomy for Pragmatic Inference: Q-based and R-based Implicature, in Schiffrin, Deborah (ed.), *Meaning, Form and Use in Context: Linguistic Applications*, Georgetown University Press, Washington, pp. 11-42.

Levinson, Stephen (1983), *Pragmatics*, Cambridge University Press, Cambridge.

Levinson, Stephen (1989), 'A Review of Relevance', *Journal of Linguistics*, vol. 25, no. 2, pp. 427-55.

Oleksy, W. (1989), *Contrastive Pragmatics*, Amsterdam.

Searle, John R. (1969), *Speech Acts*, Cambride University Press, Cambridge.
Searle, John R. (1983) *Intentionality*, Cambridge University Press, Cambridge.
Sperber, Dan and Wilson, Deirdre (1986), *Relevance, Communication and Cognition*, Blackwell, Oxford.
Wilson, John (1990), *Politically Speaking*, Blackwell, Oxford.

The Concept of Work in Europe

WOLFGANG TEUBERT

Introduction

In our modern Western culture, work is more than just occupation or activity.[1] It certainly ranks among the top values upon which our societies are built. The first sentence of the first article of the Italian constitution of 27 December 1947, states explicitly that "Italy is a democratic republic founded on work."[2]

Not everywhere and not always has work been regarded as highly as in the Italian constitution. Even in our own societies, we now and then encounter people who prefer the pleasures of idleness to the challenges of diligent labour. Apparently, work is not an anthropologically universal human characteristic. So far, a gene responsible for a drive to work has not been identified. On the other hand, however, the major part of the population of any society does work.

But what is work? For the successful manager, practically all she or he does is work; managers are fully convinced that they easily average a sixty hour working week. Reading the *Financial Times*, jetting first class to customers, entertaining clients in expensive restaurants, 'working' out in a fitness studio, getting intoxicated in a karaoke bar with colleagues - all is work, performed as a duty to the company. In the eyes of the manager, a normal factory or clerical worker only works 35 hours a week, which is half of the executive's own work load. Plus, those meagre 35 hours include countless tea breaks, private phone calls, birthday celebrations, visits to the restrooms, not to mention sickness absenteeism. But while managers have drivers to take them to the company, a secretary to buy their presents, servants to do their house work, and while they employ other people to paint their houses, repair their cars and the plumbing, the workers have to carry out these chores in addition to their jobs. Obviously, a question like "Who works harder, the manager or the factory worker?" makes little sense, since work means something different to everyone. For a teacher of the arts, reading books, going to the theatre, and even watching TV can be work, while for most of us these are just leisure activities. Is work, thus, only what we get paid for doing? Can something we really like doing be called work? Is there a moral value attached to doing something we like to do anyway?[3]

These questions are, I think, reason enough to search for the true nature of work. The only possible way to find a definition for a mental construct like work is to analyse the discourse in which concepts of 'work' and related concepts like 'labour', 'diligence', 'leisure' and 'idleness', to name but a few, occur. The changes brought about by competing social models and collective frames of mind must also be considered. For the time being, my interest is focussed on civilisation. A project that Fritz Hermanns and myself are preparing is aimed both at the history of the concepts in question and at the differences we can find today between different cultures and languages in Europe.[4]

As Mark Poster (1982) has pointed out in his analysis of Michel Foucault's concept of history, taking continuity for granted has traditionally and perhaps even naturally been our mental outlook. We believe that mainstream thinking gradually adapts to a changing environment, until, finally, a new way of viewing things is born. Foucault's method rather implies a predilection for discontinuity and non-identity. Using extra-linguistic features, he builds up a corpus, for example a corpus of medical treatises from the eighteenth century. He then attempts to establish linguistic integrity and unity by identifying recurrent propositions particular to these texts and typically absent from other corpora, e.g. law treatises from the same period. He searches for clues of discontinuity between the original corpus and other comparable corpora. In this fashion, Foucault hopes to establish a continuity which is inherent to a specific discourse. "The discourse thus can speak for itself and does not have to be absorbed by a far reaching historical phenomenology of mind" (Poster, 1982, p. 147).

Foucault's insistence on the priority of texts as historical sources is certainly justified. As we can see in early societies where no texts existed, or where we cannot read them, the study of cultural artefacts yields hardly more than guesswork. For example, our knowledge of pre-Columbian American history is only a patchwork of assumptions controlled by common-sense plausibility. The analysis of texts is thus a central task for any historian. But, in order to understand what a particular text means, we have to look at the related texts surrounding our text, i.e. the discourse in question. Then we can perceive what is new about this text, and whether this novelty was picked up by subsequent texts.

In such a discourse, we can hope to identify certain intratextual and intertextual features that allow us to speak of continuity between a sequel of texts. These features might be a particular argument structure, a small syllabus of texts to which all texts refer, or a set of collocations that yield a profile of predilections and dislikes common to the authors. However, can we wisely assume that there are such breaches of continuity between texts that would allow us to assign them to different discourses? After all, all texts have their predecessors. What from a distance may look like a revolutionary substitution of a new paradigm for an old one usually turns out to be an evolutionary development. One strain of thought, which has always been there, suddenly becomes predominant without obliterating, only repressing, the hitherto prevalent paradigm. Though some creationists remain, they are luckily outnumbered by the evolutionaries.

We have to agree with Michel Foucault that for such mental constructs as 'illness' or 'work', there is no reality outside texts. The only way to find out what work is, is to deal with the word 'work' and semantically related words, not in isolation, but in full context of the texts in which they occur. Work is thus nothing but the meaning(s) of the word 'work'. But the empirical linguistic data we find in texts do not reveal the essence of 'work' either. To count propositions in texts or corpora is insufficient; they also have to be explained and interpreted. This calls for a methodology that combines the traditional hermeneutical approach with the linguistic analysis of textual discourses. Together, these methods lay the foundation for historical semantics.

'Work' in antiquity

I would like to begin the main section of this paper by following the cherished tradition of going back to the Ancient Greeks. Not surprisingly, manual labour in classical antiquity was not highly valued in Athenian society. Xenophon put quite a characteristic statement into Socrates's mouth:

> [...] So be sure, the illiberal arts [*banausikai*], as they are called, are spoken against, and are, naturally enough, held in utter disdain in our states. For they spoil the bodies of the workmen and the foremen, forcing them to sit still and live indoors, and in some cases to spend the day at the fire. The softening of the body involves a serious weakening of the mind. Moreover, these so-called illiberal arts leave no spare time for the attention to one's friends and city, so that those who follow them are reputed bad at dealing with friends and bad defenders of their country. In fact, in some of the states, and especially in those reputed warlike, it is not even lawful for any of the citizens to work at illiberal arts.[5]

Xenophon did not misinterpret Socrates here, since in Plato's *Theaetetus*, Socrates is even more outspoken. Here, he finds that philosophers are those,

> [...] who have not grown up like serfs, but in quite different, not to say contrary, circumstances. Now this, oh Theodorus, is the way of each one individually: the one whom you call a philosopher is truly brought up in freedom and leisure, and goes unpunished though he seems simple and useless when it is a matter of menial offices, even though he should not, for instance, know how to tie up a parcel that has to be sent on, or how to prepare a tasty dish [...]; the other way is the way of those who know, indeed, how to perform all those things well and smartly, but on the other hand do not even know how to wear their cloak like a gentleman, and still less how to praise the good life of gods and men in harmonious phrases.[6]

Was this view of manual labour also prevalent in the Roman Republic? Sometimes it seems just so. Seneca, for example, wrote in a letter to Lucilius that, "Work is not a good. Then what is a good? The scorning of work."[7] However, in the same letter we also find quite a contradictory statement about *labor*, which has become one of the favourites in any book of quotations, namely, "Work is the sustenance of noble minds."

What does Seneca really mean? Clearly, his text needs interpretation. Seneca wants to tell his rich, young playboy friend Lucilius that work, or toil, is not a virtue in itself. Only if the goal is to do honourable things, then work becomes a virtue. Of course, Seneca uses *labor* not in its literal sense. He is not writing about paid manual labour, which is the main literal meaning of this word in classical Latin, but rather about such acts of labour as the peace negotiations in Bosnia represent, to give a contemporary illustration.

Today, the question concerning the nature of work cannot be separated from morality, from virtue and vice, from good and evil. As we have seen, this has not always been the case. The general understanding in antiquity was that work, here meaning manual labour, was not meant for the gentlefolk. There was no moral value attributed to this kind of work, which was left to slaves or other people without property.

Discourse and meaning

Our two quotations from Seneca already cast light on the fundamental and irresolvable problem with which our research will be concerned. There is no Archimedean point, either for lexical expressions, or for the meanings associated with them. In each of the languages involved, we find a great number of lexical expressions in this semantic field that are in some way synonymous with other expressions, and in other ways are not. In English you have 'work', 'occupation', 'labour', 'toil', 'job', 'drudgery' and 'activity', to name but a few, and there may be a similar number of German words, like 'Arbeit', 'Beschäftigung', 'Leistung', 'Tätigkeit', 'Aufgabe', 'Aktivität', 'Geschäftigkeit', etc. However, there are no mechanical rules on how to translate any one of these words, or other words for that matter, from one language into the other. The meanings of words are fuzzy by nature; they come about by social conventions which are permanently undergoing change.

Meanings are booked in dictionaries; they present rules for the correct usage of a word. But there is more to a word. A word like 'work' also expresses an attitude, such as admiration or contempt. For each of us, 'work' is connected with a prototypical image of one who works, and one who does not. We regard certain activities, usually those we do not like to do, as prototypical work, and we associate them with prototypical work situations, usually unpleasant ones. For an average German, the prototype of work would be manual labour in a factory or coal mine, the worker would be male and middle-aged, and the typical work situation would be an assembly line. We call such scenarios that accompany certain words (like 'work') concepts. Concepts have evolved through discourses held by certain members of a society, such as teachers, artists, preachers, scholars, and opinion makers. They change but slowly, sometimes by the addition of a new scenario to already existing ones, sometimes by the shifting of weight assigned to the various scenarios. Concepts also have a historical dimension. Factory work was only introduced as a new scenario about a hundred years ago, and has already become outdated. Since not the individual forms a concept, but a society does, the ensemble of concepts determines the intellectual superstructure, forming the interpretation of the world we live in. Cultural and also national identity is achieved by building up a net of communally accepted concepts of this kind.

When it comes to concepts of mental constructs for which there is not a recognized set of examples or denotations, these concepts are subject to change as long as there is an on-going discourse about them. Thus, twenty, fifty and a hundred years ago, words like the ones given above, and their equivalents in other languages, in as far as there can be equivalents, may have meant something slightly different from what they mean to us today. Quotations taken out of their context, out of their particular discourse, can give wrong impressions. I will give an example. Today, almost no-one can afford to admit that she or he is neither working nor searching for work; a leisured class does not exist any more. Many think that they can define their identity through their work. One's social importance can depend on the length of one's working day. In Stalin's office in the Kremlin the lights were never switched off at night. Contemporary rulers compete with each other over who is putting in the most working hours of devoted service to their respective countries. On the other hand, in E.M. Forster's novel *Howard's End*, the protagonists, namely the Schlegel sisters, and to some degree their brother as well, simply lived off their revenues. Being without occupation was considered to be perfectly acceptable in England until past World War II. Belonging to the leisured class was far from immoral. On the contrary, to have to work to earn one's living, be it by doing clerical work or manual labour, was considered humiliating.

Particularly at a time of social change does it make sense to take stock of the concepts at stake. Today's great concern is how to fairly distribute the small amount of work that is left across a society. In our concept of work we already find one scenario that can be applied to this new situation. This scenario was created many decades ago when men became afraid that their jobs might be taken away by women. At the time, interested parties built up the image of the devoted housewife and mother who is too busy raising children, supporting her husband, taking care of the household, and preserving the integrity of the family, to think about paid work. This image was contrasted by a negative scenario that portrayed greedy women who, in their pursuit of fur coats and sports cars, neglected their duties as housewives and mothers, thus undermining the concept of family which is the foundation of our Western society.

Today, we can safely expect a reactivation of some elements of this scenario. Striving for work is only justified when basic needs are concerned. Noble minds will search for unpaid occupation. Only very selfish people will try to take jobs away from those who need them, and only very avaricious people will refuse early retirement. Some of the familiar sayings concerning work will soon sound quite outdated, like Otto Bismarck's famous, "To youth, I have but three words of counsel - work, work, work."[8] Bismarck, by the way, knew quite well how to indulge in leisure.

One of the themes of language philosophy is to search for the Archimedean point as a point of reference for the meaning of words. As we know, the question never has and never will be settled, whether the idea, e.g. the mental construct of a chair, precedes the actual chair, or if we come up with the idea of a chair by looking at a number of devices used for sitting. For a concept like work, we can only hope to approximate its true nature if we believe in the precedence of Platonic ideas. But what if we were Aristotelian nominalists and thought that 'work' is just a name used to classify a certain set of incidents? Which properties could be considered as essential, which would just be contingent? How do we account for conflicting views concerning the attendance at an exhibition? Where does leisure end; where does work start? Without a doubt, the concept of work has changed greatly in the course of history. To show how it has developed over time can help to set us free from the limitations of today's meanings.

As unsettled as the old question of meaning is, any distinction between meaning and concept is also as arbitrary and open. About twenty years ago, Hilary Putnam (1975) in his famous study 'The Meaning of "Meaning"' presented a highly seminal proposal. He drew a line at the knowledge base that one can expect of an average layman in respect to words belonging to standard vocabulary. For the noun 'work', this knowledge would be something like: 'physical or mental effort directed to some end or purpose; toil; labour'.[9] Putnam calls this kind of knowledge 'stereotypical' knowledge, and he sets it apart from the conceptual knowledge that the expert has about the real nature of things. For Putnam, a stereotype is "a conventional idea [...] of what an X looks like or acts like or is. Such a conventional idea is associated with 'tiger', with 'gold', etc., and [...] this is the sole element of truth in the 'concept' theory [of meaning]" (Putnam, 1975a, p. 169). The language community defines the extent and intent of these opinions. "English speakers are *required by their linguistic community* to be able to tell tigers from leopards; they are not required to tell elm trees from beech trees" (Putnam, 1975a, p. 168). Stereotypes can be right or wrong; thus, the idea could actually be erroneous that all tigers are striped. Average speakers of a language can err; to know what the case is one needs an expert. According to Putnam (1975a, p. 146), the criteria associated with some terms "are known only to a subset of the speakers who acquire the terms, and whose use by the other speakers depends upon a structured cooperation between them and the speakers in the relevant subset."

However, even the expert does not necessarily possess absolute truths. For example, back in 1750, she or he would have known more than a lay person about the criteria that have to be fulfilled for a correct reference or denotation of the expression 'water', but, for instance, she or he did not know then that the denotation of the expression 'water' is H_2O. Due to this lack of knowledge, she or he may have erroneously defined substances which do not fulfil the conditions of H_2O as water.

Erroneously? Putnam (1975b, p. vii) holds that "[...] statements of science are in my opinion either true or false [...] and their truth or falsity does not consist in their being highly derived ways of describing regularities in human experience." Truth or falsity, that is Putnam's tenet, does not depend on human perception at all, existing independently of all observation, solely by the agreement of a fact with a statement. Thus, Putnam proves to be a 'metaphysical realist' in the tradition of Plato and medieval scholastic realism. Of course, he is not dealing with expressions like 'work', 'sloth' or 'leisure'. In his aforementioned article, 'The Meaning of "Meaning"', his arguments all focus on expressions for natural kinds, such as lions and tigers, gold and water, elms and beeches. Natural kinds, as the expression implies, seem to exist quite naturally, independent of our experience and discrimination. We accept them uncontroversially; they seem to correspond to universal, language-independent concepts. A natural kind possesses a specific set of essential properties, and you can name exactly those properties which make the thing what it is. For natural kinds there are experts. But it is the language community as a whole that decides which sense or senses a purely mental construct like 'work' has.

If I do not like Putnam's metaphysical realism, why then did I propose a distinction between meaning and concept? Well, it seems that even if there are no experts for mental constructs like 'work', the distinction is still useful, for it allows us to differentiate between the knowledge the average speaker employs when she or he is using the word, and the knowledge that can be found in the repositories and archives of language use which have been created by the language community as a sort of communal memory. By concept, I wish to refer to the underlying ideas, beliefs, emotional, attitudinal and moral values connected with a word. Speakers will to some extent recall these once their attention is directed at them, but they do not necessarily always and never fully have them at their command. There is more to a word like 'work' than just the collection of a dozen words or so that make up its definition as found in an average one-volume dictionary. What I mean by concept then is the sediment of what the language community as a whole remembers about the different contexts in which the word has been used and is being used, what kind of predications one can make about it, and what other concepts it can refer to.

I hope it becomes clearer why I have said above that to understand the concept of work we have to unscroll and interpret the discourse on work that has taken place in history, to the extent that it still is remembered or can be reconstructed today. Obviously, what I call a concept here is neither the *real* meaning of 'work', nor is it an objective representation of meaning. All it is and all it can be is an interpretation of what goes on in the world, an interpretation, however, that enables us to get a better grasp on reality. Ernst Gombrich (1959, p. 307) has taught that "there is no reality without interpretation," and this lesson applies to language even more than to art.

That objectivity is neither possible, nor desirable will become clearer when we look at the concept of discourse more closely. The term 'discourse' has been used in any variety of senses; and even in linguistics, discourse is the magic word for at least two domains of research. We will not concern ourselves with discourse analysis here, i.e. the analysis of spoken language, of symmetrical and asymmetrical dialogues, of rules and repertoires for turn-taking and related issues. Our usage of discourse has its place in the fairly young discipline of historical semantics which is evidently greatly influenced by Michel Foucault's work.

By discourse we mean a collection of all the texts that fulfil certain criteria which have to be made explicit. Obviously then, a discourse does not exist in any ontological way. The researcher him- or herself lays down the criteria which he or she hopes will constitute the relevant discourse for the research object chosen. Thus, the discourse is always defined *a posteriori*. The criteria can be subject matter, a selection of authors, a restriction on certain languages, certain types of speakers, for example, only white male protestants, certain forms of publication, a particular segment of time, etc. All texts conforming to the parameters set by the researcher are part of the discourse; and they together form a virtual corpus. Usually the researcher will not be able to actually lay her or his hands on this corpus - many texts will have been lost, just like most oral communication. Also, there usually is not enough time, nor are there enough means to search in all the libraries around the world. Moreover, the virtual corpus will consist of countless duplications and redundancies. On a topic such as the concept of work, presumably a large majority of texts is nothing but a collection of paraphrases of a relatively small canon of authoritative writings. This syllabus would form the core of an actual corpus on work.

Work in modern times

What makes the concept of work so fascinating to us is the importance that today is attached to working. Ethically, work has become the prime moral value of our Western culture. Work, or the lack thereof, is used as the prime argument when inequalities in property distribution are being justified or when the limits of social welfare are being defined. Conservatives and Marxists, Protestants, Catholics and Jews, individualists and environmentalists, they all hold work in the same high esteem. However, most of us will take an afternoon off, given the chance. Our attitude towards work is ambiguous and contradictory, but one generalization that can safely be made is that we prefer others to work for us, to ourselves working for others.

As we have seen, work in general, and particularly paid work and slave labour, was held in contempt in antiquity. Work bore no moral merits. Work was regarded as a curse, not a blessing. This attitude was not immediately changed by Christianity, as many historians today believe. Until the sixteenth century, the Church did not require its clientele to believe in the intrinsic values of work. Work in the Middle Ages was mainly discussed in terms of economy, and the economy was not one of the favourite topics of the day.

Were there, thus, no semantic battles about one's attitude towards work during the Middle Ages? To find out, we have to look at the centres of ideological and philosophical warfare, such as the early universities like Bologne, Oxford, Paris, etc., which were, of course, under the joint supervision of the urban episcopate and the worldly powers. Equally important were the monasteries, where eminent figures like St. Bernard of Clairvaux molded the appearance of a whole era. For monks and nuns, there was an endless discussion on how to divide up their time between the numerous obligatory activities. Therefore, if we want to discover how the concept of work changed in medieval times, we should take a close look at the rules of the monastic orders. At this time, criticism of a political and social situation was expressed by founding a new order. Thus, we have to interpret the rules laid down by each founder as an implicit condemnation of the customs practiced by the already established orders. By analysing the statements on work, leisure, and also on related concepts such as property, we can reconstruct these particular semantic battles.

At least at first glance, work did not seem to be one of the favourite virtues of occidental monastic life. Though today, the Benedictines are associated with the exhortation *ora et labora,* this modern emphasis on work was not reflected in the old rules of the sixth century. Chapter 48 of the Benedictine rules deals with manual labour (*de opera manuum cotidiana*). Work here is not treated as having value in itself, but as a therapy against idleness (*otiositas*). However, the monks are reminded not to become discontented (*non contristentur*) if local conditions of poverty force them to gather the harvest themselves, for then they live by the work of their own hands (*labore manuum suarum vivunt*) like the early fratres and apostles. Still, they should not overextend themselves in deference to the pusillanimous ones. Working time is specifically limited to eight hours during summer and six hours during the winter months, six days a week. The abbot's responsibilities included making sure that the monks did not feel oppressed by the hardships of toil (*violentia laboris*), which in extreme cases might have driven them into flight.[10]

Caritas was an important Franciscan value, and according to their rules from the thirteenth century, the Franciscans perceived work as a necessary precondition to enacting charitability. However, even for the Minorite movement did work not play the same central role as it does today in similar, more recent grassroots movements, such as those of the Amish, Mennonites or Hutterites. The principal Franciscan values were poverty, simplicity, humility, self-denial, non-aggression and chastity. Work was only a secondary virtue.[11] It remains to be seen whether there were other medieval orders where work was more significant.

In modern times, we find a rapid increase in the literature on work. In the age of the Reformation, the old division into *negotium* and *labor* was given up. *Negotium* used to refer to the occupations of the free citizens owning enough property not to have to sell their labour. For occupations in the liberal arts or in the service to the country, an *honorarium* was received instead of wages, implying that there existed "an incommensurability between performance and recompense, and that the performance [could not] 'really' be recompensed."[12] *Negotium* was something one wanted to do for its own sake. *Labor*, on the other hand, was alienated work, work done for others in order to receive a wage. By giving up this distinction, two goals could be reached. The primary goal was to give a moral basis to the distinction between the owning and the propertyless class. For this purpose, a high moral value had to be attached to work. Thomas Carlyle has expressed this idea innumerable times of which I quote but three instances:

> Blessed is he who has found his work; let him ask no other blessedness. The "wages" of every noble work do yet lie in Heaven or else nowhere.

The best worship, however, is stout working.[13]

If this attitute was commended by the church, accepted reality still looked quite different. How labour and the workers' attitudes towards labour have been, and still are understood by management, is shown by the following statement by a psychologist working for industry:

> Regarding the nature of work, the orthodox view accepts the Old Testament belief that physical labour is a curse imposed on man as a punishment for his sins and that the sensible man labours solely in order to keep himself and his family alive, or, if he is fortunate, in order to make a sufficient surplus to enable him to do the things he really likes. Regarding the conditions of work, it is assumed that improving the conditions of a job will cause the worker's natural dislike of it to be somewhat mitigated, and, in addition, will keep him physically healthy and therefore more efficient in the mechanistic sense. Finally, regarding the motivation of his work, the carrot and stick hypothesis asserts that the main positive incentive is money, the main negative one is fear of unemployment. (Brown, 1954, p. 186)

It seems that the most important achievement of the Calvinistic movement was to put the disowned class into a state of moral inadequacy. The Calvinist master ideologists knew, or thought they knew, that labour in exchange for a wage, in most cases, was seen as a punishment by the workers, and that, most naturally, the workers disliked their work. Yet, nevertheless, they demanded that commitment to work was to be voluntary, and that work had to be performed with conviction and for work's own sake. The lesson to be learnt was that those who became rich were the ones for whom work was the highest moral commitment, and those who hated their work justly remained poor. The second objective of the new gospel of work was to build up the attitude that work bears its eschatological merit in itself. Asking for better working conditions or higher wages could only forsake chances for a better life after death. As J.G. Holland put it, "To labor rightly and earnestly is to walk in the golden track that leads to God."[14]

That economy and morality, imposed by religion, are but two sides of the same coin, can be seen in the following statement by George F. Baer, President of the Philadelphia and Reading Railway, in a letter from 1902. He wrote:

> The rights and interests of the laboring man will be protected and cared for - not by labor agitators but by the Christian men to whom God in His infinite wisdom has given the control of the property interests of the country.[15]

Max Weber (1988, pp. 17-206), among others, has pointed out the particular affinity between capitalism and Calvinism, and other Protestant denominations. Still, it seems doubtful whether a genuinely Protestant morality gave rise to capitalism, or whether capitalism instrumentalized the new Christian paradigm by infecting its value system with a new work ethic. The transition from a feudal to a bourgeois society made it necessary to create a new explanation for the unequal distribution of property. The concept of work provided property with a new justification.

Up until the seventeenth century, occupation was the theoretical backbone of property. According to this theory, which is mainly attributable to Cicero, private property does not exist originally. Property only came into existence when individuals or groups began to settle down permanently. At this point, formerly uninhabited land was occupied and claimed as property. This claim to land also held for the claim to goods. To claim what did not belong to anyone in particular was perfectly acceptable and legal. Once claimed, other goods could become appropriated by exchange, purchase, rent or other agreement. The early colonial empires were based on this premise.

However, by the seventeenth century, the occupation theory could no longer satisfy the common idea of justice. There were no more unclaimed lands or unappropriated goods; but still, the new bourgeois class quickly accumulated more wealth, while the majority of the populace remained poor. Manfred Brocker (1992) has argued convincingly that the occupation theory could no longer serve as justification for existing inequalities. A new paradigm was found in John Locke's theory of work, which he laid down in his *Two Treatises of Government* (especially in Chapter 5 of the Second Treatise). Here, the right to own external objects is obtained by work, not by occupation. This theory made property inviolable to criticism. Occupation was now replaced by entrepreneurial activity. In the old paradigm, the acquisition of property was based on luck. This concept encompassed a moral obligation of the rich towards the unlucky majority. In the new paradigm, the poor themselves were responsible for their plight. If only they worked harder or with greater motivation, they would not need to suffer. The rich were now no longer obliged to share their wealth with the poor. In spite of its inherent deficiencies, John Locke's theory is still the backbone of all Western civil law.

Needless to say, this modern view of work is now reflected in the new Catholic Catechism of 1993. Work is a 'duty', whereas, not surprisingly, entrepreneurial activity is called a 'right'. Whenever it is economically feasible, the Catholic Church does not seem to hesitate to take a protestant stance.

The discourse of work

The discourse of work, where we would be able to observe this change of paradigm and reconstruct the development of the many facets of this concept, would have to be assembled on the basis of a rather large number of parameters. These include the subject fields of economy, ethics and religion. Philosophical investigations, primary school textbooks and sermons are equally important. The corpus must contain texts addressed to the owning class and the disowned class. There is a conservative and a liberal audience. Some speakers refer to their audience by the personal pronoun 'we', others utilize 'you'.[16] National, regional and cultural differences have to be taken into account. The socialist and Labour movements have to be represented.

There are some practical ways to reduce the material. Concerning reflective or theoretical texts, we can safely leave out those that have not been quoted by others; and the required margin here can be set rather high. As to the texts used for instruction and the moral improvement of the underprivileged, there are widely accepted collections of quotations, of stories, and of fables. These collections have the additional advantage that they are updated by every new generation and, thus, document changes in the concept of work by undergoing subtle alterations of their compositions.

To reduce the discourse further to a size that can be managed by standard corpus technology and methodology, it is acceptable to concentrate on eras which we can expect to have been particularly important for the evolution of today's concept. For the concept of work, it might be advisable to leave out antiquity. Important eras for shaping the Judaeo-Christian Western world as we know it today, and for their impact on the concept of work, might be the following:

- The eleventh to the fourteenth century, as represented in the rules of monastic orders. Here we will find the medieval interpretations of work.

- In the seventeenth and in the eighteenth centuries the ideological and philosophical foundation for our contemporary world was laid. The movements of sentimentalism and enlightenment defined our understanding of emotion versus reason. But most important for us is the change in the paradigm of property as described above.

- During the last quarter of the nineteenth century important clashes occurred between the Socialist and the Labour movement on one side and government and industry on the other. The impact of Marxism and Socialist ideology on the twentieth century is, I think, much stronger than has been acknowledged so far. A new Catholic doctrine on social ethics which was highly influential on the European Continent was created, since only with the advent of the labour movement did the view begin to be accepted that there are other causes to poverty than just indolence. Because capitalism now had to compete with the Socialist ideology, better living conditions for workers had to be provided, and above all, the existence of a 'social question' had to be acknowledged. There was never a time when work was more important. Evidence of the semantic battles fought then can be found in the texts of parliamentary debates and in texts included in school books.

- In the early 1970s, when civil rights were strengthened for the last time, democracy was given more room and the living conditions of the underprivileged were improved. The 1968 student movement obviously had a strong influence on the general political atmosphere. As an alternative to standard patterns of alienated work, new concepts were discussed, focussing on environmental concerns, on social problems, group therapy, rehabilitation work, child rearing and related issues, and finally on self-fulfillment ('grief work', 'memory recovery', 'identity work', etc.). In an affluent society, wages were now considered to be an aspect of inferior importance. This new concept reshaped the general attitude towards work.

- In the early 1990s, since the collapse of the Socialist bloc, governments and industry gradually seem to be falling back on the old tenets of early industrialization. At the same time, markets have ceased to expand, and less work is available for an ever growing population. As the standard of living deteriorates, a redistribution of property is taking place that will have to be justified in terms of a new morality. Work again will have to be redefined.

Such a selection of eras is governed by certain preliminary hypotheses on the history of the concept of work. It may later become apparent that other eras will be more revealing to our analysis.

Conclusion

The discourse that I have sketched out here will show, I think, that there is no 'true nature' of work. This, by itself, is not surprising. The view that the meaning of a word is nothing but an arbitrary convention by the language community is as old as the opposite view that somewhere, in the early history of humankind, or in the distant future, or on some higher level not yet accessible to us, there is a language where all the words have true meanings. Umberto Eco (1994) has explored the history of the human endeavour to find and define such an ideal language. This ideal language would mirror reality as it is. A correct sentence then would also be a true sentence. We would be safe from all ideological distortion that today still dims our vision. This is the view of metaphysical realism, but this is not how language works.

As for visual perception, it has been shown many times that humans are atuned to take an image for reality. We do not see the reality that surrounds us. We see only images, and we interpret these images as reality. Only by taking these images for reality will we avoid problems when we attempt to interrelate with our environment, with whatever is outside of us. What we see is just what we have been taught to see. Looking at the world around us, we are not able to perceive what there is in its infinite complexity until we reduce it to something familiar, something we were educated to recognize. So, instead of nature, we see a landscape, a gestalt that reminds us of similar landscapes we came across before. This is why people looking at paintings do not see a canvas with colour pigments on it, but a landscape. They see an image they have learned to interpret as reality. A romantic landscape is a mental construct, just like work is a mental construct.

Viewing pictures is similar to using language. We take a text not to be a chain of words with arbitrary meanings, but to mean something real. If there is a noun, then there must be a certain ontological reality which is the denotation of this noun. By focussing on concepts like 'work', we can show that humans create reality by using language, just as the painter creates a landscape by painting an image of nature. Without paintings, photographs, landscaped gardens, and, most importantly, without texts on landscapes, there would be no landscape, just nature or scenery. Without the concept of work there would be no work, just activities.

Painting creates images, and using language produces concepts. The human mind will transform both into reality by performing an act of interpretation. Therefore, language can, and has been, used to create the illusion of reality, of some unalterable essence behind the word, which the language community is always free to redefine by introducing a new meaning, a new scenario. However, not every member of the language community can contribute to the discourse on work with an equal chance of success. Only a few members will be quoted by others and will, thus, determine the discourse.

A new meaning will not obliterate the old meanings. It will just widen the range of the concept. Is there something, some attribute or attributes that we find in all the meanings, some common denominator, some essential property? I do not think so. What keeps the many meanings of 'work' together, is Wittgenstein's (1977) idea of family resemblance. Some meanings of 'work' share certain aspects or properties with other meanings, but not all meanings share one common aspect. To present the ensemble of meanings of the word 'work' and its counterparts in other European languages will have to be taken up in future research.

Notes

1. I am very grateful to Katerina Piro for her highly competent, efficient and thorough revision of my text. It is English now - it was not before.

2. *Die Verfassung der EG-Mitgliedsstaaten*, 1990, p. 207.

3. In Immanuel Kant's view whatever is fun cannot be virtuous at the same time. In his *Critique of Practical Reason* he relentlessly pursues the theory that the human natural bend is contrary to natural law, and adding another twist, he argues that only those actions that are carried out against one's natural inclinations can qualify as moral actions. This was too much for even Kant's followers. Goethe's peer, Friedrich Schiller, ridiculed him in

these verses: "How willingly I'd serve a friend, but alas, I do so with pleasure, and so I am often worried by the fact that I am not virtuous" (cf. Pieper, 1963, p. 15).

4   cf. Hermanns, 1993.
5   cf. Moseé, 1969, p. 25.
6   cf. Pieper, 1963, p. 36.
7   Labor bonum non est. Quid ergo est bonum? Laboris contemptio. cf. *The Home Book of Quotations*, 1967, p. 2235.
8   cf. *The Home Book of Quotations*, 1967, p. 2230.
9   cf. The Winston Dictionary for Schools, 1954.
10 The complete text of the rule translated Latin to German and explained by Georg Holzherr, Abt von Einsiedeln, 1993, pp. 235-45.
11 cf. Feld, 1994, pp. 189-214.
12 cf. *Katechismus der Katholischen Kirche*, 1993, pp. 2427-9.
13 cf. Pieper, 1963, p. 41.
14 cf. *Home Book of Quotations*, 1967, p. 1063.
15 cf. *Home Book of Quotations*, 1967, p. 1065.
16 These two categories of addressees are reflected in our alternative conceptions of morality. The one talks mostly about duties and is based on the idea that we are born in a state of amorality and that we will behave irresponsibly unless taught otherwise. In this view, people by nature are lazy; they can be brought to work only by the fear of eternal punishment. This view is usually prevalent when we look at others, at people outside our peer group. For ourselves we reserve a more benign view. Texts that are addressed at ourselves, e.g. the Déclaration des droits de l'hommes, the Declaration of Independence and the programmes of liberal parties throughout the world talk only about rights, not about duties. Following Adam Smith, they take for granted that the common good is best achieved if everyone follows his own interests. It seems that both conceptions can easily coexist, both in a society and in an individual person.

References

Brocker, Manfred (1992), *Arbeit und Eigentum*, Wissenschaftliche Buchgesellschaft, Darmstadt.

Brown, James Alexander Campbell (1954), *The Social Psychology of Industry*, Penguin, Baltimore.

Eco, Umberto (1993), *La Ricerca della Lingua Perfetta nella Cultura Europea*, Laterza, Roma.

Feld, Helmut (1994), *Franziskus von Assisi und seine Bewegung*, Wissenschaftliche Buchgesellschaft, Darmstadt.

Gombrich, E.H. (1959), *Art and Illusion. A Study in the Psychology of Pictoral Representation*, Phaidon, London.

Hermanns, Fritz (1993) 'Arbeit. Zur historischen Semantik eines kulturellen Schlüsselwortes', *Jahrbuch Deutsch als Fremdsprache,* no. 19, pp. 43-52.
Holzherr, Georg, Abt von Einsiedeln (1993), *Die Benediktsregel. Eine Anleitung zum christlichen Leben,* Benziger, Zürich.
The Home Book of Quotations (1967), 10th ed., Greenwich, New York.
Katechismus der Katholischen Kirche (1993), Oldenburg, München.
Moseé, Claude (1969), *The Ancient World at Work,* Norton, New York [= *Le Travail en Grèce et Rome* (1966)], Presses Universitaires de France, Paris.
Pieper, Josef (1963), *Leisure the Basis of Culture,* Pantheon Books, New York [= *Muße und Kult* (1948)], Kösel Verlag, München.
Poster, Mark (1982), 'The Future according to Foucault. The Archaelogy of Knowledge and Intellectual History' in LaCapra, Dominick and Kaplan, Steven L. (eds), *Modern European Intellectual History. Reappraisals and New Perspectives,* Cornell University Press, Ithaca, London, pp. 137-52.
Putnam, Hilary (1975a), 'The Meaning of '"Meaning"' in Gunderson, Keith (ed.), *Language, Mind and Knowledge,* University of Minnesota Press, Minneapolis, pp. 131-93.
Putnam, Hilary (1975b), *Mathematics, Matter and Method. Philosophical Papers, vol. I,* Cambridge University Press, Cambridge.
Die Verfassung der EG-Mitgliedsstaaten (1990), Beck-Texte, Deutscher Taschenbuchverlag, München.
Weber, Max (1988*), Gesammelte Aufsätze zur Religionssoziologie I,* Mohr, Tübingen.
The Winston Dictionary for Schools (1954), Winston, Philadelphia.
Wittgenstein, Ludwig (1977), *Philosophische Untersuchungen,* Suhrkamp, Frankfurt/Main.

The 'other' Europe on the Threshold of the Twenty-first Century: The Political and Cultural Consolidation of the Baltic States' New Sovereignty?

FRANCIS KNOWLES

Introduction

This paper reviews recent developments, and their ramifications, in the uneasy evolution of the new states which have arisen on formerly Soviet territory. It looks at them specifically in terms of the new (socio-geo)-linguistic modalities which are currently establishing themselves in the various polities that have come into being. In this account the general underlying theme is the former Soviet Union (FSU) but attention focuses on Estonia and Latvia, given that the 'Soviet legacy' there is particularly difficult to overcome (cf. Gerner and Hedlund, 1993). Lithuania is mentioned only in passing by virtue of the fact that post-war Russian settlement there never approached the proportions seen in the other Baltic republics. The homogenizing commonalities of their Soviet and Russian 'big brother' experience, lasting some forty years, are now - hopefully! - over and constraints affecting the emergence and growth of differentials are but slight. The motive force behind the tensions which exist and which are difficult to relax is identity in both an individual and corporate sense. Feelings of identity tend to correlate very strongly with choice of language in public discourse but language itself is 'raised' well above the level of a mere means of communication to the status of an icon, a badge of ethnicity and a public and often confrontational profession of 'belonging' to one community rather than or even to the exclusion of another (cf. Knowles, 1993). For speakers of the new primary languages of state a natural development is to call for the cleansing (that is, de-Sovietisation-cum-de-Russification) of Estonian and Latvian - both language and thinking? - , accompanied by a back-to-roots campaign in the area of what are, in the Baltics, vibrant national 'folk-cultures'. Russian speakers are also confronted by many problems: how to learn the relevant national vernacular to enfranchize themselves, not just politically but economically as well. Given that 'Soviet' culture, even though it was articulated and expressed vicariously via Russian, apparently had no tap-roots at all, a second significant difficulty for these Russian-speaking settlers or transferees is how to find and how to re-interpret almost in a regionalized way their own culture, expressed via Russian, potentially linking it up with the centuries-old Russian presence in the Baltic area.

Establishing and making progress from a new starting point

So the Baltic states of Estonia, Latvia and Lithuania are now once more sovereign bodies politic (cf. Lieven, 1993; Thomson, 1992). They re-emerged, in 1991, from fifty years of vassalage, unwillingly entered into in the summer of 1940 as a result of a secret protocol incorporated into the infamous Soviet-German Non-aggression Pact of August 1939. Soviet overlordship initially lasted for less than a year, being overturned by the outbreak in June 1941 of hostilities between Nazi Germany and the Soviet Union. After this brief but very brutal period in their history, the Baltic states returned to Soviet 'ownership' after the Red Army had pushed west on its victory march towards Germany. As in 1940, when thousands of supposedly 'undesirables' were arrested and either liquidated or exiled by OGPU (the forerunner of the KGB, the secret service) as forced labourers to the GULAG, so it was just over four years later. The full story of these terrible happenings is only now beginning to be told. A crude estimate of the impact of the war on the population of Latvia, for instance, is that one third of the entire population became war casualties in one way or another, by death, deportation or flight.

The post-World War II consolidation of Soviet power in the Baltic states was influenced by a number of factors: the availability, in spite of war damage, by comparison with the Soviet Union of a good industrial and agricultural infrastructure; the presence of a - once again, by Soviet standards - highly skilled and trained industrial labour force; the asset represented by a long-standing expatriate community of Russians, in the Estonian cities of Narva and Tallinn but mostly in the Latvian cities of Riga and Daugavpils; the strategic and military significance of the new and huge Soviet presence along the southern Baltic littoral, stretching without interruption from Leningrad to just short of Lübeck.

However, perhaps the most important long-term factor affecting the size and composition of the Baltic republics' populations during the last 50 years was the Soviet government's credo rather than *ukaz* of stimulating labour mobility in the grand national interest, in both the civilian and military sectors. The growth of new and the refurbishing or resiting of old industrial plants in the Baltic republics, notably in Latvia, acted as a pull factor and hence attracted a large inflow of labour on both a forcible and voluntary basis. Between 1965 and 1990 only two quinquennia show a less than the annual average of 10 per cent inflow of settlers from other Soviet republics. The largest proportion of these settlers were of Russian nationality and language but many other Soviet nationalities were involved too, with distinctly tangible numbers of Byelorussians and Ukrainians. In 1970 it is recorded that four fifths of the new immigrants to Latvia were doctors, teachers, engineers or artisans with an average age of 25 years. The rapid and extensive development of this new industrial infrastructure also led, of course, to urbanization and to a palpable depopulation of the countryside. In Latvia's case, the most extreme, two thirds of the population lived in the countryside in 1940; by 1959 just over half of the country's population lived in towns and cities. By 1990 approximately seven out of ten inhabitants of Latvia were living in towns or cities. In 1979 one in ten Latvian families had been residing at their current address for less than two years and only one person out of three in Estonia, Latvia and Lithuania had never changed their address since being born (cf. Zvidrin'sh et al., 1986).

Over the years a distinct tendency was observed in Latvia in the area of inter-ethnic marriages. By the time Latvia achieved its independence more or less two out of every five marriages contracted were ethnically mixed. This works out at about 10,000 such marriages being entered into annually. The personal linguistic arrangements involved in this phenomenon have never been properly described in their Soviet setting whatever these arrangements were, the likelihood is that they will now be in turmoil. We still need personal descriptions of all this!

Once Gorbachev's *perestroika* policy got under way in the late 1980s the whole question of immigration was, for genuine or mischievous reasons, elevated to the top of the political agenda by politicians and officials in many of the then Soviet constituent republics, not least in the Baltic republics. 1988, in particular, was the year when the genie was well and truly let out of the hitherto hermetically sealed nationalities bottle. Vacillation, temporization, diffidence, not to say outright dithering on Gorbachev's part during the early months of that year created a situation in which senior figures in the republics' party structures began to speak out, without fear, in conformity with the requirements of *glasnost*. Russians too began to openly question the usefulness, even refer to the counter-productivity of the then still proclaimed but mendacious ideology that the Russians were merely *primi inter pares* within the Soviet family of peoples. There were calls for a psychological *perestroika* on this question. Public admissions were even made to the extent of stating that "the Russians who had become accustomed to the role of being benefactors now find themselves on an equal footing with the other nationalities" (Yuri Polyakov, in *Novosti*, 25 March 1988].

These political developments moved forward apace, with Baltic writers and spokespersons in the vanguard. Initially, the running was made by various members of the 'native' intellectual elites in Estonia, Latvia and Lithuania, followed at some distance behind for reasons - all too easy to understand! - by holders of senior public office. In addition to expressions of frustration about the lop-sidedness of the nationalities 'equation', claims were also made that the Baltic republics' economies were also being short-changed in the internal market in terms of the economic return on offer for the value of their output. Concern about the inadequacies of cultural institutions with regard both to their remit and their performance also became much more open and much more widespread. Each in their own way - alongside equally resourceful, enthusiastic and fearless 'replicators' in many other constituent republics of the USSR - the new political vanguards, as yet unelected, in the Baltic republics called for many immediate and fundamental changes. They did not call, however, for outright independence, but rather for a decentralized Soviet Union which would operate via genuine economic reciprocity in the internal commodities and services market, with properly quantified economic benefits to flow back to the territories owning raw materials or freely granting the exercise of usufruct on various kinds of fixed asset etc.

There were also calls for the indigenous languages of the Baltic republics to be granted their due place as languages of state and for various other icons of statehood to be established, such as seats at UNO, national-territorial military formations, sports teams etc. etc.

Half-way through the year, the 19th Conference of the Communist Party of the Soviet Union (CPSU) took place, most memorable for the way in which the debates of the nationalities question were conducted (cf. Nahaylo and Swoboda, 1990). There was no longer any need for delegates to express their thoughts in a roundabout way. Plain speaking was definitely the order of the day in a situation where those nominally in charge were battling to regain and assert control of the ever-evolving day-to-day agenda. Boris Pugo, the leader of the Latvian Communist Party, sounded off about the Moscow-based and -inspired bureaucracy which had entangled what was anyway a command rather than a demand economy, using this as a backdrop to call for a much greater degree of independence for the constituent republics. This, of course, would involve new legislation (*Pravda*, 1 July 1988). Pugo was followed to the rostrum by his counterparts from Estonia and Lithuania, who spoke in very similar terms and tones. The latter speaker emphasised the urgent need to repair deficiencies in the language legislation (*Pravda*, 8 July 1988). Although the main onslaught was made on the stagnation and sclerosis of the Soviet economy, a distinct sub-text was drawing a picture of what changes were needed to allocate a much higher priority to the matter of ethnic diversity, cultural institutions and to the status of indigenous languages in the titular republics and analogous settings.

The Soviet legacy

It is clear from what has been said above that the linguistic practicalities attendant upon living in the Soviet Baltic republics were made unnecessarily complex by various political mythologies to which ordinary people were intended to subscribe. The question of schooling and language of instruction was a thorny one throughout the existence of the Soviet state. For quite large numbers, an education delivered in Russian rather than in a different indigenous native language was often seen by parents as a sound choice for their children, given that a knowledge of Russian was - correctly, at the time - viewed as the prime component of upward professional and social mobility. When the Soviet state imploded, the number of children being taught in Russian exceeded the total number of children whose native language was actually Russian. In Estonia and Latvia this excess was only slight, at about 1 per cent of the school population, in Lithuania it was approximately 1.25 per cent.

Statistically, according to the [last] Soviet census taken in 1989, 96 per cent of Estonians were 'loyal' to Estonian as their native language. The figures for Latvians and Lithuanians, *mutatis mutandis*, were 95 per cent and 98 per cent, respectively. Forty-four per thousand ethnic Estonians reported that Russian was their native language. The figures for Latvians and Lithuanians, *mutatis mutandis*, were one in 20 and 18 per thousand, respectively. Only one per thousand ethnic Estonians reported a native language other than Estonian or Russian. The figures for Latvians and Lithuanians, *mutatis mutandis*, were one in five hundred and one in two hundred, respectively. In this latter instance, the Latvian respondents may well have cited either Latgalian or Livonian, two minority languages spoken in the country, the former a Baltic language, the latter a Finno-Ugric language. The Lithuanian respondents would have almost certainly reported a knowledge of Polish, by virtue of links with or partial acculturation by the Lithuanian Polish community which comprises approximately 9 per cent of the population of Lithuania.

The efforts of the CPSU ideologues and administrators had for years been directed to achieving this sort of result and many others like it. Prior to the Great October Revolution both Lenin and Stalin had given much thought to elaborating a theory and an action plan which would make it possible to create a unified proletariat dedicated to Marxist values and action, but also able to overcome the immense handicap of a large multilingual and multiethnic population. The maxim was, in brief, that all things in both public and private life could, if necessary, be national or ethnic (i.e. stated in a minority language) in form but must be socialist in content (cf. Knowles, 1989). The elaboration, after the foundation of the Soviet state, of the necessary political and administrative apparatus to achieve this aim was quite impressive, given the limited resources available; both policy and practice were, however, open to being suborned in favour of other more pressing political and practical initiatives. The chief aims of the exercise may, for our purposes, be formulated in terms of a conspiracy theory, a hidden agenda dictated by raison d'état. The items in plain print represent the major political objectives, those in italics detail the practical subordinate goals and tasks involved:

> *To accelerate the controlled development of functionally retarded languages*
> To break up any non-Soviet cultural hegemonies
> To connive at the retention of innocuous cultural pluralism
> To consolidate ethnic communities in a socialist framework
> To counteract demographic pressures
> To develop Soviet 'patriotism'
> To develop Soviet cosmopolitanism
> To emphasize super-power achievements and aspirations
> *To establish Russian as a second(ary) native language*
> *To establish self-confident, but controlled language 'ecologies'*
> To foster 'internationalism' inside the USSR
> To foster the Soviet image outside the USSR
> *To homogenize modes of thought and expression*
> *To marginalize ethnic languages*
> *To maximize the effectiveness of information-handling*
> To maximize the impact of Marxist-Leninist values
> To realign the minorities' cultural realia or to expunge them if necessary
> To relieve the logistic problems of the body politic
> *To standardize as many linguistic subsystems as possible, notably terminologies*
> *To widen the scope for linguistic interaction between Soviet citizens*

It was this policy and its practicalities - including large-scale official duplicity and mendacity - which, after long years of disrepute, finally met its Waterloo at the 19th Conference of the CPSU.

Ethno-linguistic mechanisms and the Baltic peoples' reaction to them

The ethno-linguistic 'facts on the ground' in any particular country or location are the result of the confrontation of people as individuals and in groups with the socio-economic and political system within which they live. Sometimes this system is stable, all too stable; at other times, it can change out of all recognition in a relatively short space of time. The current state of the territories which used to comprise Yugoslavia is perhaps the most shocking example in modern times of a cataclysmic development. Fortunately, such events are rare. People themselves - if left to themselves - are usually characterized by a high degree of inertia *corporately*: they cannot radically change their ways, habits and customs and *totally adjust* overnight just because a new political system has come into existence. This does not mean to say that rapid *psychological* adaptation to new circumstances is impossible; it is just that such an adaptation tends to drag and lag. Certain things cannot, after all, change: a population cannot, by an act of will - unless it be to launch a civil war - change its age-structure with immediate effect. Any such change, however large or small, is nothing more than the sum of decisions taken by individuals, even if legislative coercion is involved. Actual personal behaviour normally takes time to change, and change is often the evolutionary outcome of experience rather than decision-making. The demographic processes, say, of family formation or of migration are relatively long-term phenomena, often measured by the traditional generation gap of 25 years. Even 'catalysts' such as inter-ethnic marriage or close-quarters cohabitation of two communities normally separated by language, religion, socio-economic class, colour etc. need time - often lots of time - to achieve the effect of harmonizing and eliminating potentially divisive and dangerous differentials. This can happen only when the majority of people involved have reached their own personal psycho-social accommodation with new circumstances and neighbours.

Political scientists, sociologists, psychologists and sociolinguists are all vitally interested in the gamut of problems which arise when issues of language, of language loyalty and of ethnicity manifest themselves. All are concerned to identify change and to plot its course. Yet all, naturally enough, adopt a different viewing angle. The primary focus for the political scientist is the examination of the political conditions in which a given change is or is not possible, alongside the political actors and their statements. The sociologist focuses on social change and on any functional adaptations a society makes as it evolves and becomes subject to various types of influence. Not unimportant are the social belief systems which appear to have an important bearing on events as they unfold and on changing opinions about them. The psychologist wishes to obtain some insight into the process of psychological and behavioural change in its various phases. In this particular instance the sociolinguist is interested more than anything else in changes which appear to be language-driven and in the nature of those changes. Is there, for instance, a particular discourse community which appears to have an influence on events which is not proportional to its numerical strength and to the type of its members?

The latest developments

The current situation in the Baltic states offers specialists in all four academic profiles a conundrum, the description - never mind solution! - of which requires a subtle combination of this wide-ranging expertise. A good starting point for tackling the conundrum which lies before us is the question of identity in the sense of personal identification with a coherent and cohesive group of people, statements or ideas. This identification may be articulate or it may be inchoate; it may be intellectual, it may be emotional or visceral. All those to whom developments in the current situation in Latvia and Estonia matter in a highly personal sense are really being summoned by events not just to identify but to proclaim their identification, to 'stand up and be counted'. This applies crucially to the Russian L_1 speakers, who intuitively identify with the great mass of Russians in Russia and elsewhere. However, by definition, the Estonian and Latvian Russians are not 'standard' Russians in any sense. Yet more is involved than identifying as an act of self-definition and of definition for others. The position could scarcely be more complex or fraught with the danger of adverse consequences. All the residents of Estonia and Latvia have, in one way or another, to 'out' their allegiance. The main question is whether they, notably the Russian speakers, will do so after proper and mature reflection and whether they will be diverted, intimidated or needlessly and excessively emboldened and antagonized by the 'dirty tricks' which have already been played or which they suspect are being kept in reserve. The ethnic Russians in Estonia and Latvia are easy hostages who can be and often are blamed at any moment for the actual and perceived woes of the last fifty years, if not the last 500 years. The bogey mobilizing the Estonians and Latvians is the age-old fear of the annihilatory advance of Russians, their language and culture which has been going on for centuries. Conversely, the Estonians and Latvians must fear inwardly that their languages and cultures, distilled, codified and utilized on the level of society rather than of isolated communities, have survived a hundred years of this positive internal development but are still at risk of being swamped and drowned. Perhaps they should take heart from the collective experience over the last fifty years which tells them that their languages and cultures have indeed been robust enough to withstand unrelenting political, economic and cultural pressure from a numerically very powerful adversary which, until the recent political realignment, had been gradually eroding prospects for any ongoing viability of Estonian or Latvian statehood. If the populations of ethnic Russians in Estonia and Latvia were to continue to increase at the rate witnessed over the last twenty years and if no other external events were to impact strongly on the demographic evolution, by the year AD 2017 (the centenary of the October Revolution) the Latvians would have become a minority population in their own homeland (Latvians 40 per cent, Russians 47 per cent, others 13 per cent), and the Estonians would be struggling to maintain a slender numerical superiority over the Russians (Estonians 48 per cent, Russians 44 per cent, others 8 per cent). If ethnic solidarity at election times were the name of the game, the communities of 'Others' could easily become the power-brokers (cf. Knowles, 1989; Valentej et al., 1985).

About one other factor there can be no doubt: the 'wedding' of language and culture is very tightly bonded in the cultures of all three Baltic states. This means that any economic, political or military attempt by outsiders to encroach is likely to ignite hostilities, ranging from a Gandhi-type non-violence to guerrilla or even open warfare; similarly, any inclination of fellow-citizens towards a more politically cosmopolitan frame of reference is virtually certain to be branded by the extreme right as treason. The whole political struggle revolves around the need to preserve language and culture, lest the demise of its bearers robs the world of more ways of looking at it.

It is furthermore necessary to point out that the objective of responsible politicians in Estonia and Latvia should be to clarify to everyone's satisfaction an operationally adequate but robust distinction between ethnic allegiance and national identity. The latter has been more in the firing line and at risk of hopeless entanglement because of friction between bearers of different national identities, because of differing views among the Russian-speaking populations and because of the initial internationalization of the conflict.

The current situation in Estonia

Despite the presence of so many similarities between the situations of Russian speakers in Estonia and Latvia, developments have taken a different course in the two countries. Both 'sides' in Estonia have injected a reasonable dose of pragmatism into their mutual dealings and, despite residual animosities and ongoing Estonian governmental irritation with the Russian government's indolence or duplicity in honouring undertakings given, any forecast must contain warnings of serious difficulties, probably not, however, going as far as deadlock. The whole issue revolves around the status of the Russian speakers, of course. On the linguistic side, Estonian has, naturally enough, become the official state language. However, the use of other languages is not forbidden in the mass media or in those areas where ethnic minorities are to be found in considerable numbers. Yet, public signs are now almost exclusively in Estonian and according to the statute book fines may be imposed on those not using Estonian when required to do so. If people do use Estonian, but it is ungrammatical, fines may still be payable! Furthermore, some 10 per cent to 15 per cent of Estonian military service personnel are stated to be incompetent in Estonian and, what is more, are reported to have divided loyalties. These reports obviously refer to Russian speakers. Among this community are some 11,000 military pensioners from the formerly Soviet, now Russian armed forces. Various suspicions are rife about this group of people, naturally.

The entire community of Russian speakers, alongside representatives of other ex-Soviet ethnic groups, were given the deadline of 12 July 1994 to submit applications for registration as residents of Estonia. Some 60,000 Russians in Estonia had by then already opted for Russian citizenship. The vast majority of the 400,000 people 'on the ground' but not qualified for full Estonian citizenship failed to observe this deadline. The Estonian government had no option but to extend the deadline until 31 July 1996 but it has also amended - for those who arrived in Estonia after July 1990 - the mandatory period of residence needed prior to application for full residential status from two to five years, plus a one-year period of 'marking time' pending the outcome of any application once submitted. The Estonian government has also just placed a new law on its statute book which neither acknowledges nor recognizes the concept of dual citizenship. In spite of all these political and legal machinations, a major survey, taken at the end of 1994, among the Russian-speaking population has shown that almost nine out of ten Russian-speakers report either no or only slight problems vis-à-vis Estonians; 93 per cent of the Russian-speaking community in Estonia wish to stay and make their future there. The Far Right was very badly beaten in the March 1995 General Election in Estonia, whereas some confidence-building success has been achieved by the Russian parties, amalgamated under the name 'Our Home is Estonia'. Border controls with Russia have been eased and some 'trouble-making' Russian-speaking politicians have even been deported to Russia.

The current situation in Latvia

In Latvia the story is subtly different. It appears that many Russian-speakers in Latvia either cannot successfully jettison their residual Soviet culture or successfully come to terms with things after having done so. The overall success of the Latvian Russian speakers' efforts to define exactly what old cultural values to retain and what new cultural values to adopt will undoubtedly also define or confine to a great extent their prospects of finding happiness and fulfilment in their new socio-political milieu. The problem is a difficult one because choices need to be made - how? - about the right 'admixture' of totemic ingredients on the level of ethnicity: East Slavonic supranational identity or just Russian? Where too are the monuments, both physical and metaphysical, of this new culture? How can the benefits of this culture be imbibed? And how can it operate without tension in the minds of Russian speakers who are increasingly seeing the political need to learn and the pragmatic social advantage of learning Estonian or Latvian?

In Latvia there are, unfortunately, other problems to be solved before civic harmony can make a natural appearance. Because of the above-mentioned visceral fears among the politicized right and, one must assume, in other quarters as well, proposals have been made for the introduction of punitive legislation apparently aimed at the long-term disenfranchizement of the Russian-speaking community. This legislation is concerned with the terms and conditions as well as with the process of acquiring Latvian citizenship. The relevant bill appears to set a deplorable new standard of legal chicanery designed either to deny outright the acquisition of Latvian citizenship by Latvia's Russian speakers or to make them attempt to clear such a difficult obstacle course that hardly any applicants could possibly succeed. Their status in Latvia would then be so prejudicial that many - so the bill's proposers must be hoping - would seek repatriation to Russia.

The proposed hierarchy of categories of people who may be considered for conferment of Latvian citizenship is as follows:

1. people of ethnic Latvian (or Livonian) parentage, living in Latvia but not yet naturalized
2. citizens of the ex-USSR (or their descendants), qualified under the 1919 Latvian citizenship law but still remaining unnaturalized
3. people of non-ethnic Latvian stock, residing in Latvia on 17 June 1940
4. people forcibly deported to Latvia during World War II ('Great Patriotic War') (Belorussians, Greeks, Jews, Lithuanians and Poles)
5. people who have successfully completed a Latvian language course and have accumulated five years residence prior to applying for residency
6. members of a 30,000-strong group of ethnic Estonians or Lithuanians who have accumulated five years' residence prior to applying for residency
7. people who have been married to ethnic Latvians for at least ten years and who have accumulated five years' residence prior to applying for residency
8. current residents who have performed outstanding services to the Republic of Latvia

These provisions would admit a further 230,000+ people to Latvian citizenship. It is also proposed to operate an additional quota system based on ten years' residence and a proven command of basic Latvian. It should be noted that the actual administrative process (which commenced in April 1995) of naturalizing the 400,000 people eligible among the 700,000 non-Latvian residents is expected to proceed - according to semi-official announcements - at a rate of only 2,000 persons per annum!

This bill has rightly been subjected to severe criticism by many Western politicians, including President Clinton, who appealed to the Latvian government during his visit to Riga on 6 July 1994 "not to deny others the justice and equality you fought so hard for and earned for yourselves, for freedom without tolerance is unfulfilled". Although there has been a shift to the right in thinking on the Latvian citizenship issue, there are counter-pressures on Latvian politicians which may relax the situation. Latvia has applied for membership of the Council of Europe and is expecting to become an associate member of the European Union in the fairly near future. These intentions cannot be fulfilled until there is overall satisfaction on and agreement about the issue of ethnicity and the methods used to defuse the acrimony and provide an equitable basis for the integration of the very large Russian community (including over 60,000 military pensioners along with their families!) into Latvian political and civic life. This is not an easy task. For instance, in Riga, Latvia's capital, one half of the population are Russian-speakers, whereas Latvians make up only slightly more than one third of the population of their country's capital city!

Conclusion: Future prospects?

Hand in hand with the solution of the newly reborn Estonian and Latvian states' socio-political problems, must go a determined effort to establish a high standard of linguistic usage for all citizens. This will involve a number of discrete tasks, some of considerable complexity: (i) the realignment of technical terminology, which may require the de-Russification and sanitization of tendencies which have established themselves over the last couple of generations; (ii) preparing for and withstanding the onslaught of Western economics and business 'newspeak'; (iii) the publication of teaching manuals and reference works for Estonian and Latvian, respectively, needed by residents of all ages and by foreigners of all ages too; (iv) the identification and description of different functional varieties of Estonian and Latvian for study and use, say, by doctors and social workers; (v) a charitably condoning but not condescending attitude to fellow citizens and residents whose ability to learn and/or use Estonian or Latvian, respectively, is limited because of factors such as age, state of health etc.

Estonian and Latvian, like all other fully-fledged languages, have evolved over centuries, not just as vehicles of communication but also as instruments available to individuals in the community to enable and help them to relate to the world and particularly to other fellow human beings of the same kith and kin. Estonians and Latvians are, just like people of any established nationality, formed, behaviourally conditioned, even subliminally prompted to a very considerable extent by the view of the world available to them via the cultural prism and its associated language which their society has developed, through both its travails and triumphs.

Be all that as it may, for this account the right note to end on is a positive one: the primeval fears felt down the last 50 years by speakers of Estonian and Latvian that their languages were being encroached upon and threatened in their very existence can now be laid to rest. At the root of these fears was the nightmare of the possible cultural and linguistic death of their communities, with its simple consequence: certain experiences of and insights into the human condition would then, quite literally, have become ineffable.

References

Gerner, Kristian and Hedlund, Stefan (1993), *The Baltic States and the End of the Soviet Empire*, Routledge, London.

Knowles, Francis (1989), 'Language Planning in the Soviet Baltic Republics' in Kirkwood, Michael (ed.), *Language Planning in the Soviet Union*, Macmillan, London, pp. 145-73.

Knowles, Francis (1993), 'From USSR to CIS and Beyond: Visceral Politics vis-à-vis Ethnolinguistic Realities' in Ager, Dennis et al. (eds), *Language Education for Intercultural Communication*, Multilingual Matters, Clevedon, pp. 131-58.

Lieven, Anatol (1993), *The Baltic Revolution*, Yale University Press, New Haven and London.

Nahaylo, Bohdan and Swoboda, Victor (1990), *Soviet Disunion*, Hamish Hamilton, London.

Naselenie SSSR 1988 (1989), Finansy i Statistika, Moscow.

Thomson, Clare (1992), *The Singing Revolution. A Journey through the Baltic States*, Michael Joseph, London.

Valentej, Dmitrij I. et al. (1985), *Demograficheskij Entsiklopedicheskij Slovar'*, Sovetskaja Entsiklopedia, Moscow.

Zvidrin'sh, Pyotr P. et al. (1986), *Naselenie Sovetskoj Latvii*, Zinatne, Riga.

'Den festen Kern festigen': Towards a Functional Taxonomy of Transnational Political Discourse

NIGEL REEVES

Introduction

It has become a commonplace to observe that the United Kingdom and the United States, contrary to the view consistently fostered by British politicians since the Second World War of a special relationship between two countries of kindred spirit, are rather two peoples divided by a common language. In its surface meaning this adage refers to the different colloquialisms, metaphors, everyday lexis and even pronunciation characterizing British and American English. But at a deeper level it refers to the different value sets that underlie and inform these two, broad national varieties of English. The cultures that have shaped these varieties are far from identical. Indeed, when one considers the original religious reasons for many of the early settlers leaving Britain, the War of Independence and of course the migrations of the poor and disadvantaged from imperialist, industrialising Britain during the 19th century, especially from Ireland, Wales, Scotland and the provincial extremities of England, we can see why American culture evolved from a deliberately chosen set of new values, where privilege, inherited titles and status, religion, in short, social and political distinction by virtue of birth were rejected in favour of the notion of the self-made man. True, Victorian economic Liberalism had a great deal in common with American industrial entrepreneurialism - but in Britain it was absorbed into an aristocratic, hierarchical mould, with the nouveaux riches assimilated in their values into the world of the landed rich.

Does this suggest that language, with its grammatical techniques for segmenting reality and its semantic networks for interpreting that reality and communicating those interpretations, only reflects and is, therefore, secondary to the world of experience? And that historically evolved cultural values determine perceptions of human reality while the articulation, transmission and reception of those perceptions in language are also fundamentally value - and therefore culture-determined?

Language and culture in transnational political discourse

The essays in this volume, with its provocative title *Conceiving of Europe - Diversity in Unity*, could provide evidence to support that view from within political discourse. The differing meanings attached to central political terms like 'region', 'subsidiarity', 'Europeanness' are, for O'Donnell, the consequence of conceptual reinterpretations by domestic political elites for their own power political purposes within their own ideological traditions. For Good, 'state/Staat', 'citizen/Bürger', 'Federalism/Föderalismus', 'market economy/soziale Marktwirtschaft' refer to different concepts, formed in different historical experience. The powerful determinant influence of historical experience are also illuminated by Teubert in his exploration of the changing value attached to the term 'work' and its equivalents from the Ancient Greeks to today's work-driven executive. As values slowly change in response to experience, so the meanings of terms change. But their meanings still derive from the cultural reality as the prime influence. And we see in van der Walle and in O'Donnell how the media can foster their readership's existing perceptions of national difference through the use of stereotype in political and sports reporting alike (whilst suggesting that their concern is objective truth).

While these examples would support the argument that political, social and economic concepts are culture-bound and that lack of equivalence between languages, particularly in the case of apparently identical faux amis, can lead to unwanted misunderstanding, Musolff, Schäffner and Good point, on the other hand, to the manipulative possibilities of political metaphor both within and between languages and countries or cultures.

For Musolff, 'federalism' and the metaphors that emerged to capture conceptions of an integrating Europe, specifically aspirations to a Single Currency - transmit (and thus preserve) implicit national cultural values (a conservative function) but which is creative, changing perceptions and shaping opinion - *two tiers, two speeds, fast and slow tracks, overtaking, convoys*, are not necessarily used for purposes of graphic illustration or precision. On the contrary, the evocative vagueness of metaphor is a device used by politicians to give themselves room for manoeuvre, without obviously having to lie - a theme taken up by Good, who shows how language can be used to cover discrepancies between action or outcome and promise.

Schäffner illuminates, moreover, how the elaborative possibilities of metaphor assist the accommodation of difference in diplomacy, allow for the development of dissension in political and media-based debate and are adapted or replaced as circumstances move on.

This work suggests then, a second function of language in transnational political discourse which is not to transmit and preserve (implicit) national cultural values but which is creative, changing perceptions and shaping opinion.

From 'fester Kern' to 'hard core'

An interesting example of how choice of metaphor could be used to present a critical German proposal for pushing forward European integration in a negative light was the British media reception of the CDU/CSU policy document on this topic, inspired by Wolfgang Schäuble and released to the public in September 1994. A subtle recasting of a key metaphor significantly shifted the tone and thrust of the document, as reported in British newspapers. The document argued for the formation of an inner group of closely integrated EU member states which would lead the way to wider EU integration by adoption of a Single Currency in strict adherence to the monetary convergence criteria laid down in the Maastricht Treaty. This inner group is referred to in the German original as 'ein fester Kern', as is mentioned by Schäffner earlier in this volume.

'Kern' is a positive word in German. It suggests solidity, sincerity, even wholesomeness (i.e. non-adulterated) as does the less common English metaphor 'kernel'. British English prefers 'heart', again a very positive term with its connotations of life force, warmth, being at the centre, as well as of core. It was, as Schäffner points out, John Major's favourite term for expressing to European colleagues his desire to contribute intimately to the European idea, to be inside not outside, to be with them 'at the heart of Europe'.

The CDU/CSU document had argued that with the extension of the EU to the North and with active proposals for its extension to the East, it was in the interests of Germany for a stable centre to be created, institutionally and, economically (specifically in monetary terms) and in respect of joint defence and foreign policies that could be translated into decisive action.

In the total of fourteen typed pages of the statement, 'fest' appears once on its own as an adjective and five times as part of 'ein fester Kern'; 'festigen' appears twice, 'Verfestigung' [der EU] once, 'Festigung' [des Kerns] once. In all cases the meaning revolves around notions of firmness and making firm. This concept of a firm centre for the European Union is flanked by notions of stability. Terms including the root element 'stabil' ['stable'] appear ten times: 'stabil', Stabilität', 'Stabilisierung', 'instabil', 'stabilitätsgefährend'. Closely related are items referring to strength and strengthening: 'Stärkung', three times, and once each, 'starkes Zentrum', 'starkes Europa', 'stärker' ['stronger'], 'Stärke [Deutschlands]'.

In the German political, economic and business cultures such reassurance is not only prudent but arguably necessary. In these cultures, as a response to a century of discontinuity and turbulence, essential spoken and unspoken values include political continuity (which becomes obvious in the slogan 'keine Experimente' ['no experiments']), stability and reliability, with the D-Mark and the 'Grundgesetz' [Basic Law] as the symbols of those values and the proof of their realisation. There are no more striking demonstrations of this than the admittance of the former German Democratic Republic into the Federal Republic as 'neue Bundesländer' ['the new Federal States'] in accordance with the existing Western 'Grundgesetz' and, secondly, the rapid introduction of the D-Mark into the East under the economic and monetary union of July 1990.

The D-Mark has proved itself the soundest or hardest of the currencies of the European Union. The strict monetary and fiscal convergence criteria for a Single European Currency represent criteria of prudence fostered for four decades by the Bundesbank, the German Central Bank, and largely followed by the Federal Government.

The last thing that the Bundesbank, the German Government and the German people would want is for the achievement of the D-Mark to be dissipated in inflationary fiscal policies followed by other member state governments and loose money supply controls dictated by a European Central Bank Board that bows to the habitual approaches and realities of historically less stringent economic regimes (such as those in Belgium, Italy and the United Kingdom).

It is in this political-cultural context that the CDU/CSU document twice (only) shifts from the term 'fester Kern' to 'harter Kern' (italics are mine - N.R.):

> Auch im Währungsbereich gibt es bereits den kräftigen Ansatz eines *festen Kerns* der Fünf. Sie entsprechen (gemeinsam mit DK und IR) am ehesten den Kovergenzkriterien des Maastrichter Vertrages. Dies ist deswegen so bedeutend, weil die Währungsunion der *harte Kern* der Politischen Union ist.
> [In the currency sphere there are already the beginnings of a firm core formed by the Five. They meet (together with Denmark and Ireland) most closely the convergence criteria of the Maastricht Treaty. This is of great importance because the Monetary Union is the hard core of the Political Union.]

But reading this translation will immediately suggest how the tone of the passage is altered when 'harter Kern' is translated as 'hard core'. The inescapable connotations of this term in English are hard core pornography, hard core recidivism and hard core terrorism. 'Hard core' is associated with people and things that are immoral and incorrigible.

British papers reporting on the document (e.g. *The Times*, 2 September 1994, *The Financial Times*, 5 September 1994) did not reproduce the German. The concept of the firm centre was nowhere to be seen. Instead the English reader, deprived of any original text, could only read of this 'hard core' of EU member states which an inner policy committee of the CDU/CSU intended would form a new inside grouping. In much the same way as the 'community charge' in the UK instantly took on anti-democratic characteristics once dubbed by Opposition MPs and the media as the 'poll tax', the concept of stabilizing a threateningly unstable EU was discredited. Indeed, *The Times*, pre-conditioned its readerships's response by entitling its article on the CDU/CSU document 'German vision of Europe shunts Britain into siding'.

The CDU/CSU document's deliberate attempt to try and bring the UK government over to its point of view and join the 'firm centre' was modified:

> Die Vorschläge zur Herausbildung eines Kerneuropa und zur weiteren Steigerung der deutsch-französischen Zusammenarbeit bedeuten nicht, daß die Hoffnung aufgegeben wird, daß Großbritannien seine Rolle "im Herzen Europas" and damit in seinem Kern übernimmt.
> [These suggestions for the formation of a core Europe and for the further intensification of Franco-German cooperation do not mean that hope has been abandoned that Britain will assume her role "in the heart of Europe" and thus in Europe's centre (= core).]

Taking up Major's own metaphor of the heart, the document subtly shifts that metaphor into the context of its own central metaphor, the 'kernel' or 'core'. But *The Times*, which actually records this sentiment, does not reproduce the original passage. Instead, it quotes Karl Lamers, a CDU spokesman (speaking English?) who provides a variant by mentioning John Major directly but omitting any statement that links 'the heart' to the 'Kern'.

This example is interesting for two reasons. Our starting point was the argument that political (social and economic) concepts, when transferred across languages, can change their meaning because they are received in a culture with different historical experience. Moreover, that this process can be deliberately instigated.

When politicians use metaphors to grasp and to convey complex political ideas, these ideas become particularly vulnerable to such change. The change can simply be determined by the cultural experience of the host or 'target' country or language. The journalist with limited knowledge of the system and history of the source language and culture could unwittingly translate the metaphor inappropriately, in just the way that a concept may be transferred as an apparent equivalent without explanation of its different reference in the source culture. But as we can also see from our example, carelessness or lack of knowledge does not lie far from deliberate manipulation. In either case the political perceptions of nations can be modified or directed. This is especially insidious when, as is almost inevitably the case for British readers, they have no access to original statements and texts in the source language.

But the transformation of the 'feste Kern' into the 'hard core' not only illustrates the creative or manipulative use and function of language in transnational political discourse. It illuminates a paradox characteristic of the tension in Europe between unity and diversity.

While evidence of economic convergence remains elusive except for a minority of economies that literally lie geographically in the 'heart' of continental Europe, Kelly-Holmes, also in this volume, discerns a certain cultural convergence brought about by the forces of post-industrial, consumer society, and expressed quintessentially in the discourse of advertising. Yet advertising, while taking advantage of this convergence, which is driven by the proximation of consumer lifestyles, may reinforce the use of national stereotypes at the same time and, thus, preserve earlier, simplistic notions of national self-identity on the part of the target audience for the advertisements. The discourse of national and transnational advertising can thus be seen to exert both a conservative and a creative (and certainly manipulative) function close to the functions of conceptual faux amis and metaphors in transnational political discourse.

The evidence, gathered in this volume, points, then, clearly to the continuation of a deep-seated diversity of identities in the European Union. This diversity is rooted in differing value sets and in the continuing need to perceive one's own identity through its distinction from other nationalities. The unity brought about by shared consumer life-styles, by an increasingly close nexus of legal and political ties, and by economic integration (if not convergence!) will not create a European 'national' identity any more than the United Kingdom has removed the sense of Welshness of the Welsh or of the Scottishness of the Scots!

The 'public perception loop'

The national governments of Europe and the members of the European Parliament that are elected by the peoples of Europe cannot afford to neglect their voters' desire for a continuing sense of national and cultural identity, as some learnt painfully in the Maastricht Treaty debate and the following referenda - or parliamentary debates in the case of the UK and Germany. At the same time, these voters are also the customers of the national newspapers and the viewers of national, satellite and cable television. The media cannot survive without customers. While their editors and correspondents are, like all of us, children of their age and of their culture, they must appeal to the way those customers perceive the world if they are to retain their consumer loyalty. But the media also shape that perception of reality by virtue of the simple fact that it is effectively only through the media that those who are not political leaders, diplomats or captains of industry can know directly at the macro-level what is happening. The media's daily presentation, i.e. interpretation, of political, economic and social reality can hardly be separated out by the readership from the reality itself, as the rush of events continues and the events and ideas remain distant from and inaccessible to the readership except through the media. At best the discerning reader could, given time that few have, read a range of newspapers each day to gain different perspectives on the same events. Few indeed are able , not just for reasons of time, but for reasons of linguistic ability and difficulty of access, to read of those events in newspapers from several European countries. Moreover, (closing the information loop), politicians themselves often start the day by a survey of newspaper reports relevant to their interests. Locked into this loop are the stereotypes and metaphors, to take just two prominent linguistic techniques for interpreting reality. Thus, voters, customers of the media, politicians, industrialists and the other decision-makers at national and transnational level, can be caught in a self-generating circuit of perception-building founded in language.

Towards a functional taxonomy

As Musolff, O'Donnell and Schäffner all suggest, the inherent multivalence of the metaphor (and the inherent simplification of stereotype) as a model of reality is exploited by politicians and media commentators not simply in order to understand and to grasp an elusive present. Both devices are also deployed in order to persuade, to shape perceptions of future reality, and to result in action.

The function of stereotype is to reinforce group identity. It, therefore, fulfils a *conservative* function of language in national and transnational discourse. The future is 'secured' through constraining change, in the European context, through preserving a perception of national diversity and superiority of the reader's own nation.

The function of metaphor, as a figurative model of present and of future political structures is more complex. It certainly has a *descriptive* function, that is, graphically to represent a multi-faceted and/or dynamic political phenomenon and, thus, convey an interpretation of the phenomenon to an audience. And since the audience is locked into the viewer-reader/voter/politician/media commentator/viewer-loop it also has a *perception-shaping* function. Within this function it can influence positively or negatively, and so it can affect *concrete decisions leading to future implementation* or *non-implementation of the notion it embodies*. Metaphors, furthermore, because of this multivalence and their openness to adaptation and transformation, as shown by Musolff and Schäffner and my own example of the 'fester Kern', change and become elaborated (or attenuated), while their originally attached value judgements can be radically changed or uncoupled. This chameleon-like quality of political metaphor endows it with *its function in diplomacy, negotiation and in parliamentary public debate*. It will, however, be evident that its advantage in leaving room for manoeuvre in the political arena is matched by the disadvantage that, once released into the 'public perception loop', it can no longer be controlled by its originator, a little like the fate of Goethe's 'Zauberlehrling', the sorcerer's apprentice. The fundamental paradox lies in the metaphor's multi-functionality, which cannot be avoided. It has simultaneous functions of appearing to describe a reality, while being presented in the context of political persuasion and, thus, serving to help to implement, or to block the future implementation of, or to discontinue a political process. And this multi-functionality is open to exploitation in one direction or another by the actors in the 'public perception loop'.

In counter-distinction to politics, science can set up constructs of relationships which it seeks to compare with the corresponding segment of physical reality by means of measurement, verifying or falsifying that construct. Politics has to use concepts (and their terms), metaphors and stereotypes as frames for the organization of knowledge about political reality, as Schäffner argues. These frames are culturally rooted and usually value-based - and if not initially value-based - they still attract the recipient's own value associations. Thus, in contrast to scientific models that also purport to describe or are used to verify or falsify a description of reality, the conceptual metaphorical or stereotypical construct impacts upon the reality that prompted its creation. This effect is particularly pronounced in transnational (and therefore transcultural and translingual) political discourse. The impact, as argued before, can be conservative or creative.

If this analysis of the functions of metaphor particularly, but also of stereotype and of transnational political concept, is correct, it raises an epistemological question. How precisely does language relate to political action? In how far can political reality be separated from its perception through the medium of language?

Clearly there are coercive realities such as punishment for infringement upon the law which no longer involve communication. In non-democracies, the political function of language is relatively restricted and of course tightly controlled through censorship. But in open, democratic societies, as is suggested by the very term 'parliament', which means 'the place for talking', political discourse and political action are intimately linked. In the Information Society the 'public perception loop', as I have termed it, has become a central part of the political process. And the enormous complexities of a political project like European integration, which touches upon the sensibilities of so many historically rooted cultures as well as languages, add to the difficulty of objective perception. Metaphor and stereotype may be amongst the few techniques available for trying to picture a future development, techniques often resorted to when orthodox terminology seems ineffectual or inadequate in the transnational context. But even as these techniques are used, they already themselves add to the perceptual multivalence and thus fluidity of the situation. And since that fluidity cannot be grasped or 'frozen' without language, we can assert that the *process* leading to political action is inseparable from the language used in forming that process.

By way of conclusion - in search of a *fester Kern*

So, while, to ring a change on my opening adage, Europe is a Union of fifteen peoples divided by twelve languages, the political realities that are promoted and disputed in those languages also have to be perceived through those languages. Not only are the perceptions subject to perpetual modification through political and media presentation in any given language, they are also coloured by underlying, historically determined values, and these are the expression of cultures that outnumber, of course, even the languages of the Union.

Conservation, deriving from national cultural value-sets, is in constant conflict with the creation that is necessary for change, while what may be intended as description, when interpreted, can be an agent for either conservation or creation. Language is the battle-ground. Concept and term, metaphor and stereotype are among the weapons. Small wonder that the German conservative parties, the CDU and CSU, would like to secure an island of stability in the European Union and thus 'den festen Kern festigen'.

Contributors

Colin Good is professor of German at the University of Durham. His main interests lie in the application of insights from linguistic theory to political and ideological texts. His other interests include sociolinguistics of German, translation theory and interpreting. He is the author of *Die deutsche Sprache und die kommunistische Ideologie* (1975), *Presse und soziale Wirklichkeit* (1985), *Newspaper German. A Vocabulary of Commercial and Administrative German* (1995).

Helen Kelly-Holmes lectures in German in the Department of Languages and European Studies, Aston University (Birmingham, UK). Her main research interest is in advertising and other discourses of the market, particularly in an intercultural context.

Francis Knowles is Professor of Language in the Department of Languages and European Studies at Aston University (Birmingham, UK). He is a Slavist (Russian and Polish) by training. His research interests have three foci which overlap to a considerable extent. These are, firstly, computer-assisted linguistic research, involving corpus analysis, terminology and lexicography; secondly, the sociological, ethnic and demographic dimensions of linguistic studies and, finally, the general question of data analysis, empiricism and evidentiality in research.

Frank Liedtke is a reader (Privatdozent) in the Germanistic Institute at Heinrich Heine University Düsseldorf, Germany. His main research interests are linguistic pragmatics, language and society, and contrastive linguistics. He is the co-editor of *Begriffe besetzen. Strategien des Sprachgebrauchs in der Politik* (with Martin Wengeler and Karin Böke, 1991), and *Die Sprache der Adenauer Ära* (forthcoming).

Andreas Musolff is a senior lecturer in German in the German Department at the University of Durham. His publications include *Kommunikative Kreativität. Karl Bühlers Zweifelderlehre als Ansatz zu einer Theorie innovativen Sprachgebrauchs* (1990), and articles on the history of linguistics, on political discourse, and on the theory of metaphor in journals such as *Sprache und Literatur in Wissenschaft und Unterricht*, *Sprachreport*, and *Mots. Les langages du politique*. His current research interests include cross-lingual metaphors and historical semantics.

Hugh O'Donnell is a reader in the Department of Language & Media at Glasgow Caledonian University. His main research interest is in popular culture and the processes of mediation in the press and on television. He has worked extensively in the field of sport and national identity. His publications include *Sport and National Identity in the European Media* (with Neil Blain and Raymond Boyle, covering the 1992 European Championship in Sweden). Other areas of interest include representations of monarchy in different European countries, and a current large-scale project examining the explosive growth of domestic soap opera in Europe.

Nigel Reeves is Professor of German in the Department of Languages and European Studies at Aston University (Birmingham, UK). His main research interests are language education, particularly in the context of management and of overseas trade, German business culture, and technologically-based distance language learning. His publications include *Business Studies, Languages and Overseas Trade* (with D. Liston, 1985), *Linguistic Auditing. Identifying Foreign Language Communication Needs in Corporations* (with C. Wright, 1996), and articles in journals such as *The Annals of the American Academy of Political and Social Science*.

Christina Schäffner is a lecturer in German in the Department of Languages and European Studies at Aston University (Birmingham, UK). Her research interests are political discourse, metaphors, intercultural communication, and translation. Her publications include *Gibt es eine prototypische Wortschatzbeschreibung?* (ed., 1990), *Le concept de l'Europe dans le processus de la CSCE* (co-edited with Christiane Villain-Gandossi, Klaus Bochmann and Michel Metzeltin, 1990), *Language and Peace* (co-edited with Anita Wenden, 1995) and articles in journals such as *Discourse & Society*, and *Target*.

Wolfgang Teubert is a graduate of Heidelberg University. His doctoral dissertation *Valenz des Substantivs* was published in 1979. He is the head of the Department of Language Change at the Institut für deutsche Sprache in Mannheim, Germany. Currently he is mainly engaged in the organisation of a European language resources infrastructure. His main fields of research are corpus linguistics and historical semantics. He is the editor of the new *International Journal of Corpus Linguistics*.

Michael Townson is Professor of German and Head of the School of Applied Language and Intercultural Studies at Dublin City University. His main interests lie in German language and linguistics, and he has published on the interaction of language and politics and on the socio-cultural history of German. He is the author of *Mother Tongue and Father Land* (1992).

Lieve van de Walle received a PhD in Linguistics from the University of Antwerp. Presently, she is teaching English at the Hogeschool Limburg. Her current research interests include Sanskrit Linguistics, European discourse, politeness and the intersection of linguistics and literature. She is the author of *Pragmatics and Classical Sanskrit* which appeared in the series *Pragmatics & Beyond* (1993), and published in various conference proceedings.